Ventures
in Policy
Sciences

Policy Sciences Book Series

A Series of Studies, Textbooks, and Reference Works

Edited by YEHEZKEL DROR
Hebrew University of Jerusalem

PUBLISHED

Yehezkel Dror
Design for Policy Sciences, 1971

Yehezkel Dror
Ventures in Policy Sciences, 1971

Harold D. Lasswell
A Pre-View of Policy Sciences, 1971

Beatrice K. Rome and Sydney C. Rome
Organizational Growth through Decisionmaking, 1971

Walter Williams
Social Policy Research and Analysis, 1971

IN PREPARATION

Benson D. Adams
Ballistic Missile Defense

Joseph P. Martino
Technological Forecasting for Decisionmaking

Ventures in Policy Sciences

CONCEPTS AND APPLICATIONS

Yehezkel Dror

The Hebrew University of Jerusalem
The World Institute, Jerusalem, Israel

ELSEVIER

NEW YORK   OXFORD   AMSTERDAM

ELSEVIER NORTH-HOLLAND, INC.
52 Vanderbilt Avenue, New York, N.Y. 10017

ELSEVIER PUBLISHING COMPANY, LTD.
Barking, Essex, England

ELSEVIER SCIENTIFIC PUBLISHING COMPANY
335 Jan Van Galenstraat, P.O. Box 211
Amsterdam, The Netherlands

International Standard Book Number 0-444-00106-9

Library of Congress Card Number 78-158632

Manufactured in the United States of America

TO MY SONS

Asael, Otniel, Itiel

Contents

Preface

This book is devoted to the advancement of policy sciences, through exploration of some central policy sciences concepts and through their application to real issues and problems. Thus, this volume constitutes an integral part of my trilogy in policy sciences, which includes also a general introduction to policy sciences (*Design for Policy Sciences,* New York: American Elsevier, 1971) and a comprehensive treatise on policymaking (*Public Policymaking Reexamined,* San Francisco: Chandler Publishing Co., 1968). But in structure and contents, the present volume stands by itself, providing a concrete and operational approach to policy sciences.

The unique feature of this volume is its attempt to move back and forth between theoretic exploration of policy sciences concepts and their detailed application to reality. This characteristic reflects the personal interests of the author, who has divided his time during the last seven years between academic teaching and research at The Hebrew University of Jerusalem, consultation to the government of Israel, and applied study and policy analysis at The Rand Corporation in the United States.

This volume is based on papers written during that period—for academic purposes, as consultation reports, and as policy studies. I have revised all papers in light of the present state of my thinking. Also, I have unified the concepts and increased mutual complementarity and redundancy to what I regard as a useful level. Specially written introductions and comments serve to unify the volume and to integrate it.

The main mission of this volume is to try to convey some contents and implications of policy sciences through selected concepts and applications. I hope that for this purpose its mosaic structure will prove useful. My intention in this book is to try to overcome the double dangers facing policy sciences—namely, (1) escape from the hard tests of reality into Grand Theory, and (2) proccupation with immediate applications without guiding theory—by tying in theory and practice, concepts and applications.

This book is mainly directed at those who are already policy professionals and those who are studying to become policy professionals. I hope it may be interesting and useful to planners, systems and policy analysts, management scientists, environmental engineers, budget analysts, economists, applied behavioral scientists, organizational advisors, and similar professionals, and to students preparing themselves for active professional contributions to better policymaking. The even broader population of academics, professionals, and practitioners looking to science for help in improving policymaking may also like to move along the way to policy sciences provided in this volume.

I owe a great debt to many friends and colleagues who directly and indirectly contributed to my work, as reflected in this book. In particular, I am indebted to many senior politicians and executives in Israel who made me a minor partner in some of their endeavors and who thus provided me with invaluable opportunities to learn and to experiment, while trying to do my share for my beleaguered country.

Great also is my gratitude to The Rand Corporation, which afforded me a unique opportunity to participate in its pioneering activities in policy sciences. The names of my friends and colleagues at The Rand Corporation who educated me in applied policy sciences are too many for enumeration here. But I want to express my particular thanks to the President of The Rand Corporation, Dr. Henry Rowen, and to the Head of the Social Science Division, Dr. Fred Iklé, who invited me to join The Rand Corporation and who provided me with projects and assignments full of interest and of learning opportunities.

I regard conventional expressions of gratitude to one's family as an intrusion of privacy, and, therefore, will not delve into the partnership of my wife in my work. But I want to make an exception in respect to my three sons, Asael, Otniel, and Itiel. They suffered for seven long years from father deprivation without the benefits of participatory democracy—and the end is not yet in sight. Their willingness to let their father work in the time which rightfully is theirs and the constant challenges they posed to their father's fuddling attempts to rely on policy sciences for educational family decisions are a main cause for whatever merits this book may have. My only justification for giving priority to policy sciences over three wonderful boys is that, for their sakes and the sake of children all over the world, policy sciences is urgently needed.

YEHEZKEL DROR

CHAPTER 1

Some Basic Concepts: A Glossary

COMMENTS

Concepts are essential tools of thought and communication. Therefore, unavoidably, all attempts at new thoughts involve some new or renewed concepts (though new concepts, by themselves, are no proof of innovative thinking). At the same time, conceptual and terminological innovations involve costs in terms of communication. Therefore, identification of a preferable balance between conceptual innovations, which aid thought and expression on one hand, and terminological conservatism, which aids communication on the other hand, is a difficult task. This task is especially hard for scholars of policy sciences, who stand before the contradicting needs of a novel approach, which requires new concepts as essential tools for its task, and the needs for easy communication between persons coming from different disciplines and between scholars and practitioners.

To try to handle this dilemma, I do not hesitate to propose new concepts whenever I regard them as useful tools for policy sciences; But I try to keep terminological innovations to an essential minimum. Also, every new concept is both defined and demonstrated through repeated usage.

Further to aid the reader who comes from different disciplines while also introducing him to some of the main concepts of policy sciences—whether new or borrowed—I am commencing this book with a short glossary. The terms included in the glossary are explained again and again in the text and are repeatedly used throughout the volume. The terms are also covered by the index. Nevertheless, I think the reader will find it useful to initiate his perusal of the book by carefully considering the glossary and referring to it whenever he has doubts about any of the concepts used throughout this volume.

Glossary

ADMINISTRATIVE REFORM—Directed change of main features of an administrative system. To qualify as an administrative reform, the directed change must rate high on at least one of the following dimensions and at least medium on a second of these dimensions: comprehensiveness, innovativeness, and criticality.

1

ADPF, ALTERNATIVE DOMESTIC POLITICAL FUTURES—Alternative futures of internal politics, including also the political institutions and the public policymaking system.

ALTERNATIVE FUTURES—Hypothetical states of the future which are regarded as having some probability of realization, within an explicated time horizon.

CONFLICT SYSTEM—A system composed of actors and/or multiactors who are, to some extent, in conflict with one another. Usually, in a conflict system, the relations between the actors/multiactors are, in part, cooperative relations and, in part, conflict relations.

CONTROLLING MAN—Man who exerts dominance over his environment, over social institutions, and over the very nature of human beings.

COUNTERFACTUAL ALTERNATIVE FUTURES—Hypothetical states of the future which depend on assumptions that contradict present perception of facts (including laws of nature), and which, therefore, have—to the best of our knowledge—zero probability of realization.

DELPHI METHOD—A prediction method which tries to utilize the opinions of experts who interact without personal contacts. Opinions submitted by the participants are circulated, so that these participants may revise their predictions after knowing the opinions and arguments of other participants. This procedure can be repeated several times. Convergency of opinions is regarded as increasing the reliability of the prediction, because it represents consensus arrived at without interpersonal dynamics.

DROR LAW (APHORISTIC) NO. 1—"While the difficulties and dangers of problems tend to increase at a geometric rate, the number of persons qualified to deal with these problems tends to increase at an arithmetic rate."

DROR LAW (APHORISTIC) NO. 2—"While human capacities to shape the environment, society, and human beings are rapidly increasing, policymaking capabilities to use those capacities remain the same."

EFFECTIVENESS—Extent to which direct goals are achieved. Because of neglect of costs, an alternative can be effective and inefficient.

EFFICIENCY—Cost-benefit ratio. Because of the neglect of absolute sizes, an alternative may be very efficient and very ineffective. Or net benefit.

FACET DESIGN—A research tool developed by Louis Guttman, based on decomposition of a phenomenon into the factors of which it is the product.

FUTURES STUDIES—Study and research on alternative futures.

LOOKOUT FUNCTION—Search for policy issues which are not recognized as such because of unawareness of possible developments and their significance.

MEGA-METAPOLICY—Megapolicy and metapolicy.

MEGAPOLICY—Master policy, a policy providing guides for a set of discrete policies. Megapolicies deal with overall goals, assumptions on futures, risk evaluation, degrees of innovation, etc.

METACONTROL—Control of controls, control of the control system.

METADECISION—Decision on how to make decisions, that is, decisions dealing with the characteristics of the decision system.

METAEVALUATION—Evaluation of evaluation, that is, evaluation of the evaluation system.

METAPOLICY—Policy on policymaking, that is, policy dealing with the characteristics of the policymaking system.

MIN-AVOIDANCE—A megapolicy oriented towards avoidance of the worst of all possible situations. In min-avoidance, the effort is directed toward moving from the worst possible to the worst plus one, and so on.

MULTIACTOR—Any unit composed of more than a single individual, for example, a group, an organization, a country.

NOVADESIGN—Design anew, as contrasted with redesign, which involves changes in an existing system.

PLANNING—The process of preparing a set of decisions for action in the future, directed at achieving goals by preferable means.

POLICY ANALYSIS—An approach and methodology for design and identification of preferable alternatives in respect to complex policy issues. Policy analysis provides heuristic aid to better policymaking, without any presumption to provide optimization algorithms.

POLICY ANALYSIS NETWORK—A morphological decomposition of an issue into subproblems, bringing out the relations among them and with relevant variables. The structure of a policy analysis network should serve as a heuristic program for alternative innovation and preferable-alternative identification. Any policy analysis network is provisional, to be constantly iterated.

POLICY INSTRUMENTS—Futures-shaping variables which can be reset.

POLICY SCIENCES—A new supradiscipline, oriented towards the improvement of policymaking and characterized by a series of paradigms different in important respects from contemporary "normal" sciences.

POLITICAL FEASIBILITY (of an alternative)—The range of probabilities that within a given time a particular policy alternative will receive sufficient political push and support to be approved and politically implemented (i.e., all necessary political steps for implementation have been taken— nevertheless these may be insufficient for actual implementation, even though essential).

POLITICAL FEASIBILITY DOMAIN—The range of alternatives which are politically feasible.

POLITICAL LEVERAGE—Ability of an actor (or multiactor) to influence, *inter alia,* policies and their implementation.

POLITICAL LEVERAGE DOMAIN—The space of effective political action within which an actor is able, with a certain probability, to affect reality through political means.

PPBS, PLANNING-PROGRAMMING-BUDGETING SYSTEM—A method first utilized in the United States Department of Defense under Robert McNamara for relating multiyear planning with budgeting by programs and with analysis.

PREFERABLE (VERB "PREFERIZE")—An alternative which is clearly superior to all known alternatives, but which is not necessarily optimal.

PRIMARY UNCERTAINTY—The condition of uncertainty when the dimensions of possible results are unknown (in contrast to "certainty and secondary uncertainty").

SCENARIO—A series of possible developments leading from the present to an alternative future.

SECONDARY UNCERTAINTY—The conditions of uncertainty when the dimensions of possible results are known, but their probability distributions are unknown (in contrast to "certainty and primary uncertainty"). This is equivalent to the term *risk* as used in the theory of games.

SETTING (of policy instruments)—Changing of position of policy instruments, manipulating them—but without the negative connotations of the latter term.

SEQUENTIAL POLICYMAKING—Policymaking by phases combined with parallel implementation of different alternatives, coupled to constant learning, which permits abandonment of the less promising alternatives after a relatively small investment of resources.

SOCIETAL DIRECTION SYSTEM—The units who engage in conscious efforts to influence societal policies or who do so, in fact. The public policymaking system is a main part of the societal direction system. Delimitation of the societal direction system is a matter of degrees, to be decided according to purposes of inquiry.

SUBOPTIMIZATION—Attempts to deal with a complex issue by breaking it down into subissues, each one of which can be "optimized" by itself.

SYSTEM—A number of entities (actors, multiactors, processes, symbols, and more) who interact in some patterned modes (including a maintained random pattern). The delimitation of a system depends on the relative intensities of interactions and on the purposes of the delimitation.

TACIT KNOWLEDGE—Knowledge which is not explicated and often cannot be explicated.

TACIT THEORY—Unexplicated believed-in explanations of behavior and other phenomena.

TARGET AREA—The phenomena at which a policy is directed.

ULTRASTABILITY—Stability of the laws regulating change, that is, of the change patterns.

Part I is devoted to an initial presentation of the fundamentals of policy sciences. The first chapter explores the basic ideas of policy sciences, its unique paradigms, and some of its implications. The second chapter exercises the general concepts of policy sciences through a generalized application to long-range decisionmaking in the United States National Aeronautic and Space Agency. The third chapter deals with research needs of policy sciences, by proposing a series of problems for study by policy research organizations.

PART I

The Fundamentals of Policy Sciences

CHAPTER 2

Policy Sciences: Developments and Implications[1]

COMMENTS

This chapter presents the basic idea of policy sciences, as a new supradiscipline distinguished by a set of unique paradigms. Some of the central concepts of policy sciences are explored and some possible implications of the development of policy sciences are indicated. To illustrate the range of policy sciences implications, special attention is devoted to changes in adult and school education necessary for preserving and strengthening democracy, as essential concomitants to novadesign of the policymaking system.

This chapter thus provides a set of ideas, a concept package, and a series of implications, all of which are elaborated, examined, and applied throughout this volume.

The Need for Policy Sciences

From the point of view of human action, much of scientific knowledge can be divided into three main levels: knowledge relevant to the control[2] of the environment; knowledge relevant to the control of society and individuals; and knowledge concerning the control of the controls themselves, that is, *metacontrol.*

Knowledge about control of the environment, as supplied by rapid progress in the physical sciences, is the most highly developed one. Knowledge of the control of society and individuals is much less advanced, but at least the behavioral sciences constitute recognized components of science, receive significant support, and do show some signs of progress. Least developed of all and scarcely recognized as a distinct focus for research and study is metacontrol knowledge, that is, knowledge of the design and operation of the control system itself.

---

[1]This chapter is based on a paper prepared for the International Joint Conference of the American Geographical Society and the American Division of the World Academy of Art and Science, on "Environment and Society in Transition: Scientific Developments: Social Consequences: Policy Implications," New York City, April 27-May 2, 1970.

[2]I am using the term *control* in the sense of regulating, governing, shaping, directing, and influencing. *Monitoring* is one subelement of control, in the broad sense in which I use the latter.

Scarcity of knowledge concerning the design and operation of the social overall control system—which I call the societal direction system[3]—has characterized humanity since its beginnings. While some progress has taken place in the mechanics of control and micro-control systems of some social components (such as corporations), the essential features of the societal direction system continue to be beyond penetrating understanding and, even more so, beyond conscious and deliberate design.

This blind area in human knowledge has always caused suffering and tragedy, in terms of human values. But, from a longer perspective, the weaknesses of the societal direction system did not matter very much, as long as the operations of that system did not constitute an important variable in shaping human destiny. When most variables shaping human and social fate were beyond influence by the societal direction system because of the absence of powerful policy instruments, bad decisions on the use of the few available instruments (or, to be more exact, "instrument images") had only very limited impact on basic reality and therefore could not cause long-range harm.

It is this insignificance of societal direction systems for the long-range fate of humanity which is changing, thanks to rapid progress in the knowledge of policy instruments which permits control of the environment, society, and individuals. New knowledge supplies increasingly potent instruments for use by humanity. The nuclear bomb and ecology poisoning techniques and materials are but weak illustrations of the powerful policy instruments supplied by modern science. Presetting of the gender of children, weather control, genetic engineering, stimulation of altered states of consciousness, and emotional controls—these are only some examples of the more powerful capacities for controlling the environment, society, and individuals which the progress of science is sure to supply in the foreseeable future.[4]

It is the growing gulf between the capacity to control the environment, society, and individuals on one hand, and the knowledge of how to design and operate societal direction systems so they can use these capacities, on the other hand, which constitutes the major danger to the survival and development of humanity. The emergence of *controlling man,* who exerts dominance over his environment, over social institutions, and over the very nature of human beings, makes it absolutely essential to improve societal direction systems so as to use wisely the powerful instruments at his disposal.

[3]Comparable terms are *central guidance cluster* as used by Bertram Gross and *societal control centers* as used by Amitai Etzioni. See Bertram M. Gross, *The State of the Nation: Social Systems Accounting* (London: Tavistock Publications, 1966), pp. 72-73, and Amitai Etzioni, *The Active Society* (New York: Basic Books, 1968), p. 112.

[4]For a careful discussion, see John McHale, *The Future of the Future* (New York: George Braziller, 1969). For longer-range and more speculative explorations, see Gordon Rattnay Taylor, *The Biological Time Bomb* (New York: Signet Books, 1968); and Burnham Putnam Beckwith, *The Next 500 Years* (New York: Exposition Press, 1967).

I use on purpose the term *wisely* to emphasize the multidimensionality of required changes in societal direction systems. Urgently needed, for instance, are new values and belief systems which meet the new global role of controlling man. Scientific knowledge cannot supply new values and belief systems,[5] though perhaps some of the conditions of value innovation can be studied and consciously encouraged. But science can and should supply knowledge on preferable designs and patterns for the rationality components of societal direction systems, including rational means for improving the designs and patterns of the essential extrarationality components. Especially important is improvement of the public policymaking system, which constitutes the dominant component of the societal direction system as a whole.

In short, a main problem faced by humanity can, I think, be summed up in what I aphoristically called the Second Dror Law:[6]

While human capacities to shape the environment, society, and human beings are rapidly increasing, policymaking capabilities to use those capacities remain the same.

A large number of dispersed efforts to develop knowledge relevant to policymaking improvement do take place. These include work under the auspices of a number of new disciplines, approaches, and interdisciplines, such as operations research, praxeology, systems analysis, organization theory, cybernetics, information theory, theory of games, organizational development approaches, strategic analysis, futures studies, systems engineering, decision theory, and general systems theory. Also important is some work in new directions within more traditional disciplines, especially economics, some branches of psychology, and some parts of political science.[7] This work supplies important insights, promising concepts, and stimulating ideas. But, in general, present endeavors to develop scientific knowledge relevant to the improvement of policymaking tend to suffer from the following weaknesses:

[5]For somewhat different and stimulating views, see Hasan Ozbekhan, "Toward a General Theory of Planning," in Erich Jantsch, ed., *Perspectives of Planning* (Paris: OECD, 1969); and Erich Jantsch, "From Forecasting and Planning to Policy Sciences," *Policy Sciences* 1, no. 1 (Spring 1970): 31-47. Completely unacceptable, in my opinion, are the naive proposals made from time to time by physical scientists to achieve deliberate and systematic value innovations aimed at the long-range future through quasi-rational mass movements. See, for instance, Gerald Feinberg, *The Prometheus Project* (Garden City, N.Y.: Doubleday, 1969).

[6]For the First Dror Law, see p. 2.

[7]For selected bibliographic references to relevant work until 1967, see "Bibliographic Essay," in Yehezkel Dror, *Public Policymaking Reexamined* (San Francisco: Chandler, 1968), pp. 327-56. For a survey of more recent relevant literature, see Yehezkel Dror, *Design for Policy Sciences* (New York: American Elsevier, 1971), Appendix.

1. Micro-approach, with applications to some types of decisions, but very limited relevance to the policymaking system as a whole.

2. Disjointedness, resulting in fragmented views limited to single dimensions of policymaking. Thus, systems analysis is quite isolated from organization theory, operation research from psychology of judgment, and decision theory from general systems theory.

3. Preoccupation with the rationality components of policymaking, with little attention to the fusion of rationality with extrarationality and the improvement of the latter.

4. Incrementalism, with nearly complete neglect of the problems of policymaking systems novadesign (i.e., design anew), as distinguished from slight redesign.

5. Narrow domain of concern, which neglects consideration of possible improvement needs and improvement possibilities of some critical elements of the policymaking system, such as politicians.

6. Sharp dichotomy between the behavioral approaches, which study some segments of policymaking reality, and the normative approaches, which design abstract, rationality-based micro-decision models—thus preventing a comprehensive approach to understanding and improvement of the policymaking system as a whole.

7. In the normative approaches: strong dependence on metric quantification and therefore inability to handle qualitative variables.

8. In the behavioral approaches: lack of interest in prescriptive methodology and jumps between lack of interest in application and partisan advocacy.

9. Fixation on conventional research methods; therefore, inability to utilize important sources of knowledge (such as tacit knowledge of policy practitioners) and difficulties in designing new research methods to meet the special problems of policymaking study and improvement (e.g., social experimentation).

I could go on adding additional items to the list of inadequacies of most contemporary efforts to build up policymaking knowledge, but I think the problem goes beyond a shorter or longer list of discrete weaknesses. The problem is not one of accidental omissions which can be easily corrected. Rather, I think that the overall lack of saliency of contemporary scientific endeavors to the improvement of policymaking reflects a basic incongruity between the paradigms of contemporary sciences in all their heterogeneity and the paradigms necessary for building up policymaking-relevant scientific knowledge.

To put my opinion into a positive form, it seems to me that in order to build up a science of policymaking, we need a new type of science based on a new set of paradigms.[8] Following the pioneering suggestion of Harold D. Lasswell,[9] I propose to call this new area of study, research, teaching, professional activity, and application *policy sciences;*[10] but the name does not really matter.

As a matter of fact, policy sciences is at present in *status nascendi* and, it is to be hoped, approaching a taking-off stage. Among the signs of its emergence are the following:

1. The already mentioned proliferation of research and study of various policymaking issues within new and traditional disciplines. This testifies to widespread interest and serves to build up important, though disjointed, subcomponents of policy sciences.

2. The invention and development of new types of policy research organizations which in effect engage in the development and application of policy sciences. The Hudson Institute, the Urban Institute, parts of the Brookings Institution, the new Woodrow Wilson Foundation, the Institute for the Future, the Rand Corporation, and The New York City Rand Institute illustrate this trend in the United States.

3. The self-education of outstanding individual policy scientists who, thanks to personal multidisciplinary background, accidents of opportunity, and interest in application of scientific methods to acute problems, got into the pioneering of policy sciences and thus have demonstrated the feasibility of policy sciences and its promises.

4. The recent establishment of new university programs devoted to policy sciences, with or without the use of that term. In the United States alone, more than ten such programs were initiated in the period 1967 to 1970.

5. The rapidly increasing number of conferences, books, periodicals, "invisible colleges," and similar expressions of professional activity and interest devoted in effect to the advancement of policy sciences as a whole or of some of its major aspects.

These are some of the signs of search, concern, experimentation, and interest which, I think, indicate the emergence of policy sciences. Nevertheless, at

[8]My terminology follows Thomas S. Kuhn, *The Structure of Scientific Revolutions* (Chicago: University of Chicago Press, 1962).

[9]The concept of "policy sciences" was first proposed in 1951 by Harold D. Lasswell, in Daniel Lerner and Harold D. Lasswell, eds., *The Policy Sciences: Recent Developments in Scope and Methods* (Stanford: Stanford University Press, 1951). For recent versions of Lasswell's views, see Harold D. Lasswell, "Policy Sciences," in *International Encyclopedia of Social Sciences* 12:181-89, and Harold D. Lasswell, "The Emerging Conceptions of the Policy Sciences," *Policy Sciences* 1, no. 1 (Spring 1970): 3-14. The subject will be extensively treated in a forthcoming book by Harold D. Lasswell, *A Pre-View of Policy Sciences.*

[10]To emphasize both the multiple dimensions of policy sciences and the integrated orientation of policy sciences, I propose to use its plural form *policy sciences,* but to regard the concept grammatically as singular.

best, we are only in the first stages of the required scientific revolution, and there is no assurance that it will be successful in bringing forth a viable and significant new kind of science. The challenge may be beyond our intellectual abilities, charlatans may discredit the idea of policy sciences before it really gets started, political culture may inhibit the efforts, or the conservatism of "normal" scientists may choke it. Even if policy sciences does emerge as a new type of scientific endeavor, it is doubtful to what extent one can predict now its future characteristics and implications. Therefore, the following exploration of the new paradigms of policy sciences and of their applied implications should be regarded as a normative forecast, directed at least as much at shaping the future as at foreseeing it.

Subject to this qualification, I think that preliminary examination of some of the unique paradigms of policy sciences, as I see them, will serve to illuminate both the current effort and the urgent need. It will also serve as a basis for examining some applied implications. As our analysis is a rough one, mistakes in some specifications do not matter. It is the overall *Gestalt* of policy sciences in which we are interested.

Some New Paradigms of Policy Sciences[11]

It seems that the main paradigmatic innovations to be required of and expected from policy sciences can be summed up as follows:

1. The main concern of policy sciences is with the understanding and improvement of macro-control systems—and especially public policymaking systems. In addition to overall improvement-oriented study of such systems, the main foci of policy sciences include, for example, (*a*) policy analysis, which provides heuristic methods for identification of preferable policy alternatives; (*b*) alternative innovation, which deals with the invention of new designs and possibilities to be considered in policymaking; (*c*) master policies (or megapolicies), which provide postures, assumptions, strategies, and main guidelines to be followed by specific policies; (*d*) evaluation and feedback, including, for instance, social indicators, social experimentation, and organizational learning; and (*e*) improvement of metapolicy, that is, "policy on policymaking," through redesign and novadesign of the public policymaking system, its organizational components, selection and training of its personnel, and reconstruction of its communication and information network. While the main test of policy sciences is better achievement of considered goals through more effective and efficient policies, policy sciences as such is in the main not directly concerned with the substantive contents of discrete policy problems (which should be dealt with by the relevant normal

[11]This and the following section lean in part on Yehezkel Dror, "Prolegomenon to Policy Sciences," *Policy Sciences* 1, no. 1 (Spring 1970): 139-80. For a more extensive discussion, see the author's *Design for Policy Sciences,* op. cit. [in footnote 7].

sciences), but rather with improved methods, knowledge, and systems for better policymaking.

2. The traditional boundaries between disciplines, and especially between the various behavioral sciences and decision disciplines, must be broken down. Policy sciences must integrate knowledge from a variety of branches of knowledge and build it up into a supradiscipline focusing on public policy-making. In particular, policy sciences is based upon a fusion between behavioral sciences and analytical decision approaches. But it also absorbs many elements from decision theory, general systems theory, organization theory, operations research, strategic analysis, systems engineering, and similar modern areas of study. Physical and life sciences are also relied upon, insofar as they are relevant.

3. The usual dichotomy between pure and applied research must be bridged. In policy sciences, integration between pure and applied research is achieved by accepting the improvement of societal direction as its ultimate goal. As a result, the real world becomes a main laboratory of policy sciences, and the test of the most abstract theory is in its application (directly or indirectly) to problems of policymaking.

4. Tacit knowledge and personal experience must be accepted as important sources of knowledge, in addition to more conventional methods of research and study. Efforts to distill the tacit knowledge of policy practitioners and to involve high-quality policymakers as partners in the up-building of policy sciences are among the important characteristics distinguishing policy sciences from contemporary "normal" sciences.

5. Policy sciences shares with normal sciences a main involvement with instrumental-normative knowledge, in the sense of being directed at means and intermediate goals rather than absolute values. But policy sciences is sensitive to the difficulties of achieving "value-free sciences" and tries to contribute to value choice by exploring value implications, value consistencies, value costs, and the behavioral foundations of value commitments. Also, parts of policy sciences are involved in invention of different "alternative futures," including their value contents. Furthermore, "organized creativity" —including value invention—constitutes important inputs into parts of policy sciences (such as policymaking system novadesign and redesign, policy design, and policy analysis), and the encouragement and stimulation of organized creativity is therefore a subject for policy sciences. As a result, policy sciences should seek to breach the solid wall separating contemporary sciences from ethics and philosophy of values and build up an operational theory of values (including value morphology, taxonomy, measurement, etc., but not the substantive absolute norms themselves) as a part of policy sciences.

6. Policy sciences is very time sensitive, regarding the present as a bridge between the past and the future. Consequently, it rejects the a-historic ap-

proach of much of contemporary behavioral sciences and analytical approaches. Instead, it emphasizes historic developments on one hand and future dimensions on the other hand as central contexts for improved policymaking.

7. Policy sciences does not accept the take-it-or-leave-it attitude of much of the contemporary behavioral sciences, neither does it regard petition signing and similar "direct-action" involvements as a main form of policy sciences contributions as such (in distinction from scientists acting as citizens) to better policymaking. Instead, it is committed to striving for increased utilization of policy sciences in actual policymaking and to preparing professionals to serve in policy sciences positions throughout the societal direction system (without letting this sense of mission interfere with a clinical and rational-analytical orientation to policy issues).

8. Policy sciences deals with the contribution of systematic knowledge and structured rationality to the design and operation of societal direction systems. But policy sciences clearly recognizes the important roles both of extra-rational processes (such as creativity, intuition, charisma, and value judgment) and of irrational processes (such as depth motivation). The search for ways to improve these processes for better policymaking is an integral part of policy sciences, including, for instance, possible policymaking implications of altered states of consciousness. (In other words, policy sciences faces the already-mentioned paradoxical problem of how to improve extrarational and even irrational processes through rational means.)

Some Implications of Policy Sciences

Any policy sciences the *Gestalt* of which resembles the image conveyed by the policy sciences paradigms previously offered will have far-reaching implications. Of relatively minor importance are various implications for the organization of science, its research, and its teaching. These include, for instance, the transfer of some major research and teaching functions from universities to policy research organizations; the participation of experienced politicians, executives, and similar policy practitioners in scientific activities; novel teaching designs; and new career patterns involving transitions between abstract policy sciences research, long-range policy research, and policy analysis of pressing issues—accompanied by movement between universities, policy research organizations, and a variety of new roles in various branches of government and in public, quasi-public, and private organizations.

These are implications of much importance for academia. But from an overall social point of view, the critical significance of policy sciences is in the basic changes which it brings about in the age-old dilemma of *scientia et potentia,* knowledge and power. These, in turn, have far-reaching implications for the exercise and structure of social power, that is, for politics.

The relevant unique feature of policy sciences is that policy sciences presumes to deal with the internal processes of policymaking and presumes to tell the policymakers how to arrive at decisions. This is a degree of penetration into the innermost processes of politics removed by a step-level function from the contributions of contemporary "normal" sciences to policymaking. Contemporary normal sciences supply inputs to be taken into account in policymaking and sometimes propose solutions as stipulated outputs of policymaking; but contemporary normal sciences do not open up the black box of how policy decisions are made and do not claim to develop scientific models for rewiring the box.[12]

In blunt language, the more policy sciences indeed does develop, the more should the policymaking system be redesigned to avail itself of policy sciences knowledge and the more should politics be reformed to permit full symbiosis between political power and policy sciences knowledge. The basic roles of elected politicians in a democratic society will not be impaired. Indeed, the critical functions of value judgment, interest presentation, consensus maintenance, and trans-scientific judgment will not be weakened, but will actually be strengthened, thanks to clearer presentation of alternatives, better control of implementation, more reliable feedback, fuller explication of tacit theories, and similar contributions of policy analysis. Essential, however, are policymaking arrangements which will assure that policy sciences knowledge will be correctly appreciated and taken into account, and that both its underutilization and its overutilization will be avoided.

Somewhat to concretize this general idea, let me present some implications for changes in the policymaking system which seem to result from initial work in policy sciences.[13] To provide variety in my illustrations, some are presented as a short enumeration while others, which are less technical, are discussed at some length:

1. Pervasive utilization of policy analysis for consideration of issues, exploration of alternatives, and clarification of goals.

2. Encouragement of explicit megapolicy decisions, in distinction from discrete policy determinations. Explicit megapolicy decisions (including mixed megapolicies) are needed on the following issues, among others:

[12]Some exceptions are provided by political science and public administration, both classic and modern. However, the relevant work in political science tends to suffer from one or more of the following characteristics, which make them inadequate surrogates for policy sciences: (a) mainly ideological orientation; or (b) mainly technical orientation, dealing with administrative efficiency; (c) focus on specific components of the policymaking system, without an overall systems view; (d) absence of empiric basis; or (e) absence of decision theory basis.

[13]For a detailed discussion of some of these recommendations and their policy sciences theoretic bases, see Yehezkel Dror, *Public Policymaking Reexamined*, op. cit. [in footnote 7], esp. Part V, pp. 217 ff.

degrees and locations of acceptable innovations in policies; extent of risk to be accepted in policies and choice between a maximax approach and/or maximin approach and/or min-avoidance approach;[14] a preferable mix between comprehensive policies, narrow-issue-oriented policies, and shock policies (which aim at breakthroughs accompanied by temporary disequilibration); and a preferable mix between policies oriented toward concrete goals, toward a number of defined future options, and/or toward building up resources better to achieve as yet undefined goals in the future.

3. Encouragement of comprehensive megapolicies, in which discrete policy issues are considered within a broader context of basic goals, postures, and directives.[15]

4. Systematic evaluation of past policies in order to learn from them for the future. For instance, methods and institutions should be established to provide periodic independent audits of the results of legislation.

5. Better consideration of the future. Special structures and processes should be designed to encourage better consideration of the future in contemporary policymaking. This includes, for instance, dispersal of various kinds of "look-out" organizations, units, and staff throughout the policy-making system and utilization of alternative images of the future and scenarios in all policy considerations.

6. Search for methods and means to encourage creativity and invention in respect to policy issues. This may involve, for instance, no-strings-attached support to individuals and organizations engaging in adventurous thinking and "organized dreaming"; avoidance of their becoming committed to present policies and establishments; and opening up channels of access for un-

[14] I use the term *min-avoidance* to refer to policies directed at avoiding the worst of all possible situations. One important advantage of such a megapolicy concerns support recruitment: it is often much easier to achieve agreement on ills to be avoided than on operational positive formulations of "good life" to be realized.

Some success in min-avoidance would constitute a significant improvement over reality. However simple this may sound, human capacities to approximate mini are amazing. Still well worth reading in this connection is Walter B. Pitkin, *A Short Introduction to the History of Human Stupidity* (New York: Simon and Schuster, 1932). Recent policies around the world could provide a long second volume for such a history.

[15] President Nixon's First Annual Foreign Affairs Message, *United States Foreign Policy for the 1970s: A New Strategy for Peace,* as well as the Second Annual Foreign Affairs Message, well illustrate such an effort. It is relevant to observe that this innovation in comprehensive megapolicies is closely related to the existence of a new type of policy-making-improvement-oriented policy analysis unit in the White House, namely, Dr. Kissinger's staff.

Preparation of similar megapolicies for, say, urban problems would require more than establishment of a parallel urban policy analysis unit in the White House. The basic concept package and integrative framework have first to be developed. Among the urgent tasks awaiting policy sciences is work on overall policy concept packages, on integrative problem mappings, and on issue taxonomies.

conventional ideas to high-level policymakers and to the public at large. Creativity and invention may also be influenced within policymaking organizations by institutionally protecting innovative thinkers from organizational conformity pressures. Requiring careful study also are creativity-amplifying devices and chemicals, and arrangements for their possible use in policymaking.

7. Establishment of a multiplicity of policy research organizations to work on main policy issues. Some of these policy research organizations should work for the central government, some for the legislature, and some for the public at large—diffusing their findings through the mass media of communications.

8. Development of extensive social experimentation designs and of institutions able to engage in social experimentation (including reconsideration of involved ethical problems). It seems quite clear that social experimentation is essential for finding solutions to present and emerging social issues. For instance, new experimental cities may be needed to develop suitable habitations for the many million additional Americans expected by the year 2000. Careful social experimentation requires invention of new research designs and of new legal-political arrangements. Also important and very difficult is the requirement for a political and social climate in which careful research and experimentation on social institutions is encouraged. (As a United States illustration, a change is needed in the attitudes which expressed themselves, for instance, in the legislative prohibition of studies on the operation of juries.)

9. Institutional arrangements to encourage "heresy" and consideration of taboo policy issues, such as the possibilities of long-range advancement of humanity through genetic policies and of changes in basic social institutions, such as the family.

10. Improvement of one-person-centered high-level decisionmaking. Even though of very high and sometimes critical importance, one-person-centered high-level decisionmaking is very neglected by both contemporary research and improvement attempts. This in part is due, one one hand, to difficulties of access and, on the other hand, to dependence of such decisionmaking on the personal characteristics and tastes of the individual occupying the central position, and the consequent difficulties in improving such situations. Thus, neglect of the study and improvement of one-person-centered high-level decisionmaking is illustrated in the lack of suitable research methods, conceptual frameworks, and instrumental-normative models in contemporary normal sciences. With the help of the novel approaches of policy sciences, one-person-centered high-level decisionmaking can be improved. Many conditions of better decisionmaking can be satisfied by a variety of means, some of which may often fit the desires of any particular decisionmaker; for example, information inputs, access of unconventional opinions, feedback from

past decisions, and alternative predictions can be provided by different channels, staff structures, mechanical devices, and communication media. This
multiplicity of useful arrangements provides sufficient elasticity to fit the
needs, tastes, preferences, and idiosyncrasies of most, if not all, top decisionmakers.

11. Development of politicians. The idea of developing the qualifications
of politicians is regarded as taboo in Western democratic societies. But this is
not justified. The qualifications of politicians can be improved within the
basic democratic tenets of free elections and must be improved so as to permit
the required new symbiosis between power and knowledge. Thus, for instance,
politicians need an appreciation of longer-range political, social, and technological trends, need capacities to determine megapolicies, and should be
able to critically handle complex policy analysis studies. One possible approach to the problem is to encourage entrance into politics of suitably qualified persons and to vary the rules of presentation of candidates to permit
better judgment by the voter. Other less radical proposals are to establish
policy sciences programs in schools where many future politicians study (such
as law schools), and to grant to elected politicians (e.g., members of a state
legislature) a sabbatical to be spent in self-developing activities, such as
studying and writing. Suitable policy sciences programs can be established
at universities and at special centers, for active politicians to spend their
sabbaticals in a productive and attractive way.

12. Advancement of citizen participation in public policymaking. Here,
modern technology may be very helpful by providing tools for much better
presentation of policy issues before the public (e.g., policy analyses of controversial issues on television and citizen involvement through active participation in policy games through cable television) and for more intense
participation of the public in decisionmaking (e.g., systematic opinion polling
with the help of home computer consoles).

13. Education of adults for more active roles in public policymaking. I just
mentioned the intensification of citizen participation in public policymaking
as one possible policy sciences' recommended improvement. But in order
for increasing citizen participation to constitute in fact an improvement,
changes in the quality of that participation are needed. At the very least are
needed more knowledge of policy problems, better understanding of the interrelations between different issues and various policies, and fuller realization
of the longer-range consequences of different alternatives. Also highly desirable are better value explication and sensitivity to value trade-offs, increased
propensities to innovate, and capacities to face uncertainty.

The slogan of "enlightened citizen" as a requisite of democracy has been
with us for too long to be taken seriously. Nevertheless, increasing demands

for citizen participation based on both ideological reasons and functional needs combine to make "citizen enlightenment" a hard necessity. Indeed, because of the growing complexity of policy issues, increased quality of citizen contributions to public policymaking is essential in order to preserve the present level of citizen participation in public policymaking. In other words, if the quality of citizen inputs into public policymaking remains as it is now, meritocracy may well become the only chance for survival. Therefore, building up the policy-contribution capacity of citizens is essential for continuous viability of democracy.

This is the challenge facing adult education from the point of view of public policymaking improvement. To meet this challenge, radical novadesign of adult education is required.

To concretize, let me mention these main policy-sciences-related directions for novadesign of adult education:

a. Policy sciences must develop new formats for presenting and analyzing public issues in the mass media of communication in ways conductive for the formation of informed individual opinions. For instance, policy issues should be presented in the form of policy analysis networks, with clear alternatives, explicit sensitivity analysis, uncertainty explication, and assumption visibility. Techniques are required for presentation of such programs on television in ways which combine audience appeal with improvement of citizen comprehensions of complex issues.

b. Training tools which are simultaneously interesting and beneficial must be developed. Such tools include, for instance, cases, projects, policy games, and individual policy-exploration programs. In particular, policy games and individual policy-exploration programs are very promising. Based on computers and brought to each house through cable television and home computer consoles, suitable games and policy-exploration programs should be able to combine education for better policymaking with inputs into on-going policymaking.[16]

c. Incentives for participation in policy-oriented educational activities must be provided. Hopefully, increased opportunities to participate in public policymaking together with the availability of clearly relevant learning opportunities will provide basic motivation. This may be the case all the more because of the possibility—illustrated by the proposed techniques—to combine the useful with the attractive. But additional incentives may be necessary. Competitive games and exercises may provide one set of incentives; public attention and dramatization may provide a second set of incentives. If this does not work out, reservation of some special opportunities to participate in

---

[16]E.g., see Stuart Umpbley, "Citizen Sampling Simulation: A Method for Involving the Public in Social Planning," *Policy Sciences,* 1, no. 3 (Fall 1970):361-375.

public policymaking (other than the basic rights of voting, expression of opinion, etc., reserved of course for all) for those who do undergo a set of learning activities might prove necessary in some circumstances in the longer run. However, adoption of suitable programs in schools—as soon discussed—should make such distasteful distinctions unnecessary.

These are only some illustrations which point out the possibility for re-design of education to serve, *inter alia,* the needs of increasing citizen partici-pation in public policymaking. This is a problem in need of much research and creativity.

14. Preparation of children for future roles in public policymaking. On a more fundamental level, preparation for increased participation in public policymaking must take place before maturation. The best location to prepare the citizen for increased policymaking roles is in school, when the necessary knowledge and capacities should be developed as a basic part of the equip-ment needed by every citizen in a modern democratic society.

The necessary knowledge to be conveyed and capacities to be developed at school include, among others, some knowledge and understanding of the social system and of social dynamics; a feel for alternative social futures; the ability to handle uncertainty and probabilities; basic skills in logic and seman-tics; an understanding of the elements of policy analysis and the capacity to handle problems with the help of policy analysis networks; a tolerance of ambiguity; an appreciation of the main concepts of social sciences, economics, and decision theory and their application to policy issues; and the ability to search for information on new problems and issues and absorb that informa-tion within one's frame of appreciation.

This is a formidable list which may look prohibitive, unless we bear in mind that no technical skills and professional knowledge are aimed at. Some familiarity with fundamental concepts, some appreciation of their use, and, most important of all, some skill in application of the knowledge and con-cepts to concrete issues as a main mode for making up one's mind—this is all that is aimed at.

Even so, this is an ambitious program which can only be approximated through far-reaching changes in school teaching. Much of the required knowl-edge and capacity should be developed through new approaches and novel teaching methods in traditional subjects. Thus, the study of history should include the history of policy issues, should be problem oriented, and should be supplemented by treatment of alternative futures. As another illustration, mathematics should be taught as a problem-solving approach, with emphasis on probability theory, Boolean algebra, and theory of games. Some new sub-jects also have to be added, devoted explicit to policy problems and policy analyses. In the new subjects and in the new contents of the traditional sub-jects, new teaching methods play a major role. Such new teaching methods include, for instance, gaming, computer interaction, and internships. Existing methods such as projects and essays can also be very useful, if adjusted.

All this depends on the development of policy sciences knowledge, which can serve as a basis for suitable teaching material and teaching methods. Here we meet another innovative facet of policy sciences: it should not constitute esoteric knowledge monopolized by a few initiated; instead, conscious and intense efforts must be made to transform at least the basics of policy sciences knowledge into forms that can be widely communicated to different policy-making actors, to the interested broad public, and even to school children.

Lest the impression created by these illustrative policy sciences implications for redesign of policymaking is that most of the burden of change lies on politics, the public, and education, let me add a word on implications for the scientific community which goes beyond the earlier-mentioned reorganization of research, teaching, and career patterns.

The emergence of policy sciences leads to many requirements not only for repatterning politics, education, and the like, but also for repatterning the contributions of scientists to policymaking. At present, many of the pronouncements of scientists on policy issues suffer from serious defects, as can easily be illustrated from the debates on issues such as pollution, the nuclear test ban, [17] and ABM. These defects are related to failure to distinguish—first of all, for oneself, and then in one's pronouncements—between highly reliable scientific facts within the professional competence of the actor; doubtful scientific facts within the area of competence of the actor; issues which belong to science, but are not within the competence of the actor; and issues which are outside the domain of science, such as judgment on values to be pursued and on value priorities, judgment on risks to be taken, and judgment on time preferences and metaphysical assumptions.

As a result of the failure to make these distinctions, recommendations are often presented "in the name of science" which are based on assumptions and preferences in large part outside the domain of competence of the actor.

Even with present very limited policy sciences knowledge this state of affairs is not only regrettable, but inexcusable: knowledge in policy analysis already available permits the presentation of recommendations by scientists in formats which clearly distinguish between the different bases of their recommendations. Such formats would enable those entitled to it—whether the elected politicians or the public at large—to exercise their judgment in respect to those issues not included within the area of competence of the recommending scientist; therefore these formats should be widely used even now. When

[17]Cf. Robert Gilpin, *American Scientists and Nuclear Weapons Policy* (Princeton: Princeton University Press, 1962); and Robert A. Levine, *The Arms Debate* (Cambridge, Mass.: Harvard University Press, 1963).

policy sciences is more developed, the demand upon scientists to be self-sophisticated and self-restrained in their contributions to policymaking will become more than a recommendation; it will become, I think, a moral absolute imperative, deviation from which may well destroy democracy, science, or both. Thus, the emergence of policy sciences will be accompanied by very strict and, in some respects, restrictive demands upon scientists, not less so, and perhaps even more so, than upon politicians and other actors in the public policymaking system.[18]

Conclusion

Policy sciences holds forth the hope of improving the most backward of all human institutions and habits—policymaking and decisionmaking. It constitutes a major attempt to assert and achieve a central role for rationality and intellectualism in human affairs and to increase by jumps the capacity of humanity to direct its futures. Important first steps to build up policy sciences are being attempted now. There is no assurance that these steps will lead anywhere and that the endeavor to build up policy sciences will succeed. But the expected benefits of policy sciences and—even more so—the gloomy results of failure to advance policy sciences make this endeavor one of the more critical challenges ever faced by science. It is also one of the most difficult challenges because of the intrinsic difficulties of the subject, because of the needed revolution in scientific paradigms, and because of the far-reaching and, in many respects, radical implications. Therefore, policy sciences needs and deserves all the help it can get, including, first of all, strong support and intense personal commitment from the scientific community and from the community of policy practitioners.

---

[18]Especially vexing are the moral issues facing policy scientists. While all knowledge can be used for *good* and for *bad,* the high potentials of policy sciences require special safeguards to reduce the probabilities of misuse. This problem is beyond the confines of this chapter, but I want explicity to point it out.

CHAPTER 3

Applications to NASA Long-Range Decisions[1]

COMMENTS

The application of policy sciences and its various components to specific problems, actual issues, and real systems is a complex activity, success in which constitutes a main criterion for evaluating the significance of policy sciences as an intellectual endeavor. Before policy sciences can be put to its ultimate test, it must be nurtured and developed, and this, at best, will take at least five to ten years. But the actual quality of policymaking is often so poor that even in its present embryonic phase policy sciences can make significant contributions to the improvement of policymaking reality.

Some such contributions will be indicated in following chapters. The present chapter does not present any detailed applications of policy sciences to actual policymaking, but it serves to introduce the idea of such applications by pointing out on a very generalized level some possible directions for policy sciences applications to a relatively high-quality activity, namely, to NASA long-range decisions.

Introduction

The purpose of this chapter is to indicate some potential uses of policy sciences as an intellectual and academic basis for advancing NASA's long-range decisions. While a number of concrete NASA decision issues are mentioned, this is only for the purposes of illustration, without any claims for substantive validity. The actual application of policy sciences to concrete NASA decision issues requires detailed data beyond the scope of this exploration.

The Nature and Scope of Policy Sciences

The concept of policy sciences was first proposed by Harold D. Lasswell in 1951, but only during the last few years has there been sufficient progress in the field to justify claims for the application of policy sciences to actual issues. Although still in its emerging stages, policy sciences can be characterized as follows:

---

[1]An earlier version of this chapter was published in S. H. Dole et al., *Establishment of a Long-Range Planning Capability* (Santa Monica, Calif. The Rand Corporation, RM-6151-NASA, September 1969), pp. 96-104.

1. Policy sciences constitutes a supradisciplinary effort focusing on public policymaking.

2. Policy sciences is based on the behavioral sciences and on analytical approaches; it also draws from decision theory, general systems theory, management sciences, and similar modern areas of study.

3. Fusing pure and applied research, policy sciences is concerned mainly with improving policymaking through use of systematic knowledge, structural rationality and organized creativity.

4. In common with all applied scientific knowledge, policy sciences is instrumental-normative in principle, in the sense that it is concerned with means and intermediate goals rather than absolute values. But it is also aware of the difficulties of achieving "value-free science" and tries to contribute to value choices by exploring value implications, consistencies, and costs and the behavioral foundations of value commitments.

5. Policy sciences emphasizes metapolicies (i.e., policies on policies), including policymaking modes and systems, and policy analysis and megapolicies (i.e., master policies). While the main test of policy sciences is better achievement of considered goals through more effective and efficient policies, policy sciences does not deal with discrete policy problems as such, but provides improved methods and knowledge for doing so.

On a more operational level, four of the main components of policy sciences seem to have direct relevance to NASA long-range decisions. These are (1) policy analysis, (2) megapolicies, (3) evaluation and feedback systems, and (4) policymaking systems redesign. I will discuss each of these components separately and describe its applications to NASA long-range decisions, but it is important to emphasize the close interrelationships among these components and the necessity for treating them as synergistically related modes. Indeed, one of the main contributions of policy sciences is in providing an integrative framework for approaches, methodologies, and techniques which tend to be isolated from one another in much of contemporary management sciences, systems analysis, and planning theory.

Policy Analysis

The design of policy analysis is based on applied decision theory and systems analysis. Systems analysis is often presented in the literature in terms of methods, techniques, and tools. This is natural because the tools and techniques are tangible, explainable, and easily communicated. But systems analysis is much more important as an approach, an orientation, and even—to use an apt phrase by Sir Geoffrey Vickers—a "frame of appreciation."

Reduced to its essentials, systems analysis is an effort to apply structured rationality to problems of choice. In particular, systems analysis in its pure form involve three main elements:

1. Looking at problems and alternatives in a broad way, trying to take account of many of the relevant variables and the probable results—that is, taking a "systems" view.

2. Searching for an optimal, or at least clearly preferable, solution among available alternatives, without being limited to incremental changes.

3. Explicitly and rationally identifying the preferable alternative (or alternatives) through comparison of expected results in terms of operational goals. This is done with the help of a large set of techniques, ranging from mathematical models to human gaming and from sensitivity analysis to canvassing of experts.

To this basic framework of systems analysis, policy analysis adds at least five main elements, each one of which has direct implications for NASA long-range decisions.

1. The first of these is penetration into underlying values and assumptions and exploration of relationships with higher-order and longer-range goals. For NASA long-range decisions, this element has the following illustrative applications:

a. Stronger efforts to deal explicitly with long-range NASA goals in close relationship with national goals research, as now being pursued, for instance, by the White House National Goals Research Staff.

b. Explicit recognition and elaboration of ideological bases of space explorations, for example, as part of human self-realization and as affecting long-range human destiny.

c. Exploration of unconventional secondary goals, such as potential cooperation with the Soviet Union.

d. Changes in goal determination methodology, such as explicit construction of alternative NASA futures, closer contacts with political decisionmakers during goals deliberations, and consideration of public opinions as input into goals deliberation.

e. Systematization of goals succession and goals diversification considerations, for example, in respect to accepting completely new domestic missions, such as design of new experimental towns or novel educational missions.

2. The second main element is explicit consideration of political variables. For NASA long-range decisions, this element has the following illustrative applications:

a. Continuous and systematic political feasibility analysis with respect to alternative NASA postures.

b. Research on design and evaluation of alternative political pathways for policy approval, resource allocation, and implementation.

c. Study of social and national power implications of alternative policies and relationships to coalition needs and possibilities.

3. The third element is strong emphasis on policy alternative innovation. For NASA long-range decisions, this involves the encouragement and partial institutionalization of the search for "wild" ideas and unconventional proposals, not only with respect to technical details, but on the basic mission and structure of NASA.

4. The fourth factor is use of behavioral sciences orientations and inputs. For NASA long-range decisions, this involves, for instance:

> a. Much more attention to the behavioral sciences aspects of NASA's activities, including, for instance, development of "sociology of space activities" as an integral part of NASA's self-perception.
>
> b. Consideration of deeper social and psychological implications of NASA's activities, for example, with respect to human self-image, disenchantment versus space romanticism, and religious movements.
>
> c. On a structural level, the building up of strong behavioral sciences components as a part of NASA's planning system.

5. The fifth element is institutional self-awareness, for instance, with respect to the following:

> a. The necessity for multiplicity and redundancy of analysis and analysis units.
>
> b. Early involvement of politicians, community leaders, and so on, in the analytical activities.
>
> c. Recognition of the limits of analysis as a perceptive set for relating human reality and aspirations, particularly to so complex an activity as space exploration.

Megapolicy

Megapolicies involve determining the postures, assumptions, and main guidelines to be followed by specific policies. They make up a kind of master policy, clearly distinct from detailed discrete policies, although these two pure types are on a continuum with many intermediate cases. Megapolicies are a principal focus of interest of policy sciences and comprise a main contribution to practice.

Megapolicies have a number of dimensions, which produce a multidimensional matrix with a large number of cells, representing the different mathematical combinations of various megapolicies. Setting aside the problems of calibrating the different dimensions, some of which are continuous and some of which have only a few points, there is the possibility of generating "mixed megapolicies," in which different megapolicies can be followed in various policy instances. Whether to follow a "pure" megapolicy combination (a real cell of the multidimensional matrix) or to adopt a megapolicy mix (selecting several different cells in accordance with a predetermined pattern, including a random patterns as one possibility) is, in itself, a main megapolicy decision. There are also empty cells, because of logical contradictions, and non-feasible cells, because of behavioral conflicts. When we consider all this together, the picture becomes very complex, but not prohibitively so. We can build up the main outlines of a megapolicy matrix, identify essential conditions for each megapolicy, and find out at least some of the criteria for preferring different megapolicy combinations under various conditions.

Again, let me proceed by presenting a few important megapolicy dimensions and illustrating their applicability to NASA long-range decisions, by adding a level of explicit policy consideration:

1. *Incremental-innovative.* This dimension deals with the choice among various degrees of policy changes (defined in terms of extent of change, scope of change, and time), ranging from small incremental changes in a few policy details over a long period of time to major, comprehensive and rapid policy innovations.

With respect to NASA, the issue here is how far to go in developing goals and techniques incrementally, or whether to make efforts at major jumps, such as nuclear-propelled vehicles, acceptance of major domestic missions as an integral part of NASA's work (possibly with a change of name), or strong efforts toward international cooperation in space.

2. *High risk-low risk.* This dimension involves the degree of risk to be accepted in policymaking. Here, the pure choices are between maximax, on the one hand, and maximin or minimax, on the other hand. Also involved are preferences between "average expected value" and "lottery value" and similar choice principles with different forms of risk parameters. Another very important element of this megapolicy is selecting the principles to be followed in comparing uncertainties. For NASA, this involves, for instance, major decisions on launch-readiness states that produce an increasing number of failures with lower costs for each operation versus high-cost "fail-safe" for each endeavor.

3. *Goal oriented-capability oriented.* This dimension involves choosing between policies more oriented toward building up capabilities for the future and policies more oriented towards achieving defined goals. Sometimes these orientations go together, as when a sequential learning path can be identified, but often quite different megapolicies are required for developing capabilities or achieving direct goals.

As applied to NASA, for instance, building up capabilities for obtaining new resources and enlisting continuing support for as-yet-undefined future goals ("building up goodwill") is a clear megapolicy choice, as, to some extent, are technical activities designed mainly as experiments versus discrete goal-oriented technical missions.

Evaluation and Feedback Systems[2]

The need for evaluation and feedback is universally recognized, sometimes selectively satisfied, but almost never dealt with systematically and
comprehensively.

To build up an evaluation and feedback system as a part of a long-range
decision system, it is necessary to construct a comprehensive evaluation
matrix dealing with all the important features of activities. In NASA, this may
involve the following components:

1. Evaluation not only with respect to technical missions, but in consideration of other short- and long-range goals. These include, for example,
personnel development, organizational capabilities, political support, civil
technological spinoffs, and broad social costs and benefits.

2. Evaluation in terms of explicit ascertainment criteria, appraisal standards, and time-and-area cutoff horizons. Thus, at NASA, elaboration of
alternative standards in terms of peer-group opinions, organizational aspirations, political expectations, and planned achievements is necessary.

3. Evaluation by special groups of people who are not involved in planning
or implementation, to reduce the dangers of a single point of view and similar
learning-distorting phenomena.

4. Special processes and structures for translating evaluations into recommendations for the future.

5. Specific attention to metaevaluation, that is, continual evaluation of
evaluation itself and periodic revision of the "NASA achievement indicators"
in the light of new internal and external developments.

Policymaking System Redesign

A principal characteristic of policy sciences is intense concern with policymaking system redesign. Indeed, it seems correct to say that no changes in
the modes of policymaking are feasible without changes in quite a number
of characteristics of the policymaking system as a whole. Applied to NASA
decisionmaking, the pertinent idea is that consideration of a long-range decision method is incomplete; rather, one should think about a long-range
decision system, of which the method is only one—and not necessarily the
dominant—dimension. Other dimensions of a long-range decision system
include the following:

1. The structure of the decision system, with issues such as in-house and
outside units; relationships among planners, high-level executives, and implementation groups; redundancy assurance; and involvement with external

[2]Usually I include evaluation and feedback in the metapolicy level, that is, policymaking
system redesign. In this case, because of its special importance for NASA, evaluation
and feedback systems receive separate treatment.

power and expertise centers (e.g., scientific and political advisory bodies in the decision system).

2. The staffing of the decision system, with issues such as multi-disciplinary background, staff development, rotation with other types of units, and exchanges with the outside.

3. Output stipulations about the forms of plans, such as annual and multiple year plans, detailed plans, contingency plans, general guidelines, operation plans, resources plans, and personnel plans.

4. Interlocking with operations, including communication and participation arrangements, tie-ins with current decisions (e.g., through a PPBS design), and relationships with crisis management.

5. Interlocking with evaluation and feedback.

6. Metadecisions, that is, continual evaluation of the decision system as such and redesign with a view to learning-feedback and internal or external changes.

Conclusions

The main thrust of policy sciences with respect to NASA long-range decisions lies in sensitization to some needs and possibilities that are beyond the usual domain of decision methodologies. These include a broader approach to analysis, with attention to political variables, innovation, and value contexts; specific consideration of overall megapolicies; and conscious redesign of a long-range decision system within its organizational environment.

With regard to some of these issues, all that policy sciences can do in its present stage of development is sensitization. For some of the other issues, more concrete recommendations can be derived through detailed application of policy sciences to actual NASA conditions and problems.

A recommendation justified by even as brief an exploration as this one is that NASA should establish in-house capabilities in policy sciences in order to study more closely its possible uses in long-range decisions, and in making improvements in decisionmaking in general. An in-house capability in policy sciences will also be able to utilize NASA experience to advance the stage of knowledge of policy sciences itself, which may produce a significant spinoff contribution from NASA to the domestic and international problem areas.

CHAPTER 4

Public Policymaking Improvement: A Proposed
Area for Study by Policy Research Organizations

COMMENTS

The one most essential requisite for the advancement of policy sciences is research. Present knowledge is completely insufficient for the needs of policy sciences: hence, initiation of research is a first step on the way to policy sciences. This research must meet the unique paradigms and specific needs of policy sciences, both in subjects and in methods. Therefore, policy research organizations must fulfill a main role in policy research. Because of their experience with policy-oriented studies and their mixed characteristics as academic-scientific institutions and as policy-oriented institutions, policy research organizations enjoy significant advantages for policy sciences research. But, in order to maximize their contribution to policy sciences, significant changes are required in the orientation of some of the studies going on in policy research organizations. In particular, much more attention must be paid to metapolicy research.

This chapter presents some proposals for metapolicy research. While mainly directed at policy research organizations, the proposals also fit—with some changes—policy sciences research at universities that want to establish centers, institutes, or departments in policy sciences.

Introduction

This chapter proposes policymaking improvement as a main focus for study by policy research organizations, an increasing number of which exist, especially in the United States. These policy research organizations constitute an important innovation in government, providing a main bridge between scientific knowledge and policymaking. But, at present, most studies by such policy research organizations deal with concrete policy issues and not with the improvement of policymaking as such. There are important exceptions, such as the development of systems analysis and PPBS at The Rand Corporation; studies on evaluation in the Federal Government at the Urban Institute; and proposals for a new Constitution for the United States prepared at the Center for the Study of Democratic Institutions. In general, however, policy research organizations do not pay sufficient attention to the improve-

32

ment of policymaking, as distinguished from the improvement of discrete policies on specific issues or issue-areas.

The preferable studies to be undertaken by any one policy research organization depend on its characteristics. But, in principle, this chapter proposes policymaking improvement as a main area for study by policy research organizations.

The Improvement of Public Policymaking

My proposal distinguishes between (*a*) improving specific policies and (*b*) improving policymaking, and suggests that policy research organizations develop a series of activities directed at the improvement of public policymaking on the level of metapolicy, in the sense of policymaking on how to make policy. This is an endeavor separate from improving individual cases of policymaking by analyzing select policy issues and recommending specific alternatives.

This distinction is not always a clear one, and admittedly a main avenue for arriving at policymaking improvements is through developing new methods and approaches, while working on concrete policy issues. Similarly, the main way to try out policymaking improvements is by applying them to concrete policy issues. Furthermore, there may be significant differences between different areas of policy—such as defense, foreign affairs, research and development, education, and race relations—casting doubts on the possibility of developing policymaking improvements of very broad applicability.

Nevertheless, it seems to me that there are sufficient common elements to public policymaking to permit study focused on its improvement, which can be expected to lead to recommendations and frameworks broad enough to enjoy a large domain of applicability and concrete enough to be operational in a significant way. This hope is well demonstrated by two main contributions to public policymaking of a policy research organization, namely, PPBS and systems analysis.

The difficulties met in efforts to apply these two important contributions to broader areas of public policymaking seem to demonstrate also the need for a more systematic approach to public policymaking improvement, if we want to achieve a significant impact: it seems that because of the interdependencies of many factors and variables in policymaking, the changing of single components may have no impact or even a negative one. What is needed is a systems approach to the improvement of public policymaking.

The main, closely interdependent dimensions of such an approach should include:

a. Policymaking-systems redesign: structures, personnel, and procedures.

b. Policy postures: megapolicies on uncertainty treatment, feasibility domains, values consideration, etc., basic to large policy spaces.

c. Policy assumptions on alternative states of the future in respect to main features shared by many policy issues, such as population, technology, international situations, culture, and economy.

d. Policymaking methods, such as policy analysis, attribute sets, and evaluation frameworks.

e. Policy instruments—law, economic incentives, education, and coercion.

f. Policymaking knowledge and professionals, including policy sciences as a distinct cluster of research, teaching, and training; policy analysts as a distinct profession; and behavioral sciences, or physical science, policy advisors in organizations—a role which requires specific preparation, training, and development.

This list is general, requiring, at least in part, transformation into a series of better-defined research subjects before its significance and feasibility can be evaluated. This can be done with the help of a set of criteria for selection of study subjects.

Criteria for Selection of Subjects for Study by Policy Research Organizations

To put matters as concisely as possible, it seems to me that the following criteria (not in any order of priority) should guide policy research organizations in selecting subjects for study:

1. The subject is relevant to important problems and issues faced by the country (and the world).

2. The subject is useful, in the sense of having some possible beneficial impacts on actual behavior in the country (and the world).

3. The policy research organization has a specific advantage, or a capacity to develop a specific advantage, in respect to that subject. This involves, it seems to me, *(a)* susceptibility of the problem to intellectual analysis and application of interdisciplinary knowledge, and *(b)* relevance of experience by the policy research organization.

4. Staff members are, or will be, intensely interested in the subject and eager to work on it.

5. The subject fits the mission of policy research organization, namely, pioneering (and sometimes "heresy") contributions to the improvement of societal direction through the systematic application of interdisciplinary knowledge, structured rationality, focused research, organized creativity, and trained intelligence under conditions of both professional independence and access to information and policymakers.

6. The subject will permit the policy research organization to learn and develop, keeping it increasingly in a state of intellectual excitement and creative tension.

7. Resources (general and specific) can be mobilized for study of the subject.

Now let me try to apply these criteria to the study of public policymaking improvement in general.

Application of the Criteria to the Study of Policymaking Improvement

1. Taking into account the growing importance of public policy in trying to deal with increasingly complex and risky problems, ways of improving public policymaking are certainly a subject very relevant to highly important problems faced by every country and the world as a whole. Indeed, improvements in public policymaking may result in many better policies on diverse subjects; therefore, improvements in public policymaking may constitute a highly efficient contribution to society's capacity to deal with its problems and issues.

2. More difficult is the problem of usefulness, in the sense of probability of real and beneficial impact. Here, I recognize the many barriers to changes in public policymaking. But my impression is that by preparing a large variety of useful suggestions for policymaking improvement, some of them will become politically feasible—whether thanks to crises, fashions, leadership, or the pressure of new problems and issues. Taking into account the very high significance of improvements in policymaking, even low probability of impacts produces a high "expected value" of work in this area. Keeping in mind the nature of human institutions and my view of most social decisions as a "history of stupidity," even some improvements in public policymaking and some min-avoidance must be regarded as far-reachng progress, well deserving missionary commitment and all-out intellectual efforts.

3. The subject matter of public policymaking improvement is a very broad one, including elements requiring different capacities, skills, and experiences. In respect to many of them, existing policy research organizations have relevant specific advantages. Thus, some experience in defense studies can be transferred. This pertains, for instance, to the applications of military Command and Control systems to one-person-focused decision situations, and of systems analysis to low-level (and, perhaps, some medium-level) social problems. In respect to such issues, much readjustment is needed to meet the more complex political, ideological, and structural characteristics of nonmilitary policymaking, but policy research experience is a specific advantage.

My impression is that the specific advantage of policy research organizations is, and potentially can be, much broader. Experienced "think tanks"—with a highly qualified, multidisciplinary professional staff and a strong tradition of applying interdisciplinary knowledge and systematic analysis to problems, and of combining innovative thinking with solid facts—are better equipped than other research or university units to face the novel aspects of public policymaking improvements, including most (though not all) of the elements involved.

I use the term *potentially* because we have here, in part, a latent capacity, full development of which requires conscious action in respect to the policy research organization itself. In other words, a decision to direct parts of a policy research organization's efforts toward systematic study of policy-making improvement is justified in terms of their specific advantage, but also requires intense efforts to build up that specific advantage, which, in part, is already highly developed and, in part, is a potential capacity which requires much nurturing and development.

4. I have met a number of staff members in a variety of policy research organizations who are highly interested in the improvement of public policy-making and some others who became interested when the subject was presented to them. Many others prefer to work on substantive policy issues, being less interested in policymaking as a systems process or regarding it as an inappropriate subject for direct study. I cannot estimate exactly the extent of interest in such a study area. A main purpose of initial attempts should be to stimulate interest in the study of policymaking improvement as a distinct endeavor and to help in crystallizing that interest into intent and action. The direction and extent of response will indicate to what extent this criteria is met.

5. While applying criteria 1, I already, in effect, discussed criteria 5—the importance of policymaking improvement for the betterment of public action.

It seems to me that the proposed area of study is distinguished by its potential importance in pushing the mission of policy research organizations as pioneers in better public policymaking. While interest in the study and improvement of public policies is very much in fashion and receives increasing attention, few studies adopt a broad approach to the improvement of policymaking. In many respects, initiation of systematic policymaking-improvement-oriented studies at policy research organizations would, therefore, be pioneering in the double sense of *(a)* being first and *(b)* guiding the activities of many others.

6. Internally, study of policymaking improvement should interact synergetically with other activities of policy research organizations, especially studies in substantive policy issues. Emphasis on policymaking improvement may provide an additional dimension for some of these studies and a comprehensive framework for others. Also, studies of policymaking improvement will provide opportunities and require further advancement of important aspects of study capacities, including, among others: stronger integration of behavioral sciences with analytical approaches, more explicit attention to methods, higher sensitivity to political and cultural variables, and more intense treatment of organizational phenomena.

7. In respect to the recruitment of money, my knowledge is inadequate to support even a guess. Nevertheless—looking around at the many "public affairs," "social planning," "social analysis," and similarly named programs

which receive considerable support—my hunch is that a policy research organization's proposal directed explicitly at policymaking-improvement elements should be able to get financial support. Certainly, foundations should be eager to support such studies, which are not very expensive and promise large spin-over benefits.

The problem of finding the required additional staff, especially in the more traditionally oriented disciplines (such as political science, history, and depth psychology), may be very difficult. Concentrating on bright young Ph.D.'s and providing them with accelerated learning opportunities at the policy research organizations themselves, may well be the preferable approach.

My conclusion is that by all criteria, public policymaking improvement is a very appropriate focus for study by policy research organizations. To further strengthen this conclusion, it is necessary to examine the proposal in comparison with other research alternatives competing for limited resources (especially, time of professional staff, attention, and resources recruitment). This cannot be done in the abstract. Instead, let me make one more argument: the study of public policymaking and its improvement is not only an appropriate subject for policy research organizations; it is more than that, being, in fact, an essential subject for study, if policy research organizations want their substantive policy studies to have a significant impact.

It is very difficult to have significant policy recommendations (other than low-level Operations Research or very specific and limited policy proposals) adopted within the relationships which can be expected to prevail in most contacts between a policy research organization and a public agency, unless the decisionmaking characteristics of the relevant public agencies are, first, well understood, and, second, themselves subjected to change. Hence, my claim that systematic study of policymaking improvement is not only worthy of attention by policy research organizations, but is essential for successful contributions by policy research organizations to substantive policies.

Some Operational Proposals

I shall try to concretize my proposal to engage in the study of public policy-making-improvement by presenting a few operational projects for study by policy research organizations. But let me emphasize the illustrative character of the following proposals: many perhaps better projects are excluded and some of the included ones may be inappropriate or not feasible.

Keeping that caveat in mind, here are some illustrations of potential projects in the area of policymaking improvement, presented in no conscious order of logic or priority:

1. *Improvement of one-person-centered high-level decisionmaking.* Even though of very high and sometimes critical importance, one-person-centered high-level decisionmaking is very neglected both by research and by improve-

ment attempts. This, in part, is due, on one hand, to difficulties of access, and, on the other hand, to dependence of such decisionmaking on the personal characteristics and taste of the individual occupying the central position and the consequent difficulties in improving such situations. Nevertheless, one-person-centered high-level decisionmaking can be improved, because many needs of better decisionmaking can be satisfied by a variety of means, some of which may often fit the desires of any particular decisionmaker. Thus, for example, information inputs, access of unconventional opinions, and feed-back from past decisions can be provided by different channels, staff struc-tures, mechanical devices, communication media, etc., which provide sufficient elasticity to fit arrangements to the needs, tastes, preferences, and idiosyncrasies of most, if not all, top decisionmakers.

2. *Civil crisis management*. Improvements in planning, analysis, and simi-lar future-oriented rationality-increasing decision methods will not do away with crises—whether nature-caused or brought about by human action and social conditions. Better crisis management is, therefore, important in the civil areas, particularly, perhaps, on the urban level.

3. *Organizational conditions of improved decisionmaking*. There is grow-ing awareness that efforts to improve decisionmaking in organizations through methods such as analysis and Planning-Programing-Budgeting can-not succeed unless accompanied by broader organizational changes. A study of the organizational conditions for increasing the utility of new decision methods would thus constitute a natural, and, indeed, essential, continuation of work in developing methods such as Planning-Programing-Budgeting.

4. *Social-environmental indicators*. The present idea of social indicators is one of the more interesting innovations in respect to social policymaking, though theoretic or applied achievements are, as yet, very few. Especially challenging are the problems of developing integrated sets of social-environ-ment indicators, which could provide systematic and reliable data on the impact of human action on the environment and perhaps some insights on the feedback of changes of the environment on human society. Work on environmental indicators in particular may well tie in with widespread inter-ests in the physical aspects of environmental pollution. A first step could be compilation of a national (and international) "pollution atlas," which would, at least, pinpoint urgent needs for additional data.

5. *Social policy experimentation*. Improvement of social policymaking urgently requires methods permitting accelerated learning through social policy experiment designs. This involves, first, frameworks and methods for evaluation of the consequences of social policies, and then more explicit setups for experimenting with different alternatives. Work on the methodo-logical issues of such social policy experimentation might thus be an im-portant project.

6. *Methods and material for teaching analysis on a professional level.* A requirement shared by all efforts to introduce more and better analysis into government is the need for better trained analysts. Indeed, there are a growing number of graduate and special (such as mid-career) university programs in analysis, public policy, social policy analysis, policy planning, public affairs, and so on, but most of these are still in an experimental stage. What is needed is a new approach to the teaching of analysis, whether as a special concentration or as part of graduate training in behavioral sciences, architecture, city planning, law, and other more traditional professional subjects. Such a new approach must deal with curriculum, teaching methods (e.g., projects), degree requirements (e.g., a thesis on an applied project in a policy research organization), teaching material (e.g., texts and cases), and preparation of teachers.

A survey of the contemporary teaching of analysis, an analysis of the problems of teaching analysis, proposals of curricula and teaching methods, and preparation of some of the required teaching material—these are among the components of a project in this area.

7. *Methods and material for developing the capacity of school pupils to understand and analyze social problems.* Quite different from the last suggestion, but similar in some respects, is the proposal to work on methods and material to be used at primary and secondary school levels to encourage the analytical capacities of pupils, especially in respect to social problems. Though this suggestion is often stamped "essential" for enlightened democracy, very little has been done to prepare children for their role in the "problem-solver state."[1] Progress in the teaching of mathematics, physical sciences, and, to a lesser extent, behavioral sciences has not been accompanied by advances in the early conveyance of an analytic frame of mind and of ability to face intellectually and emotionally the complexities of social problems.

8. *Policymaking case studies.* All improvement of policymaking depends on understanding policymaking reality. Preparation of teaching material for training in policy analysis also often requires empirical studies—for cases, realistic projects, and fact-based texts. Therefore, it is necessary to engage also in much behavioral study of policymaking—especially in the form of cases where a policy research organization enjoys specific advantages in familiarity with the material and access. Especially worthwhile may be current study of on-going policymaking, particularly under innovative conditions; for example, a "participant observation" study of the position occupied by Henry Kissinger and his staff, may provide insights of extreme importance

---

[1] See Philip M. Burgess and James A. Robinson, "Political Science Games and the Problem-Solver State," in Sarane S. Boocock and E. O. Schild, eds., *Simulation Games in Learning* (Beverly Hills, Calif.: Sage Pub., 1968), pp. 243-249.

for better understanding of the higher-level policymaking system and possibilities for its redesign, if such a study is feasible.

A quite different illustration related to widespread interests in public health and pollution, in addition to policymaking, is the problems posed by the findings on the health hazards of smoking. The identical and limited nature of the problem may make it a perfect instance for a cross-national study of policymaking, which may contribute much to sharpening one's sensitivity to the basic characteristics of any particular national policymaking system.

9. *Policy analysis methods and frameworks.* Certainly, a main interest for study—whether as part of a broader program in policymaking improvement or by itself—is policy analysis methods and frameworks. Essentially, what we are interested in here is a broadening of the methods of systems analysis to deal better with more complex and intensely "political" problems. This includes, for instance, explicit treatment of political feasibility, both as an independent and as a dependent variable; broader consideration of values and ideologies; treatment of diffuse social attributes; and consideration of time and uncertainty when concepts such as "discount rate" and "expected value" do not apply.

10. *Sets of policy-relevant assumptions.* All policymaking is based on large varieties of assumptions, usually tacit, unexamined, oversimplified, and inconsistent (between policy and policy and, often, also in respect to single policies; sometimes such inconsistency may be desirable as a hedge against uncertainty, but there seems to be too much of it). Therefore, development of sets of explicit assumptions in more sophisticated form (multiple, open-ended, carefully defined margins of validity, etc.) can constitute an important contribution to policymaking (if the dangers of such assumptions being too static and being taken too seriously are avoided).

For some policy research organizations, it may be particularly suitable to try to develop sets of alternative states-of-the-future—international, national, sectoral, regional, and city-wide, as may best fit in with other projects. Despite the increasing interest in futures studies (which is becoming too much of a fashionable subject) and some significant relevant work, only insufficiently sophisticated and comprehensive sets of alternative futures are available; these are, therefore, urgently needed, the better to sensitize policymakers to the dimensions of the future.

11. *Policy issues taxonomies.* Some morphological ordering of policy issues in the form of multi-dimensional topological structuring of policy spaces is urgently needed to systematize policy research. Interdependencies between different policy issues and various policy studies could both be clarified through policy issues taxonomies. A consideration of the present mixup of terms such as *urban problems, environmental problems,* and *race problems* and of contemporary tendencies to neglect interdependencies between differ-

ent problem areas does indicate the potential benefits of systematic policy issues taxonomies. At the same time, the provisional and tentative nature of any problem taxonomy should be emphasized: constant changes in issue formulation reflect social change, while improvements in issue formulation are a main avenue towards better policymaking. Therefore, any policy issue taxonomy must be regarded as an aid to dynamic reformulations and not as a rigid conceptual framework into which reality is to be fitted.

12. *Policy-instrument analysis.* The usual order of policy formulation is to start with problems and try to deal with them with the help of policy instruments traditionally used in that problem area. But, in reality, policy instruments mainly developed in respect to one policy issue may be very useful for other policy issues, as illustrated by the utilization of negative income tax in social welfare policies. Therefore, systematic study of main policy instruments and of their characteristics independent from specific policy issues may be very useful by providing sets of instruments, the utility of which, in respect to specific policy issues under detailed conditions, can then be investigated separately. Focused study of policy instruments such as law, various forms of economic incentives and economic structural arrangement, coercion, communication, education, and so on, is, therefore, a very promising area for policymaking improvement studies.

13. *Comprehensive policymaking system studies.* In many respects the most challenging type of policymaking-improvement oriented study—which includes as elements most of the other proposed study subjects—is comprehensive policymaking system studies. In such studies, a broad (thought not all-inclusive) policymaking system is analyzed and evaluated and sets of interrelated improvement proposals are developed. Such studies can be part of a broader country, state, or city study or can be a separate study—of a territory and/or of a policy area (e.g., foreign policymaking, federal Research and Development policymaking, educational policymaking in a state).

Such comprehensive policymaking system studies would serve as a climax for policymaking improvement studies. To engage successfully in such studies, many other elements of policymaking improvement studies—such as are presented in this chapter—must achieve a high level of development. In such comprehensive policymaking system studies, real pioneering innovations may be arrived at and tried out. Indeed, it seems to me that development of a capacity for such studies and the undertaking of such studies should be the longer-range goals of work by policy research organizations along the lines proposed in this chapter. But even before such comprehensive studies can be undertaken, less ambitious work on the proposed lines is, I think, very worthwhile.

Futures and their roles in policymaking constitute a main focus for policy sciences. How better to identify and elaborate alternative futures, how better to take such alternative futures into account in policy-making, and how to improve the handling in policymaking of unavoidable and far-reaching uncertainty about the future—these are some key issues which cross-cut sub-divisions in policy sciences between policy analysis, megapolicies, and metapolicies, and which, therefore, deserve special attention. This part explores some of these issues. The first chapter provides a broad overview of futures studies as seen from a policy sciences perspective. The second chapter examines changes in government which are required for better taking into account of futures. The third and fourth chapters go into the substance of policy-oriented futures studies, providing designs and methods for the study of alternative domestic political futures and for the predicition of political feasibility.

PART II

A Policy Sciences View of Futures Studies

CHAPTER 5

Alternative Futures and Present Action[1]

COMMENTS

Adjustment of futures studies to the needs of better policymaking is the subject of this chapter. In order to usefully interrelate alternative futures to present action—via better policymaking—futures studies must (1) be salient to policy issues, (2) be credible, (3) be useable in policymaking, and (4) be in demand for use in policymaking. These requirements involve significant changes in futures studies, presented in this chapter in the form of fifteen guidelines for policy-oriented futures studies.

Introduction

This section looks on futures studies[2] from the point of view of policy sciences. From this point of view, improvement of policymaking is regarded as the main mission of futures studies. The policy sciences approach to futures studies does not exclude other goals for futures studies, such as satisfaction of human curiosity, and recognized socio-psychological functions of futures studies, such as reassurance and catharsis. But I do think that the main mission of futures studies should be to contribute to the improvement of policymaking and that the main test of futures studies should be its impacts on policymaking.

Looking at futures studies as a policy-oriented activity does not imply a narrow conception of its nature and scope. Contributions to policymaking can, and often should, be long-range and indirect, for instance, by broadening the frames of appreciation of policymakers and by sensitizing them to long-range perspectives. Nevertheless, looking at futures studies as contributions to policymaking does have operational implications for the contents and

[1]This chapter is based on a presentation at the International Future Research Conference, Kyoto, Japan, April 10-16, 1970. Earlier versions were published in *Technological Forecasting and Social Change* 2, no. 1 (1971): 3-16, and in the Council of Europe Series of Studies on Long Range Planning and Forecasting, study no. 2 (1970).

[2]I prefer the term *futures studies* to *futurology, futuristics, technological forecasting*, etc., to avoid both popularized connotations and technological annotations. The plural *futures* is used to avoid possible mix-ups with studies done in the future, and also to emphasize that we should always study different alternative futures.

methodology of futures studies and for the organization of futures studies as an area of study and teaching, and as a profession.

This paper is devoted to examination of some implications of a policy sciences view for the contents and methodologies of futures studies. Implications of a policy sciences view for the organization of futures studies as a discipline and as a profession and for the structural aspects of the interface between futures studies and the policymaking system will also be indicated, but the latter is left for more detailed treatment in the next chapter.

The main conclusions arrived at in this chapter are presented in the form of guidelines for policy-oriented futures studies. These guidelines do apply to policy-oriented futures studies in the aggregation, but not necessarily to each and every single study. They are intended to provide heuristic aids rather than detailed instructions. But hopefully they should serve to concretize and operationalize the concept of policy-oriented futures studies and help in their advancement.

Main Issues

A tacit assumption widely shared by futures scholars seems to be that *good* futures studies are sure to reach policymakers and to influence policymaking. This assumption is the only reasonable explanation one can offer for the surprising neglect by most futures scholars of the issues of interface between futures studies and real-life policymaking.[3] But this tacit assumption is a fallacy, because of the strength of various barriers which operate against consideration of futures studies in policymaking. Some of these barriers face all consideration of the future dimensions, whether presented in the form of futures studies, longer-range plans, or pressures by future-oriented interest groups.[4] Some barriers are more specifically active in respect to explicit futures studies. Together, the different kinds of barriers constitute a very strong insulation of policymaking from futures studies, virtually assuring zero impact by the latter unless the barriers are broken down or a way around them is laid.

[3]This generalization does not apply to policy analysts who move from concern with policy issues to interest in futures studies. Thus, the works of Herman Kahn include many bridges between policymaking and futures studies, within a broad framework of policy sciences. Especially important is the statement by Kahn and Wiener of the objectives of future-oriented policy research:

"1. To stimulate and stretch the imagination and improve the perspective.

2. To clarify, define, name, expound, and argue major issues.

3. To design and study alternative policy 'packages' and contexts.

4. To create propaedeutic and heuristic expositions, methodologies, paradigms, and frameworks.

In a broad sense of the term, four main clusters of barriers to the consideration of futures studies in policymaking can be identified: (1) futures studies are not salient to policy issues; (2) futures studies are not credible; (3) futures studies are difficult to use; and (4) futures studies are undesirable. We will present our policy sciences view of futures studies through examination of the issues created by these four clusters of barriers and of ways to overcome these barriers, at least in part.

The Saliency of Futures Studies for Policy Issues

The requirements of saliency of futures studies for policy issues include (*a*) linkage between the present and alternative futures and (*b*) relevance of futures studies for actual or potential present main policy concerns. These requirements are a matter of degree, because long-range perspectives may be salient for policymaking by sensitizing and educating frames of appreciation of policymakers, a function the importance of which I have already mentioned. But for more concrete and specific inputs of futures studies into policymaking, more than this is required. And even broader frame-of-appreciation-shaping futures studies must have some linkage to the present and some relevance to potential policy concerns.

The requirement of linkage involves some explicit casual relations between present decisions and the considered futures. When the future is independent from present decisions or when the dependencies of the future on present decisions are too vague and too uncertain to permit identification of some connecting links with some degree of assurance—then that future is not salient for present policymaking.

This is an especially important requisite because of the not uncommon

5. To improve intellectual communication and cooperation, particularly by the use of historical analogies, scenarios, metaphors, analytic models, precise concepts, and suitable language.

6. To increase the ability to identify new patterns and crises and to understand their character and significance.

7. To furnish specific knowledge and to generate and document conclusions, recommendations, and suggestions.

8. To clarify currently realistic policy choices, with emphasis on those that retain efficiency and flexibility over a broad range of contingencies.

9. To improve the 'administrative' ability of decisionmakers and their staffs to react appropriately to the new and unfamiliar." Herman Kahn and Anthony J. Wiener. *The Year 2000: A Framework for Speculation on the Next Thirty-Three Years* (New York: Macmillan Company, 1967), pp. 398-99. For detailed discussion, see pp. 399-409.

⁴The sudden upsurge of pollution concerns illustrates a related tendency. When pressures are strong enough to break through the barriers against consideration of futures, then positive feedback may occur and result in one-sided exaggerations, instead of the needed systematic consideration of different alternative futures in relation to complex policy choices.

tendency of futures studies (and of much long-range planning) to "escape into the future" by designing various states of the future which cannot be related to the present in any meaningful way. I do not wish to imply that Utopias or anti-Utopias are unimportant; they may fulfill very important social functions, including long-range effects on policymaking through changes in public values and mass opinions. But such functions of dreaming about the future must be kept distinct from the roles of futures studies in respect to policymaking. Invention of new futures is an essential element of policy-oriented futures studies, as are more "scientific" forecasts and predictions. But for policy purposes it is essential that the various normative futures as well as the forecasted futures be relatable to present decisions—either as goals to be aimed at or as expected states to be taken into account.

Relationships between the present and alternative futures can be presented in various forms, such as time curves, bands and envelope curves; scenarios; or verbal descriptions. Usually the relationship will be stochastic rather than deterministic, and conjectural rather than provable. But some time series of situations and developments which show possible relations of the alternative futures to present actions are essential (with one exception which I will soon discuss). This is the justification of the following first guideline for policy-oriented futures study:

Guideline 1. Policy-oriented futures study should explicitly relate alternative futures to present decisions (subject to Guideline 4). Some dependence of an alternative future on present action is essential for policy saliency, but insufficient by itself. If alternative futures deal with phenomena which are uninteresting in terms of the values of contemporary and emerging policymaking systems, or are trivial in terms of those values, then these alternative futures have little saliency for policymaking. This is the case even when clear links do connect these alternative futures with present decisions. Therefore, policy saliency requires that futures study should be relevant to policy concerns, actual or potential. *Actual* policy concerns are perceived issues which are recognized in policymaking, never mind if more or less adequately. *Potential* policy concerns are issues which are relevant to policy values and would be a matter of policy concern if more information were available and/or if policymaking were of higher quality. In some respects a most important possible contribution of futures studies to policy improvement is the transformation of potential policy concerns into actual policy concerns through what is called the "lookout"[5] function. This lookout function involves identification of possible developments which require present action, to inhibit undesirable futures and support desirable futures. Therefore:

[5]See Robert Jungk, "Outline for a European Look Out Institution," proposal prepared for the Council of Europe, June 1967.

Guideline 2. Policy-oriented futures study should deal with matters of actual or potential policy concern.

Guideline 3. Policy-oriented futures study should engage in "lookout," that is, identification if important policy issues, which are not recognized as such because of unawareness of possible developments and their significance. Here we reach an important exception to guideline 1, which required that policy-oriented futures studies should explicitly relate alternative futures to present decisions. When a very important policy concern is involved, the null hypothesis is also very important. Showing that the alternative futures of a very important subject of concern are quite independent from present decisions is very helpful, because it should lead to one of three conclusions (or a mix between them):

a. To initiate intense search for new ideas and new knowledge which may provide links between present decisions and alternative futures, and thus permit efforts to influence the latter; this may involve new alternative futures, new links between present decisions and given alternative futures, or a combination of both.

b. To broaden the concept of "present decisions" by transforming factors which are regarded for ideological, political, or technological reasons as beyond resetting[6] into policy instruments which are objects for present decisions.

c. To reformulate our policy concerns so as to drop for the time being efforts to influence the involved future developments and, instead, adjust to the uncontrollable.

These are extremely important conclusions with many action implications other than resignation. Even dropping efforts to influence some expected developments because we see no way by present actions to do so should at least be accompanied by careful monitoring of actual developments in order to increase probabilities of successful adjustment to the unavoidable and to be ready for interference if and when some futures-influencing instruments are discovered or invented.

The more that unavoidable futures look undesirable and the harder that adjustment to them is expected to be, the more should the search for possible links between present action and those futures be pressed. Indeed, when the unavoidable futures look very bad, we may well be ready to reconsider basic social institutions, which are usually far beyond the domain of directed change. Even basic values may in this way come to be regarded as policy

[6]I am using the terms *setting* and *resetting* of policy instruments instead of *manipulation,* which has a negative annotation.

instruments which have to be changed to handle critical future developments.[7]
Therefore:

Guideline 4. Policy-oriented futures studies should deal with alternative futures of critical issues even when no relation of alternative futures to present decisions can be identified. This is a convenient point to introduce the related, but distinct, problem of alternative value futures as an essential content of policy-oriented futures studies. Policymaking involves choice and every choice involves value judgment. This value judgment is a political function, requiring value-sensitivity testing of futures studies (to be discussed later). But acceptance of the right of whomever we regard as the legitimate political institutions to engage in dominating value judgment does not imply that this value judgment should not and cannot be improved. Improvement of political value judgement is an urgent necessity to be met in part by futures studies. Explicit examination of alternative futures and their links to the present is a main aid, by bringing out the future consequences of present value judgments. An additional and very important contribution by futures studies in this matter can be the exploration of alternative futures of values.

Basically, preference of one alternative future over others should be determined by values relevant to the time of realization of those alternative futures. Only if (*a*) values in the relevant futures are expected to be equal to present values, and (*b*) this is regarded as a satisfactory state of affairs, should present values serve as criteria for shaping the future. True, determination of desirable values for the future is a matter of judgment beyond the domain of futures studies. But such judgment should (*a*) be based on explication of the implications for the future of alternative value judgment, and (*b*) be considered within the context of future values as a whole. For that, it is necessary (*a*) to consider present value judgments as future-shaping variables, and (*b*) to explore alternative value futures. The first need should be met as part of the examination of the relation between present decisions and alternative futures. The second need can only be met by directing futures study to explorations of alternative value futures[8] (which themselves can be influenced through policy instruments which are influenced by value choices). Therefore:

Guideline 5. Policy-oriented futures studies should engage in exploration of alternative value futures. Closely related to guidelines 2, 3, 4, and 5, but going beyond them, is the requirement for exploration of alternative compre-

[7]E.g., see Hasan Ozbekhan, "Toward a General Theory of Planning," in Erich Jantsch, ed., *Perspectives of Planning* (Paris: OECD, 1969); and Erich Jantsch, "From Forecasting and Planning to Policy Sciences," *Policy Sciences* 1, no. 1 (Spring 1970): 31–43.

[8]On this problem, see Fred C. Iklé, "Can Social Predictions Be Evaluated?" *Daedalus*, Summer 1967, pp. 733-58; Kurt Baier and Nicholas Rascher, eds, *Value and the Future* (New York: Free Press, 1969); and Irena Tavirs, "Futurology and the Problems of Values," *International Social Science Journal* XXI, no. 4 (1969): 574-84.

hensive futures. To provide a broad perspective for policymaking and to increase the probability that guidelines 2, 3, 4, and 5 will indeed be satisfied, it is necessary to go beyond alternative futures of specific social institutions.[9] What are also urgently needed are alternative comprehensive futures, dealing at least in outlines with all social institutions, including the futures of politics and policymaking. Such alternative comprehensive futures are, in addition, essential as a framework for cross-impact analysis between the futures of different social institutions—a subject to which I will return later on. Therefore:

Guideline 6. Policy-oriented futures studies should try to develop alternative comprehensive futures covering all social institutions at least in outline.

The Credibility of Futures Studies

In order for futures studies to serve as useful inputs into policymaking, they should be of high quality. This is too obvious a requirement to deserve more than *pro forma* notice, were it not for the related, but distinct, requirement for clear signs permitting discrimination between higher-quality and lower-quality futures studies.

The rapid proliferation of futuristic and futurological studies and their popularity, bordering on fashionability, makes visible quality recognition signals all the more urgent. Being bombarded by hundreds of predictions and prophesies, the policymaking units cannot take any of them into serious consideration without sifting the few high-quality studies from the many nonsense hallucinations. In the absence of visible quality signs, policies will tend to quote futures studies fitting earlier arrived-at conclusions or to be influenced by a mass of futures studies operating as a pressure variable, either directly or through the mediation of the mass media of communication, independent of the quality of those studies.

Because of the propensity of the mass media to play up more extreme predictions, there may even be a negative correlation between the quality of futures studies and their impact on policymaking through pressure and opinion-shaping. Therefore, visible signs of quality are all the more essential.

The difficulties of this problem are compounded by the propensity of some highly qualified and well-known scientists to make pronouncements on futures which are completely outside their competence. Such pronouncements get much attention, thanks to the prestige of their originators, with little opportunity for examination of the bases of the predictions and for careful evaluation of their reliability.

Unless signs for identification of high-quality futures studies are developed very soon, the whole idea of futures studies may become quite discredited

---

[9]I am using the term *social institutions* in its broadest sense, including also socially relevant features of physical reality.

and the chances to use futures studies for policymaking improvement may be lost for many years. Therefore:

Guideline 7. Policy-oriented futures studies must not only be of high quality, but should be recognizable as of high quality. How this guideline can be realized is a difficult question, which brings us to the issues of professionalization and institutionalization of futures studies. Every professionalization and institutionalization of futures studies involves risks, such as some inhibition of wild ideas and some loss of contributions by brilliant individuals who do not fit institutional and professional standards. Nevertheless, for purposes of policy uses of futures studies, the benefits of some institutionalization and professionalization may well outweigh the costs. Efforts must be made to continue and provide scope for wild ideas and unconventional brilliance—both within and outside policy-oriented futures studies institutions and professions. But some institutionalization and professionalization seem essential, so that institutional affiliation and professional identification can serve as at least some indication of quality of a futures study.

This chapter, as already stated, does not go into the details of institutionalization and professionalization of futures studies and their problems. But institutionalization and professionalization are highly important for building up systematic methodological and substantive knowledge in futures studies and for training of scholars and professionals in futures studies, in addition to the needs of credibility and of transformability (which is discussed in the next section). Therefore, I want to make here one main point, to indicate some directions for thinking on this subject: In order to develop and progress, futures studies seem to need novel institutional and professional arrangements and designs, different from traditional university structures on one hand and traditional governmental structures on the other hand. In particular, policy-oriented futures studies are in many respects an integral part of policy sciences and should develop within the context of policy sciences, with due care being taken to avoid repression of some more imaginative elements of futures studies by some more rational elements of other parts of policy sciences (such as analytical approaches). This point of view has implications for the concrete forms of institutionalization and professionalization of futures studies, but the details go beyond the domain of this chapter.

The needs for and some characteristics of desirable policy-oriented futures studies institutionalization and professionalization stand out sharper when we examine the problems of transformability of futures studies into policymaking inputs.

The Transformability of Futures Studies into Policymaking Inputs

When policy-salient and credible futures studies are available, then the issue of transformability of these studies into policy inputs is reached. This involves designing futures studies to fit the characteristics of policymaking as a process and of policymaking units as structures, organizations, roles, and human individuals. But not only the design of futures studies is involved. The transformation of futures studies into policymaking inputs necessitates also redesign of the policymaking system, to increase its capacity to receive inputs from futures studies and to absorb them into the policymaking process.

A useful framework for considering the issues of transformability of futures studies into policymaking inputs is the compartment model of general systems theory.[10] In such a compartment model, futures studies and policymaking are considered as two interacting systems, which are both subsystems of society. The formulation of the problem is then how to optimize (not maximize, because too much interrelations are undesirable, for instance, by undermining the autonomy of futures studies, which is essential for high quality) the interactions between futures studies and policymaking. Such optimization will involve changes in the futures studies system, changes in the policymaking system, and changes in the direct and indirect intertransport channels between these two systems.

Enough knowledge is available for attempts to utilize such a general-systems-theory compartment model in respect to other problems of the uses of knowledge for better policymaking (e.g., see chapter 14). But I think that available experience and knowledge regarding futures studies and their possible contributions to policymaking are too meager to justify analysis in terms of such a model. Also, a general-systems compartment model of futures studies and policymaking requires close examination of the policymaking system, leading far beyond the domain of futures studies into policy sciences as a whole.[11] I, therefore, forego at present such systematic approaches, preferring to proceed more tentatively and to limit my observations and recommendations to some of the features of transformability of futures studies into policymaking inputs. But I will return to some implications of a general-systems compartment model when I reach my concluding guideline 15, which will deal with the need for broad study of the interface between futures studies and policymaking.

Having tried to provide at least some glimpses of a broad view of the issue

[10]For compartment theory see A. Rescigno, "Synthesis for Multicompartment Biological Models," *Biochem. Biophys. Acta.* 37 (1960): 463-68; and A. Rescigno and G. Serge, *Drug and Tracer Kinetics* (Waltham, Mass.: Blaisdell, 1966).

[11]An alternative systematic approach is to take some models of preferable policymaking and to examine in respect to each phase the potential contributions of futures studies and the characteristics of futures studies (methodology, contents, media, structures, personnel, etc.) necessary for realizing this potential. The interested reader can try this approach with my "optimal model of public policymaking" in Yehezkel Dror, *Public Policymaking Reexamined* (San Francisco: Chandler, 1968), pp. 163-96.

of transformability of futures studies into policymaking inputs, I will take up a few concrete items belonging to this issue, namely, those dealing with the required characteristics of futures studies.

A minimum requirement of transformability of futures studies into policy-making inputs involves communication and access:

Guideline 8. Policy-oriented futures studies must be easy to communicate to policymakers and should meet the conditions of access to policymaking. The concrete conditions of communication and access depend on the characteristics of discrete policymaking systems. For instance, in different countries policymakers are able to absorb futures studies of different levels of abstractness; and in various countries channels such as party machinery or mass media can fulfill different roles in promoting communication and access of futures studies to policymakers. Universal requirements include reduction and unification of technical jargons;[12] existence of structural communication and access channels, together with sufficient looseness to prevent monopolization and to permit unconventional communication and access; and futures studies formats which are easy to use for policymaking.

The question of futures studies formats leads us directly into the most difficult and most important issues of transformability of futures studies into policymaking inputs, and indeed into the whole cluster of issues involved in a policy sciences view of futures study. These concern the relations between futures studies methodology and the needs of policymaking.

Up till now we have discussed the implications of a policy orientation for futures studies in respect to subjects of study, quality of study, communicability of study, and access to policymakers. These all are important issues, dealing with the external characteristics of futures studies and their general direction. But up till now we have not taken up the implications of a policy orientation for the main methodological issues of futures studies. The critical question is, after a suitable subject is selected, with good arrangements for certification of quality and for satisfactory contact with the policymaking system—what are the requirements which a policy orientation imposes on the methodology of futures studies (in addition to the already discussed need to look for links between the present and alternative futures)?

Limiting the discussion to more general requirements and to the role of futures studies as a professional activity (in distinction, for instance, from advocacy roles of individual futures scholars), the following guideline seems essential:

Guideline 9. Policy-oriented futures studies should adjust their methodologies to the needs of policymaking. This includes, in particular: (a) an "alterna-

---

[12]The need to unify futures studies terminology is clearly brought out by Francois Hetman, *The Language of Forecasting* (Paris: Futuribles, 1969). This book also illustrates possibilities to explain futures studies concepts in a communicable way.

tive futures" approach; *(b) attention to cross-impacts and interdependencies between the alternative futures of different social institutions; (c) emphasis on identification of future-shaping variables; (d) examination of future developments influencing identity of variables which can serve as future policy instruments; and (e) strict explication of assumptions and rigorous value-sensitivity testing.* Let me examine these recommendations one by one.

a. An "alternative futures" approach. Policymaking involves choice between alternatives. A main potential contribution of futures studies to better policymaking is in enlarging the choice perspective through presentation of alternative futures (and, in accordance with guideline 1, links between these alternative futures and the present). The tendencies of organizations to ignore uncertainty and repress ambiguity—which we will discuss in the next section—reinforce the requisite that futures studies should emphasize the multiple possibilities of the future. Therefore, even in the unusual case where one future has a very high probability, policy-oriented futures studies should always present alternative futures—including some low-probability and even "counter-factual" ones. This should be done whenever possible with explicit estimates of probabilities of the different alternative futures (including admission of ignorance of probabilities when appropriate), with emphasis on the dependence of the probability estimates on explicated assumptions and on specified contingencies.

b. Attention to cross-impacts and interdependencies. The fragmented structure of much of policymaking and the somewhat greater bureaucratic and political feasibility of coordination in respect to future events rather than on current activities make it all the more necessary for futures studies to emphasize the intense interdependencies of alternative futures of different social institutions. Therefore, cross-impacts should be emphasized in policy-oriented futures studies. This has an implication going beyond methodology to the subject matter of policy-oriented futures studies. To provide a broad framework for examination of cross-impacts, comprehensive alternative futures are necessary—as pointed out in guideline 6.

c. Emphasis on identification of future-shaping variables. Cross-impact analysis is required to point out possible first-, second-, and third-order consequences. But these same cross-impacts also enlarge the set of future-shaping variables, by adding external variables to those which are endogenous to a delimited social institution. Policymaking is mainly concerned with attempts to increase the objective probability of desirable futures. Therefore, policymaking depends on identification of future-shaping variables. This is, I think, the one most important potential contribution of futures studies to improved policymaking: to increase the set of identified future-shaping variables, including both variables endogenous to specific social institutions and variables exogenous to specific institutions but influencing these institutions through cross-impacts. This guideline is closely affiliated with guideline 1, because we are mainly looking for future-shaping variables existing in the present. But a policy orientation is also interested in identification of future-shaping variables which themselves exist in the future—which leads us to the next item of guideline 9.

d. Examination of future developments influencing future policy variables. Policymaking is a continuous process of trying to shape the future. In addition to decisions on present actions, it also includes both present decisions on action in the future, especially in the "planning" mode of policymaking, and decisions on the timing of policymaking itself, that is, what issues to defer for decision in the future. Therefore, identification of policy instruments located in the future, which can be used to influence the further future, is important for good policymaking. Policy instruments are future-shaping variables which can be reset. The identification of the subset of present policy instruments from the set of presently available future-shaping variables is outside the domain of futures study, though futures study is relevant by continuing the search for future-shaping variables till some policy instruments can be identified or the conclusion must be reached that none can be found or invented. But the identification of future policy instruments depends mainly on futures studies: what is needed, in addition to identification of future-shaping variables which themselves are located in the future, are predictions of the features which will permit a future-shaping variable to serve as a policy instrument. These features include the feasibility and costs of resetting the variables.

I want to emphasize the multidimensionality of "feasibility and costs." Easiest (though not easy) to deal with are technological and economic feasibility and cost. Often more important and always more difficult to predict are organizational and especially political feasibility and costs. But however difficult, the future political feasibility of using various future-shaping variables as policy instruments must be investigated in order for futures studies to supply essential policymaking-improvement inputs. I regard this as so important and so neglected, as to warrant emphasis as a separate guideline:

Guideline 10. Policy-oriented futures study should explicitly deal with alternative futures of political feasibility. I will discuss the conceptual and methodological problems of the study of the futures of political feasibility in chapter 8. Here let me make only two comments: (1) the study of the futures of political feasibility is closely tied in with the study of alternative domestic political futures, and (2) alternative political feasibility futures, like alternative domestic political futures as a whole, are a legitimate and indeed essential area for directed change. Therefore, very important for long-range improvement of policymaking is identification of present policy variables for influencing future policy variables through changing future political feasibility. (The same applies also—as is more recognized—to future technological and economic feasibility.)

e. Explication of assumptions and value-sensitivity testing. This requisite is on a somewhat different level, cross-cutting all others. But it is a very important one for transformability of futures study findings into policymaking inputs. I tend to go a step further and regard this requisite as a categorical imperative to be followed by futures studies as a whole; certainly, for futures studies as a policymaking-oriented endeavor the necessity to explicate assumptions and values is a very strict one.

The reasons for this requisite are both moral and functional. Morally, the political components of society are entitled to exercise value judgments and to determine extrascientific assumptions. This is the case, independent from regime, as long as one regards the politicians as legitimate. When one regards the politicians as illegitimate, the whole idea of their contributing to policy-making gets a different slant and may be inappropriate.[13] But when one works for, let us say, some counter-establishment group—again, the right to judge values and make extrascientific assumptions belongs to whomever one regards as the legitimate decisionmakers, whether it is an individual leader or a general assembly of all members.

Functionally, nonexplication of values and of assumptions impairs the utility of futures studies as an aid for better policymaking by repressing alternatives and inhibiting explicit consideration of values and assumptions. Also, hidden value judgment will often be perceived or at least sensed by policymakers and reduce their readiness to utilize futures studies—in my opinion, rightly so.

Were it not for the widespread tendency of many so-called futures studies to accept blindly very simplistic value judgments and naive assumptions, it would be unnecessary to belabor what is a quite simple point. But a brief look at many (though not all) futures studies reveals many hidden value judgments and assumption selections. For instance, this basic methodological weakness is deeply rooted in city planning and its modern derivatives—which take the form of "the future of the city" and "the future of environment" images.

These various methodological implications of a policy sciences view of futures studies lead to a variety of methods, techniques, and tools which are necessary for their implementation. Discussion of these methods, techniques,

---

[13]We meet here the major moral issues facing all knowledge: how to encourage utilization of knowledge for good and inhibit its uses for bad. When discussing the professionalization of futures studies, safeguards against misuse of the knowledge should be considered. But I believe the solution, if one exists, can lie only in the individual moral responsibility of the man of knowledge as a conscious human being. This problem too is shared by futures studies with policy sciences as a whole.

Ventures in Policy Sciences

and tools goes beyond the confines of this chapter. But I want at least to point out the necessity to work out formats for futures study findings which serve to present these findings in a concise form which fits into policymaking. Such formats for policy-oriented futures studies findings should serve also to improve communication and access of futures studies to policymaking. Therefore:

Guideline 11. Policy-oriented futures studies require formats permitting concise presentation of findings for policymaking uses. These formats, in turn, have feedbacks for methods, techniques, tools, and even methodologies.[14] Therefore, they require careful attention and constant revision.[15]

The Desirability of Futures Studies to the Policymaking System

A distinct series of issues is posed by the undesirability of futures studies to various components of the policymaking system. The main reasons for such undesirability include possible disagreement by components of the policymaking system with policy implications of futures studies, and discord between the orientations and frames of appreciation of futures studies and those of regular organizational and political behavior.

To be more specific, let me mention some of the factors which make future-oriented studies undesirable to many of the policymaking system components:

1. A clear formulation of alternative futures tied in with present future-shaping variables imposes choices, which may be often nonincremental and which may require explicit judgment between competing values. Such choices may endanger essential coalitions, in which case it may indeed be preferable to ignore those futures studies. But more often, what is endangered are not essential coalition needs but more conventional habit-supported ones. Also endangered are widespread political and organizational propensities to "satisfice" and to limit choices to incremental change.

2. A clear formulation of alternative futures tied in with present future-shaping variables draws attention to future issues and future problems and

[14]Especially important are methodologies which integrate futures studies with policymaking. PPBS involves some such intentions, but must be supplemented with stronger future-oriented elements. "Planning" is conceptually the process by which longer-range views of the future should be locked in with present decisions. But contemporary public planning theory is ill-equipped for this task. Modern corporation planning sometimes better handles integration of futures studies with present decisions, but the problems of corporation planning are much simpler than those of public planning. On corporation planning see the comprehensive work of George A. Steiner, *Top Management Planning* (New York: Macmillan, 1969); no comparable study of public planning is available.

[15]For illustrations of attempts to build up policy-oriented methodologies, including some formats for putting futures studies findings into a form suitable to serve as policymaking inputs, see Wayne Wilcox, "Forecasting Asian Strategic Environments for National Security Decisionmaking: A Report and a Method" (Santa Monica, Calif.: The Rand Corporation, RM-6154-PR, June 1970); and table 7-5, pp. 81-2.

requires explicit judgment on the preferability of different situations dispersed in the time stream. This contradicts the usual propensity of politics and organizations to be concerned only with the present or, at best, with short-range futures—a propensity strongly reinforced by institutions such as annual budgeting and frequent elections. (These institutions may be justified by other and more important reasons, but their negative impacts on consideration of the future should be explicitly recognized, so that some counter-measures can be designed.)

3. A clear formulation of alternative futures tied in with present future-shaping variables involves recognition of uncertainty, ambiguity, stochastic relationships, and ignorance. This contradicts strong political and organizational tendencies to ignore uncertainty, repress ambiguity, assume determinism, and make believe that one knows what one is doing.

4. A clear formulation of alternative futures tied in with present future-shaping variables involves, if they are used in policymaking, formalization of expectations. These expectations, even if stochastically formulated, can serve as objective standards for appraising achievements, thus hindering political and organizational tendencies for postdecisional dissonance reduction through presentation as goals of whatever in fact happens. At the same time, good futures studies also inhibit selection of unrealistic goals, thus disturbing arbitrary goal setting as a device of support recruitment. More justified is rejection of good futures studies because they may inhibit messianic activities which are directed at very improbable goals, but which nevertheless sometimes succeed if intensely believed in and accepted with total commitment.

5. The acceptance of futures studies as an important input into policymaking involves changes in the power structure of the policymaking system, with transfer of some power to futures scholars. Such transfers of power are always resisted, all the more so when the recipients are an unknown and suspect group, composed of intellectuals, new types of scientists, and new professionals.

To generalize, good policy-oriented futures studies constitute a pressure for different policymaking and are therefore unwelcome by most of contemporary policymaking reality. The trouble here is that the better and the more convincing futures studies are, the more they will endanger established policymaking patterns and the more they will usually be undesired.

Correction of this state of affairs requires redesign and even novadesign (that is, design anew) of significant parts of the policymaking system. This is a subject belonging to policy sciences as a whole, in which futures studies can play only a minor, though important, part. What futures studies should do is to study the political and organizational conditions of desirability of futures studies to the policymaking system, an issue which merges well with study of the policymaking features necessary for good communication and access by futures study, and with study of the policymaking features necessary for capacity to put futures studies to good use for policymaking improvement. Therefore:

Guideline 12. Policy-oriented futures study should participate, as part of policy sciences, in the study of policymaking system characteristics necessary and sufficient to make good futures studies desired and used by the policymaking system.

Guideline 13. In particular, policy-oriented futures study should explore alternative policymaking system futures and identify relevant future-shaping variables.

Conclusion

In this chapter, I have already hinted several times that good futures studies and their utilization by the policymaking system may not always be an un-mixed blessing. Disruption of essential coalitions and endangering of necessary consensus are problems, though futures studies are far away from the point of overinfluences. What really worries me is the danger of self-fulfilling prophecies and the possible discouragement of human efforts to achieve the nearly impossible. For instance, the establishment of the State of Israel is a dramatic demonstration of the ability of human devotion sometimes to realize what every good and policy-oriented futures study would have regarded sixty and probably even thirty years ago as impossible. I think we should be very much aware of the human significance of such cases, even if they are extremely scarce. Therefore, self-awareness of the limitations and dangers of future studies should be an important part of policy-oriented futures studies.

Guideline 14. Policy-oriented futures studies should carefully study the limitations and dangers (such as self-realizing effects) of even excellent futures studies as an input into policymaking, explicate these limitations and dangers, and search for ways to reduce them. On a more general level, I hope this chapter at least serves to bring out some complexities of the problems of relations between policy-oriented futures studies and policymaking. Whether one agrees with my main findings and recommendations or not, I think an inescapable conclusion is that policy-oriented futures studies should be very self-conscious and pay much attention to their interface with policymaking. This can best be done by closely relating policy-oriented futures studies to policy sciences as a whole.

Guideline 15. Policy-oriented futures studies should pay much attention to the problems of interface between futures studies and policymaking, including relevant features of the policymaking system; of the communication channels between the policymaking system and futures studies; and of the content, methodology, organization, and structure of futures studies themselves. This should be done in close relation with policy sciences as a whole.

CHAPTER 6

Consideration of Futures in Government[1]

COMMENTS

Changes in futures studies so as to fit the needs of policymaking, as proposed in chapter 5, are necessary but insufficient for increased contributions of futures studies to better policymaking. Better use of improved futures studies in policymaking requires also changes in the policymaking system, including changes in government—in structure, personnel, and decision patterns. This chapter explores such necessary changes, looking at the utilization of futures studies for better policymaking on the level of involved innovations of meta-policy.

Introduction

Public policymakers have necessarily been interested in the future since the early beginnings of organized society, relying on a variety of religious, mystic, intuitive, and random devices for making hard decisions in the face of uncertainty.[2] Therefore, interest in the future as such constitutes no innovation in government. What is new are three converging and interrelated developments concerning the future dimensions of governmental activities—namely, (1) increasing necessity to take the future into account; (2) increasing possibility to take the future better into account; and (3) increasing demands to meet the needs of the future.

The creation and accelerating aggravation of very difficult public problems as a result of contemporary social and scientific developments make it essential to foresee main problems and try to deal with them well in advance, when more alternatives are available and lead time permits careful search for preferable solutions. Developments in knowledge of how to foresee probable alternative futures and how better to absorb unavoidable and extensive uncertainty by making our present actions less sensitive to unpredictable futures, do improve possibilities (relative to the rate of change) to take the future better into account. And contemporary ideologies, which combine revolutions

[1]An earlier version of this chapter under the name "The Role of Futures in Government" was first published in *Futures* 1, no. 1 (September 1968): 40-46.

[2]See Richard Lewinsohn, *Science, Prophecy and Prediction* (New York: Harper, 1961); and F. N. David, *Games, Gods and Gambling* (New York: Hafner, 1962).

61

in expectations with belief in organized public activity, do generate widespread demands to meet the needs of the future (though, often, only of the near future) by and through governmental action.

Needs, possibilities, and demands are essential requisites for better consideration of the future in governmental activities. But they are not sufficient to assure it. Given the present structures, staffing, and modes of operation of contemporary governments—Democratic and Communist, modern and modernizing alike—there is little probability that needs, possibilities, and demands can result in more than lip service to futures and, perhaps, some marginal improvements in their consideration. Governmental activities are necessarily shaped by all the characteristics of governmental systems. Therefore, the more far-reaching a change we desire in the processes of government, the more far-reaching changes are required in a variety of characteristics of the governmental system. Better consideration of the future—this is a far-reaching change in the specifications of governmental processes which (despite much talk on planning) tend to follow the precepts of "muddling through" and incremental change. Under more stable conditions and with less knowledge available, incremental change was often an optimal strategy, which still has much to recommend itself. But even if we adopt, as I think we should, a nonpresumptuous stance and limit our present ambition to achieving some more weight to futures in contemporary governmental policies, this constitutes a demand for far-reaching changes in contemporary governmental practices, requiring significant changes in some critical variables of the governmental system. In addition, changes are needed in the contents, quality, and structure of futures studies—but this is a separate subject dealt with in chapter 5.

The main required changes in government are related to the need for a new public policymaking culture, in which futures are an integral part of the appreciative framework of governmental decisions and activities. Increasing public awareness of the importance of futures for contemporary activities is an essential element of strengthening the role of futures in policymaking culture—hence, the applied political significance of public associations in futuristics, of treatment of alternative futures in mass media of communication, and of various efforts to build bridges between the work of professional futures scholars and public awareness. But changes in appreciative frameworks are difficult to achieve and diffuse cultural influences cannot be relied upon to transform deep-rooted habits of Establishments fast enough.

As sufficient transformations of public policymaking culture are difficult and time-consuming and are insufficient unless accompanied by organizational arrangements, we must also try to increase the weight of futures in government through suitable changes in a number of organizational variables of the governmental system. In particular, changes are required in (a) the structure of government, (*b*) the staffing of government, and (*c*) the patterns of governmental decisionmaking.

Futures and Governmental Structure

The basic rationale of governmental structure is division of labor. The division of labor in government is generally constructed along the dimensions of substance, type of activities, and bases of interest. Different units look after various goals and subgoals, interests and subinterests, functions and subfunctions; and a few, often weak units try to achieve some coordination, integration, and comprehensive view. This structural principle followed by all governments ignores another main dimension of activities and goals, namely, the time dimension. It is not enough to distinguish between goals of public security and increasing Gross National Product, the interests of farmers and universities, and the services of telecommunication and health—with, at best, some minor efforts to coordinate these goals, interests, and services. These goals, interests, and services also must be considered and synchronized within the stream of time, with due consideration of the mission of taking care of the future within the overall division of labor in the governmental structure.

A standard reaction to this problem is to claim that every unit in charge of any goal or activity is also in charge of the time dimension of that goal or activity: considering the future is regarded as an integral part of the job of every unit.

The trouble with this easy answer is that it does not work. One main reason why it is ineffective to combine responsibility for the present and for the future in one and the same unit is the well-documented tendency for the pressure of present problems to drive the future out of consideration, in the sense that limited resources of time and energy tend to be first allocated to more immediate needs. Another main reason for the incompatability of dealing with the present and with the future in one and the same unit is the differences in temperament, knowledge, methods, and orientations which are required for successfully looking after the present, on one hand, and trying to consider the future, on the other hand.

The conclusion that due consideration of futures in government requires special units who have, so to speak, a vested interest in the future seems to me inescapable. Only by giving to futures an organizational expression in government can the pressures of the present be somewhat contained and can the special qualities needed for more successfully dealing with the future be assured.

But setting up special "Lookout Institutes," however useful, is insufficient for solving our problem. In order for units looking after the future to serve as a countervailing force against governmental myopic fixations on the present (and, often, on the past), these units must, in part, be closely involved in current governmental decisionmaking and implementation activities.

Here, a basic organizational dilemma is faced: In order to increase the impact of futures on present policies and operations (and, often, in order to survive), special futures organizations must be in close contact with current activities and feed their specific contributions into the on-going governmental processes. But being closely involved with the present may subject the futures organizations to temptations of building up their power by becoming involved in present problems and adjusting their views of the future to present expediences.[3]

There is no short and easy solution to this dilemma. Much depends on the professional qualities and moral character of the personnel staffing both the special units "representing" the future and regular governmental organizations. Much also depends on changes in patterns of governmental decisionmaking. To these two subjects I will turn soon. On the structural level, the main emerging recommendation is to try to achieve a balance between very pure study of futures without influence on government and compromised study of futures with some influence on government, through positive redundance. A set of units working on futures dispersed throughout government and, indeed, throughout the societal direction system is needed. This set of units should range from special independent lookout institutes to single futures experts in departmental planning and policy analysis units.

I would like, in particular, to stress the need for small units dealing with futures within regular governmental organizations. Only by becoming part of the "insiders" and participating in the internal processes of the various governmental agencies, can futures achieve the desired pervasive influence on current decisonmaking.[4] Similarly, because of the multiple and differentiated structure of government, dispersal throughout the governmental system (including, also, the legislature) and throughout the societal directive system (including, for instance, parties, trade unions, and interest organiza-

---

[3]The history of the National Goals Research Staff in the United States, from its establishment in the White House on July 13, 1969, until it submitted its first report in July 1970, illustrates both the potential contributions and the limitations of central units put in charge of looking out after the future. The Presidential announcement of the establishment of the National Goals Research Staff is an excellent statement on the needs to consider futures in government. The announcement is reproduced, *inter alia,* in *Technological Forecasting* 1, no. 2 (Fall 1969), pp. 217–220.

[4]For details, see Yehezkel Dror, "Some Requisites of Organizations' Better Taking into Account the Future," in Robert Jungk and Johan Galtung, ed., *Mankind 2000* (Oslo: Norwegian Universities Press, 1968), pp. 286-90.

tions) is necessary.[5] Such a network of units working on futures will also be very helpful in strengthening coordination and integration within government by serving as an additional interunit connective tissue and by providing compatible views of alternative futures as common frameworks for contemporary action by different units.

Futures and Government Personnel

Efforts to set up futures units in government and to integrate them with regular governmental operations demonstrate at once the validity of my own substitution for Malthus' law, which I aphoristically call the First Dror Law, namely:

While the difficulties and dangers of problems tend to increase at a geometric rate, the number of persons qualified to deal with these problems tends to increase at an arithmetic rate.

Having many people talking about the future, a few doing serious work on futures, and single individuals making brilliant contributions to building up futures studies is one thing. Establishing a formalized role of "futures analyst" in government is a completely different thing, requiring types of professional training not available at present.

Here, the close dependence of introducing new types of knowledge into government on the structure of academic teaching and professional training is paramount. Having failed, after extensive search, to locate a university equipped to accept an assistant of mine for advanced study and for writing a Ph.D. in prediction methods and treatment of the future, I may be somewhat oversensitive to the issue.[6] But recognition of these areas as a distinct field of specialization and professional training on the graduate and postgraduate level seems to be an essential requisite for advancing the consideration of futures in government (as well as in industry and, indeed, in all types of societal institutions).

This does not imply that futures studies can or should be a discipline of its own; neither available knowledge nor the eclectic nature of futures studies justifies such a proposal at present or in the foreseeable future. The best place for training professional staff for work on futures is in conjunction with policy sciences and its various subdisciplines — with special care being taken to

---

[5] Our analysis applies *mutatis mutandis* to one quite widespread type of futures-dealing organizations, namely, planning units. A main reason for the failure of many national planning units is the basic weakness of the dichotomy between a single central planning unit and regular ministries. Diffusion of planning throughout the governmental structure, and the societal direction system, is essential for a viable solution.

[6] I first made this statement in 1968. A renewed search in 1970 resulted in the same negative findings.

develop also the more imaginative and creative capacities essential for work on futures. But some arrangements for university professional training in futures studies is essential.

To repeat, preparation of adequately trained professionals to staff the proposed special units dealing with futures is an essential requisite for successful establishment of such units. Establishing new positions without good personnel to fill them is an empty gesture which may well have a negative boomerang effect, bringing the idea of futures in government into bad repute. One can and should proceed by stages, setting up one or two central units for futures studies with available self-trained personnel as soon as possible. But a concerted effort to develop relevant professional training is necessary for the establishment of the required set of special units to become feasible. The training of suitable professional manpower will also press in the direction of institutionalization of looking-after-the-future as a recognized role in government (and industry) because of the demand of such manpower for suitable positions. Thus, the training of professionals in futures studies is, in all respects, a most important step in advancing the consideration of futures in governments, and in society as a whole.

The preparation of a specialized staff for working on futures is essential, but not sufficient. In order to permit communication between present governmental staff and the new professionals and to enable utilization of new knowledge and novel orientations in actual governmental processes, the present staff must understand the basics of the new knowledge and have some feeling for the new orientations. Attention to futures studies in the training of senior civil servants, both pre-entry and post-entry, is, therefore, essential. The emphasis in such training should be on the importance of consideration of futures for present policymaking and decisionmaking, on the ability to face and absorb the increased subjective uncertainty associated with efforts to take the future more and better into account, and on basic knowledge of the main tools of futures studies, to evaluate correctly potential contributions and their limitations.

Similarly needed are study days and courses for politicians, in addition to intense attention to futures studies in more systematic activities to train politicians (see chapter 20). It is also important to try to influence politicians through the mass media of communication and to get individual politicians interested in futures through personal contacts, informal meetings, and other means.

The role of the citizen as an increasingly important partner in some types of policymaking makes broader efforts to educate the public on futures also very important. Here, care must be taken to avoid the propensity toward sensationalism and to preserve the distinction between "mass movements" and futures studies. The mass media of communication bear a great responsibility in educating the citizen in correctly considering alternative futures when adopting positions on current issues.[7]

Making policymakers aware of futures and of the importance of futures for present policies is critical for useful consideration of futures in government. It is part and parcel of the broader problem of achieving a new symbiosis between knowledge and power within rapidly changing societies. Hopefully, the other proposed measures in respect to structure, personnel, and decision pattern will also — together with more interest in futures by the public — influence policymakers.

Patterns of Governmental Decisionmaking

Changes in structure and personnel are not aims by themselves; they are but tools to increase the consideration of futures in present governmental action — which, again, is an instrumental specification designed to increase the achievement of longer-range human objectives. When we reach patterns of governmental decisionmaking, we are approaching the crux of the problem of futures and government, as the main aim of the proposed changes in structure and personnel is to influence governmental decisionmaking.

In addition to shaping the decisionmaking process by varying its structural and personal determinants, it is also necessary to improve the consideration of futures in government by direct shaping of decisionmaking patterns. This can be done by introducing a number of patterns for decisionmaking, designed to reinforce consideration of alternative futures. Here, we have a number of possibilities, such as the following:

—Establishing a planning-programing-budgeting system (PPBS, in short), whereby current issues are tied in to longer-range problems and goals.
—Providing all government units with shared alternative assumptions on basic alternative states of the future (population, technology, economy, international relations, etc.) and requiring them to take these assumptions explicitly into account when analyzing present policy alternatives.
—Requiring all main departments to prepare alternative scenarios of the future implications of their present activities up to a given time horizon.
—Requiring all staff papers, position papers, White Papers, and the like, to deal explicitly with the future implications of their recommendations and to subject their recommendations to sensitivity testing in terms of alternative futures.

[7]An interesting illustration is provided by the *Governor's Commission on the Year 2000* in the State of Hawaii. During 1969 and 1970, this Commission fulfilled very important functions in increasing consideration of the future in government. In addition to preparing an important report, its activities involved extensive educational activities—including lectures before a joint session of the Legislature, the establishment of broad task forces, and the holding of widely attended conferences.

This is a technical area, further exploration of which requires detailed examination of organizational decision processes and of modern decision theories, which would carry us beyond the scope of this chapter. Particularly important are modern developments in policy sciences as a whole, which provide ideas for reshaping focal governmental policymaking patterns so as to take the future somewhat more into account. It is sufficient for our present purposes to note these possibilities and their importance.

Conclusion

Tackling the problem of futures and government requires a variety of changes in government, academic institutions, and public interests. Considerable leeway is provided by the range of required changes for adjusting orders of priority and modes of realization to actual conditions, to availability of resources, and to specific political feasibility constraints. Different combinations of various changes can be useful under distinct conditions. But there is a critical mass, below which single improvements will be corroded by the inertia of day-to-day governmental routine.

The various proposed changes which have been discussed are largely interdependent and mutually supportive. Only when an aggregative effect can be achieved, is there a good probability that together a number of changes may move government toward more and better consideration of futures, and even then, only if external conditions are favorable. In particular, public interest in futures and advances of knowledge in futures studies are essential, as is the successful management of current problems—which otherwise become acute crises, necessarily displacing futures and pushing them into the background.

CHAPTER 7

Alternative Domestic Political Futures (ADPF)[1]

COMMENTS

Politics is a main subject of policy sciences, both for behavioral study and for improvement. Recognition and explication of this fact and of its manifold implications may well prove to become an important contribution of policy sciences to the behavioral sciences and other disciplines. In respect to futures studies, the requirement to study alternative domestic political futures constitutes a main conclusion from a policy sciences view.

The study of politics from the perspective of policy sciences requires novel research designs and methods. This is illustrated in the present chapter, which explores research needs and research designs for the study of alternative domestic political futures. Particularly relevant is the attempt to connect the study of ADPF to policy sciences, by providing a scheme for transforming the findings of the study of ADPF into policy instruments.

Introduction

An amazing omission in contemporary work in futures studies is the lack of consideration of alternative futures[2] of domestic politics. Much attention is being devoted to alternative futures of the international system, of science and technology, of population and food production, of energy, of the economy, of cities, and even of families and communities. Some attention is also being paid to a few subcomponents of domestic politics, such as the executive and bureaucracy. Thus, the American Academy of Arts and Sciences Commission

---

[1] This paper is based on a presentation at the International Future Research Conference, Kyoto, Japan, April 10-16, 1970. An earlier version was published in *Futures* 2, no. 4 (December 1970): 302-311.

[2] I am using the term *alternative futures* as "hypothetical states of the future which are regarded as having some probability of realization." *Counterfactual alternative futures* are "hypothetical states of the future which are regarded as having no probability of realization." In respect to both alternative futures and counterfactual alternative futures, the time span to which they refer must be explicated.

For related uses of the term *alternative futures,* see Bertrand de Jouvenel, *The Art of Conjecture* (New York: Basic Books, 1967), pp. 18-19; and Herman Kahn, "The Alternative World Futures Approach," in Morton A. Kaplan, ed., *New Approaches to International Relations* (New York: St. Martin's Press, 1968), pp. 83-136.

on the Year 2000 did deal with the future of government, but only in a narrow sense of the term. It put forward many stimulating ideas relevant to ADPF, but the latter were not directly and comprehensively dealt with. Alternative futures of domestic politics are seldom mentioned and nearly never studied in a systematic and comprehensive way.[3]

The neglect of ADPF, despite the rapidly growing interest in futures studies and their proliferation, cannot be explained as an accidental oversight. The necessity of studying ADPF has been clearly recognized and intensely urged by the founder of modern futures studies, Bertrand de Jouvenel.[4] Nevertheless, despite the strong influence of de Jouvenel on other aspects of modern futures studies, his call for studies of ADPF remains a voice in the wilderness. Most of the exceptions are studies on different aspects of ADPF published in *Analyse et Prevision.*

As with all real phenomena, the reasons for this neglect in contemporary futures studies can be explained on the basis of study and research. But no sociology of futures study being as yet available, all explanations of the present state of the art are necessarily subjective guesses with uncertain validity and reliability. While thus recognizing the tentative character and doubtful basis of any proposition, it would seem that every explanation for the neglect of ADPF should include the following interrelated elements:

1. The taboo nature of the subject and its high sensitivity to ideologies and values. These hinder the study of ADPF both by introducing biases into the work of individual scholars and by imposing strict external constraints on whether such studies and their possible conclusions are allowed, and on the availability of resources for their support.

2. A disdain for politics by some of the leading futurists and forecasters, who therefore dislike the subject and neglect it; who delude themselves with the belief that domestic politics is a transitory phenomenon, sure to wither away with developments in science and technology; or who believe that domestic politics is a dependent variable which will adjust to changes in other dimensions of society. Especially striking is the tendency of some futures scholars and futures planners who come from physical sciences to try to skirt around domestic politics by proposing new institutions for "inventing values," which, through some hidden and unspecified *deus ex*

---

[3]We must distinguish between the implicit and explicit predictive elements, which are an integral part of every scientific study, and longer-range exploration of futures as a specific endeavor. As pointed out correctly by Benjamin Akzin, political science includes many conjectures on the future. But disjointed conjectures on a multiplicity of different facets of politics and society do not add up to systematic alternative futures of politics. See Benjamin Akzin, "On Conjecture in Political Science," *Political Studies* 14, no. 1 (February 1960): 1-14.

[4]De Jouvenel, op. cit. [in footnote 2]; and Bertrand de Jouvenel, "Political Science and Prevision," *American Political Science Review* 59, no. 1 (March 1965): 29-38.

machina mass movements, will completely transform domestic politics into an implementation tool of "rationally created" and "carefully selected" new values and goals.[5]

3. The scarcity of methods suitable for identifying, considering, elaborating, and evaluating ADPF. One illustration is the currently increasingly used Delphi Method;[6] who are the experts on domestic politics with whom to run a Delphi study? Politicians, political correspondents, political scientists—all have something to say on the subject, but they cannot be considered experts on domestic politics in the same sense as a top physicist is an expert in physics. The difficulty is not a technical one, but relates to the very nature of domestic politics, which make ADPF much harder to treat than the futures of technology and even of international relations.

4. The critical importance of domestic politics in respect to studying alternative futures in every area. This additional factor adds an important explanation for the neglect of ADPF in contemporary futures studies, and at the same time also constitutes an overriding reason for intense efforts towards its study.

Domestic politics is so important a variable in constraining and directing all aspects of society, that the cross-impacts of ADPF constitute significant and even dominant factors in the shaping of alternative futures for every subject matter. This means that the exploration of ADPF must impose strict constraints on work on various alternative futures. Therefore, a degree of intellectual discipline is required from explorers of the future, who must, at the very least, explain the naïve *status quo* of "democracy is unavoidable" assumptions adopted by many futures scholars.[7] This is likely to expose some of their basic methodological and substantive weaknesses.

5. Examination of the cross-impacts of various alternative futures of social institutions (in the broadest sense of the term, including also relevant aspects of the physical environment) on domestic problems, leading to Alternative Domestic Political Futures, many of which are quite possible but most unwelcome to us, contradicting our optimistic hopes for the future.

These five reasons, in combination, explain the neglect of ADPF in contemporary futures study. But some of them, and especially the two last reasons, also serve as compelling arguments for intense efforts to study ADPF and to examine closely the relations between them and alternative futures of other social institutions.

---

[5]See, for instance, Gerald Feinberg, *The Prometheus Project* (Garden City, N.Y.: Doubleday, 1969).

[6]Olaf Helmer, *Social Technology* (New York: Basic Books, 1966).

[7]An exception is in "Democracy is Inevitable," Warren G. Bennis and Philip E. Slater, *The Temporary Society* (New York: Harper and Row, 1968), which at least faces the issue explicitly.

If domestic politics were, indeed, a dependent variable, sure to adjust itself in a functional (i.e., *good*) way to all alternative futures of other social institutions (or, at least, to those futures regarded as more desirable), then the neglect of ADPF in futures studies would not matter very much. But, to say the least, there seems to be a high probability that (*a*) domestic politics is a main controlling variable significantly shaping the futures of most other social institutions, if not all; and (*b*) domestic politics can fail to adjust in a functional way to various alternative futures of other social institutions, with all-engulfing catastrophic results. Therefore, instead of being neglected and despite all the psychological, cultural, political, and methodological difficulties, the exploration of ADPF and their interdependencies with the alternative futures of other social institutions should be a main concern of futures studies.

One might even be justified in going one step further and postulating that any alternative future which does not at least make its assumptions concerning the salient states of domestic politics explicit should be regarded as incomplete, at best. Indeed, alternative futures which ignore relevant aspects of ADPF should be regarded as dangerous daydreaming which may well be misleading—both as a source of objective forecasts and, even more so, as a basis for policy recommendations.

Recognition of the need to study ADPF is essential, but insufficient by itself. Also necessary are designs and methodologies for doing so. The main initial task of any project for the study of ADPF is to build up, through sequential learning, the necessary study designs and methodologies. However, presently available knowledge and experience do permit the preliminary outline of a provisional study design to serve as a first approach in the construction and investigation of ADPF. Their nature and scope can thereby be made somewhat operational and concrete.

A Preliminary Design for the Study of ADPF

A basic design for the study of Alternative Domestic Political Futures includes four elements:

1. A facet analysis of domestic politics, which permits identification of the main dimensions of domestic politics and their possible permutations.

2. A cross-impact analysis of the implications of a range of alternative futures of various social institutions on the future of the facets of domestic politics.

3. A cross-impact analysis of the implications of a variety of ADPF—broken down by facets and subfacets as desired—on the futures of other social institutions.

4. An estimate of the probability of ADPF, based on the integration of autonomous ADPF predictions and the predictions of various cross-impacts on ADPF.

The facet analysis[8] should permit construction of a large range of imaginary ADPF through the combinations of various subfacets. Some of these imaginary ADPF are theoretically impossible because of inherent behavioral or logical contradictions. The remaining theoretically possible ADPF serve as a basis for the various cross-impact analyses and predictions.

Because of the practically infinite possibilities of facet and subfacet classifications and combinations, no facet analysis of so complex a phenomenon as domestic politics is definite. Additional knowledge and changes in foci of interest will make different facet classifications more valid or more significant. Nevertheless, with the help of constant iteration of the facet analysis of domestic politics and through sensitivity testing of the main findings to variations in the facet classifications, the facet design of domestic politics can be sufficiently developed for useful cross-impact analysis. (See table 7-1 page 74.)

The cross-impact analyses should permit identification of some inter-dependencies between ADPF and alternative futures of other social institutions. The matrix of cross-impacts of various alternative states of social institutions on domestic politics brings out the significance of different developments for the probability of ADPF, and the matrix of the cross-impact of different ADPF on other social institutions brings out some of the broader implications of ADPF and their influence on the probability of different alternative futures of various social institutions.

Because of the importance of initial concrete situations, cross-impact analysis should differentiate the impacts of the same alternative futures of various social institutions according to different initial domestic politics situations; this can be done country by country, or by various classifications of countries, so as to take account of specific circumstances which cannot be expressed through the facet analysis, and to provide a bridge between idiographic and more nomographic levels of analysis, which is essential for applications.[9] (See tables 7-2 and 7-3 pages 76, 77, 78.)

[8] The concept of "facet analysis" used here is as developed by Louis Guttman, "An Outline of Some New Methodology for Social Research," *Public Opinion Quarterly* 18 (1954): 395-414; and "What Lies Ahead for Factor Analysis," *Education and Psychological Measurement* 18 (1958): 497-515.

[9] On the concept of cross-impact matrices, see T. F. Gordon and H. Haywood, "Initial Experiments with Cross-Impact Matrix Method of Forecasting," *Futures* 1, no. 2 (1968): 100-117; T. F. Gordon, "Cross-Impact Matrices," *Futures* 1, no. 6 (1969): 527-31; Richard Rochberg, T. F. Gordon, and Olaf Helmer, *The Use of Cross-Impact Matrices for Forecasting and Planning* (Middletown: Institute for the Future, Report R-10, 1969); and T. F. Gordon, Richard Rochberg, and Selwyn Enzer, *Research on Cross-Impact Techniques with Applications to Selected Problems in Economics, Political Science, and Technology Assessment* (Middletown: Institute for the Future, Report R-12, 1970).

Table 7-1

Formats for Facet Analysis of Domestic Politics
and Its Use for Identification of ADPF

I. *Illustrative Format for Facet Analysis of Domestic Politics*

Primary Facets	Subclassifications into Secondary Facets, Tertiary Facets, etc.
1. Units of Sovereignty	By size: global to city By population By number of nations, cultures, races, etc. And more
2. Ideology	By intensity By various dimensions, such as right-left, tough-soft, inner-outer directed By substantive contents And more
3. Degrees of Pluralism	By types and numbers of decision centers By forms of interdependence And more
4. Cohesion and Consensus	By homogeneity vs. heterogeneity By social distance By extent and form of internal violence And more
5. Mass Participation	By subject matters By modes (e.g., elections, opinion polls, etc.) By significance And more
6. Elite Structure	By recruitment base and succession rules By rate of change of recruitment base and succession rules By turnover By homogeneity vs. heterogeneity And more
7. Size of Political Activities	By number of persons directly involved By costs By perceived attention And more
8. Social Functions	By social function By degree of control By detailedness of interference By mode And more
9. Formal Structure And more	By various traditional classifications, such as presidential versus parliamentary, multiparty versus single party, etc.

Table 7-1 (*continued*)

II. *Format for Use of Facet Analysis for Identification of ADPF*

Short Designation	Facet Combinations	Verbal Description	Imaginary/Possible
	1 2 3 4 5 6 7 8 9		

Comments: The heuristic nature of the Facet Analysis and of its use for identification of ADPF should be emphasized. The categories of classification and degrees of elaboration should be selected so as to serve the purposes of studying ADPF, rather than meeting the criteria of elegant and aesthetically pleasant taxonomies or of categorically exclusive morphological analyses. The main purpose is to help in identification of novel and possible ADPF and to provide dimensions for cross-impact analyses.

To estimate the probabilities of ADPF in respect to specific countries or groups of countries, the probabilities of various cross-impacts must be integrated with those of various autonomous developments of ADPF. This is essential because ADPF are not a deterministic product of cross-impact factors alone, but are also shaped by the internal dynamics of the involved domestic political systems. (See table 7-4 page 80.)

Avoiding Pitfalls in the Study of ADPF

Further refinement of the initial designs for the study of ADPF is, at present, inappropriate in view of the low validity and reliability of available methodologies for putting content into the proposed design. In order to build up the content of the cross-impact matrices and of the prediction scheme and so as to identify main patterns based on them, all available and forthcoming prediction methods have to be used side by side, from intuitive guess to gaming, from extrapolation to Delphi.[10] Hopefully, through constant iteration,

---

[10]Surveys of relevant prediction methods are provided in Erich Jantsch, *Technological Forecasting in Perspective* (Paris: OECD, 1967); James R. Bright, ed., *Technological Forecasting for Industry and Government: Methods and Applications* (Englewood Cliffs, N.J.: Prentice-Hall, 1968); and Robert U. Ayres, *Technological Forecasting and Long-range Planning* (New York: McGraw-Hill, 1969). The recent project of the Institute for the Future on Connecticut pioneers some methodologies relevant to the study of ADPF. See Theodore F. Gordon and Robert H. Ament, *Forecasts of Some Technological and Scientific Developments and Their Social Consequences* (Middletown: Institute for the Future, Report R-6, 1969); and Selwyn Enzer et al., *A Simulation Game for the Study of State Policies* (Middletown: Institute for the Future, Report R-9, 1969).

Table 7-2

Illustrative Format for Exploration of Cross-Impact of Selected Social Institutions' Alternative Futures on the Futures of Domestic Politics

Social Institutions	Given Assumptions		Main Predicted Impacts on ADPF		
	Conjectured Change	Other Assumptions	On Facets and Subfacets (Taken from Table 7-1, I)	On Specific ADPF (Taken from Table 7-1, II)	On Concrete Countries and Groups of Countries
	Direction, Scope, Rate, etc.	Situation in respect to other social institutions and various aspects of ADPF	To be filled in separately with different prediction methods, with alternative predictions, probabilities, time dimensions, and additional assumptions, depending on the capacity of the prediction method and the needs of analysis		
Population					
Size					
Distribution					
And more					
Science and Technology					
Mind Control					
Weather Control					
Communication					
Social Engineering					
Energy					
And more					
International Relations					
Military Threats					
Economic Cooperation					
And more					
Economy					
Raw Materials					
Production					
And more					

Table 7-2 (continued)

Social Institutions	Given Assumptions		Main Predicted Impacts on ADPF		
	Conjectured Change	Other Assumptions	On Facets and Subfacets (Taken from Table 7-1, I)	On Specific ADPF (Taken from Table 7-1, II)	On Concrete Countries and Groups of Countries
	Direction, Scope, Rate, etc.	Situation in respect to other social institutions and various aspects of ADPF			
Education Contents Distribution And more *Mass Movements* Religions And more *And more*			To be filled in separately with different prediction methods, with alternative predictions, probabilities, time dimensions, and additional assumptions, depending on the capacity of the prediction method and the need of analysis		

Comments: The heuristic purposes of the Cross-Impact analysis should be noted. The categories of social institutions and of impact ADPF, the elaboration of conjectured changes and of other assumptions, the methods for cross-impact prediction, and the degree of elaboration of these predictions all depend on the capacity of prediction methods on one hand and the purposes of the analysis on the other hand. To permit conclusions, convergence of findings by different methods, with various assumptions and with heterogeneous classifications, is necessary. Even then, conclusions can only indicate main patterns.

Table 7-3

Illustrative Format for Exploration of Cross-Impact of Selected ADPF on the Futures of Social Institutions

ADPF	Given Assumptions		Main Predicted Impacts on Social Institutions
	Conjectured Change	Other Assumptions	Social Institutions and Subinstitutions (classified as convenient)
	Direction, Scope, Rate, etc.	Situation in respect to other aspects of ADPF and various social institutions	To be filled in separately with different prediction methods, with alternative predictions, probabilities, time dimensions, and additional assumptions, depending on the capacity of the prediction method and the needs of analysis
By Facets and Subfacets (Taken from Table 7-1,I)			
By Specific ADPF (Taken from Table 7-1, II)			
By Concrete Countries and groups of Countries			

Comments: The heuristic purposes of the Cross-Impact Analysis should be noted. The categories of ADPF and of impact social institutions, the elaboration of conjectured changes and of other assumptions, the methods for cross-impact prediction, and the degree of elaboration of these predictions all depend on the capacity of prediction methods on one hand and the purposes of the analysis on the other hand. To permit conclusions, convergence of findings by different methods, with various assumptions and with heterogeneous classifications, is necessary. Even then, conclusions can only indicate main patterns.

design, methodology, and content will progress together toward better knowledge and prediction of the range of Alternative Domestic Political Futures and the variables shaping them.

The proposed design for the study of ADPF suffers from all the dangers of analytical approaches, which involve the breaking down of an overall *Gestalt* into components and elements. These can be overcome through recombination of the different components and elements into a few main patterns and through systematic movement back and forth between main patterns and detailed analytical treatment.

More difficult to overcome is the inability of even elaborate cross-impact analyses to do justice to the real-life complexities of interdependencies and interrelations. These complexities include, for instance, (*a*) the nonadditive effects of different combinations of alternative futures of various social institutions on domestic politics (e.g., the combined effects of weather control and population increases on domestic politics may be much stronger than the sum of the two factors occurring separately); and (*b*) the simultaneous impact of domestic politics on other social institutions and the impact of the latter on domestic politics.

We can design multidimensional cross-impact matrices and sophisticated mathematical structures for handling complex interrelations. But such tools are at present inappropriate for futures studies, where lack of theoretic models and of any "hard data" should make one very suspicious of complex tools that cannot but compound mistakes and build up illusions, both for oneself and for others.

Rather, one must recognize the limitations of futures studies, especially in respect to so complex a phenomenon as domestic politics, and bear in mind that even minor improvements in our understanding of the emerging future and of the variables shaping it may have far-reaching implications for the improvement of policymaking—which I regard as the most important of all the goals of futures studies.

For the purposes of policymaking, we must process the facet analysis, cross-impact matrices, and integration prediction scheme into a policy-oriented format, which clearly indicates main cross-impacts and main development directions and identifies the main policy instruments in ways convenient for policy analysis. (See table 7-5 pages 81 and 82.)

The next step is to try to use the findings of an ADPF study for purposes of improving policymaking and to revise and improve study of ADPF in the light of feedback from such attempts. It is the purpose of the design presented in this chapter to permit this next step.

Table 7-4

Format for Integrated ADPF Prediction Scheme

	Autonomous Trend (Probability Distribution by Time Periods)	Cross-Impacts (Probability Distribution by Time Periods)	Combined Prediction (Probability Distribution by Time Periods)	Comments on Reliability	Main Assumptions and Sensitivities
Concrete Countries and Groups of Countries		In terms of changes in main facets			
Domestic Politics Facets and Sub-Facets (Taken from Table 7-1, I)		In terms of main direction of change		Explanation of prediction methods and degrees of convergence of results	Explanation of assumptions and sensitivities
ADPF (Taken from Table 7-1, II)		In terms of possibilities of realization			

Comments: Care must be taken to emphasize the low validity and reliability of the predictions. Therefore, inconsistent predictions arrived at by different methods should explicitly be indicated, probability distributions should not be aggregated unless they converge, and main assumptions and sensitivities should be spelled out.

Table 7-5

Suggested Policy-Oriented Format of ADPF Study Findings

I. ADPF as Policy Goal

Target Area	Target Vector	Main Salient Variables	Possibilities to Control Variables and Side Effects	Main Policy Instruments	Comments on Validity, Reliability, Sensitivity, and Assumptions
By concrete Countries and Groups of Countries	Desired and undesired developments of facets and subfacets	Changes in other social institutions which strongly increase or decrease probability of target vector	Legitimacy, feasibility, and costs, including side effects, of resetting the main salient variables	Main salient variables which are feasible and efficient instruments for influencing probabilities of target vector	Detailed explanation of limitations of policy—instruments identification
By Facets and Subfacets (In general, or in particular countries and subcountries)	Desired and undesired directions of change				
By ADPF	Realization desired or undesired				

II. ADPF as Policy Instrument

Target Area	Target Vector	Main Salient Domestic Policies Variables	Possibilities to Control Domestic Policies Variables	Main Domestic Policies Variables to Be Considered among Policy Instruments	Comments on Validity, Reliability, Sensitivity, and Assumptions
By Social Institutions and Sub-Institutions	Desired and Undesired Changes	Changes in facets of domestic policies which strongly increase or decrease probability of target vector	Legitimacy, feasibility, and costs, including side effects, of resetting the main salient variables	Main salient variables which are feasible and efficient instruments for influencing probabilities of target vector	Detailed explanation of limitations of policy-instruments identification

Comments: This scheme is particularly sensitive to classifications, assumptions, and validity and reliability of predictions. The scheme should be worked out separately in much more detail for concrete policymaking instances. The present scheme is only intended to indicate the transformations necessary for making ADPF studies relevant for policymaking and to permit reconsideration of the proposed design for the study of ADPF in light of the needs of such transformations. I want also to emphasize an important difference between Part I and Part II of this table. Part I is designed in principle to deal with all exogenous variables influencing ADPF, and therefore can serve as a basis for ADPF-oriented policies. Part II includes only a small subset of the variables influencing various social institutions, namely, those which are a part of ADPF. Therefore, it can constitute only a subset of a social-institutions-oriented policy analysis. (For the same reason, no Integrated Prediction Scheme for other social institutions, parallel to Table 7-4, can be developed within a study focused on ADPF.)

CHAPTER 8

Prediction of Political Feasibility[1]

COMMENTS
The concept of political feasibility ties in futures studies and policy analysis; it deals with the prediction of political acceptance of an alternative, thus enlarging analysis to include political dimensions and enlarging futures studies to include policy-relevant dimensions.

This chapter examines the concept of political feasibility and then proposes a method for its study, through a combination of Delphi and some political science concepts.

The reader is invited to pay special attention to the caveats with which this chapter concludes. The dangers of self-fulfilling prophecy and conservative bias face large parts of policy sciences, especially its more analytical and quantitative components. Special care should, therefore, be taken to recognize these dangers and avoid them.

Introduction
Since policymaking is directed at influencing reality, the probability of a given policy-alternative being politically acceptable (i.e., being politically feasible) does constitute a main criterion in identifying a preferable policy, because political acceptance is one of the requirements of implementation. While there are policies which should be elaborated for reasons other than implementation (e.g., political bargaining, educational impact, tacit communication, expression of ideologies, and symbolic significance), a "reasonable" (on the level of subjective satisficing) probability of political acceptance within a defined time period should constitute a threshold which must be passed by every implementation-oriented policy-alternative before it becomes a subject for serious consideration.

While recognizing the importance of political feasibility, care must be taken to avoid a mistake widespread in practice and sometimes supported by theory,[2]

[1]An earlier version of this paper was published in *Futures* 1, no. 4 (June 1969): 282-88.

[2]Some of the writings of Charles E. Lindblom lead to such a conclusion. See especially his article, "The Science of 'Muddling Through,'" *Public Administration* 19 (Spring 1970): 79-88; and David Braybrooke and Charles E. Lindblom, *A Strategy of Decision* (New York: Free Press, 1963). His more recent book, *The Policy-Making Process* (Englewood Cliffs, N.J.: Prentice-Hall, 1968), is careful in treating agreement as a necessary, but not a sufficient, condition of a good policy.

that feasibility becomes a dominant criterion of a preferable alternative, in the sense of "the more feasible, the better." Predictions of political feasibility should play an important role in policy analysis, in limiting the range of seriously considered alternatives. But this limitation should be made explicit and based on an objective statement of the political feasibility criterion to be used—to avoid the danger either of underrating or of overrating this element of the relevant policy analysis network. Bearing in mind this caveat, it seems true that it is the neglect of political feasibility which makes so many prediction studies quite irrelevant for real-life policymaking and policy practitioners, and thus hinders significant contributions of predictions to actual policymaking.

In view of the importance of political feasibility for policymaking, it is quite surprising that it is neglected and even ignored in the professional literature, including most prediction studies. One main reason for this neglect seems to be the general tendency in much of prescriptive sciences, including prediction studies, to exclude political phenomena as either too difficult and/or too "mundane." Another main reason is the economic or physical sciences and quantitative background of most developers of decision sciences and systems analysis (who are the pioneers of applied prediction studies, rather than the more humanistic and politically oriented broad "futurists"), which excludes political science. Also important are the great objective difficulties of dealing with politics within predictions in a way which is more useful than misleading.

In this chapter an effort is made to deal with the objective difficulty by proposing some methods for more systematic exploration of political feasibility in a way operationally useful as part of policy analysis. To do so, we must first clarify the main relevant meaning of the concept "political feasibility," then investigate the variables shaping political feasibility, and finally —based on the conceptual examination and variable search—propose a method for operationalizing political feasibility as a part of prediction sets.[3]

---

[3]I am not dealing in this chapter with the related, but distinct, question of whether or how to institutionalize more systematic political feasibility predictions in the policymaking system. This is a complex problem because of the dangers of intruding on the role of the politician and the risks of reinforcing conservative bias and repression of innovative alternatives—alternatives which in the beginning often look quite unfeasible. Encouragement rather than repression of adventurous thinking and social invention is certainly a main need of contemporary policymaking. Therefore, arrangements are required for preventing their repression by political feasibility predictions and analytical methods in general—for instance, through establishing socio-organizational distance and barriers between the more invention-oriented and the more analytical-oriented functions.

The Concept of "Political Feasibility"[4]

Political feasibility—in relation to policy-oriented predictions—can be defined in three closely interdependent ways: (1) as relating to an actor, (2) as relating to a policy alternative, and (3) as relating to a policy area.

1. From the point of view of any *actor* (individual, group, organization, nation, etc.), political feasibility refers to the space of effective political action within which the actor is able, with a certain probability, to affect reality— including, among other activities, his ability to influence policies and their implementation. In this sense, political feasibility is closely affiliated with the concepts of "influence" and "power." I will use the term *political leverage* to refer to this ability of an actor to influence (among other phenomena) policies and their implementation (including, sometimes, to make and implement policies on his own). A derived term is *political leverage domain,* which refers to the action-space within which an actor has political leverage.

2. Political feasibility as regards a defined policy alternative deals with the probability (or range of probabilities) that within a given time a particular policy alternative will receive sufficient political push and support to be approved and politically implemented. ("Politically implemented" means that all necessary political steps for implementation are taken. For economic, technological, and administrative reasons the alternative may, nevertheless, remain unimplemented.)

3. In relation to a policy issue or a policy area, political feasibility refers to the range within which alternatives are politically feasible. I will use the term *political feasibility domain* to refer to this range of alternatives.

There are close logical and empirical relationships between these three definitions. Thus, logically, in order for a policy alternative to be politically feasible (in the second sense above), it must be within the political feasibility domain (in the third sense above) of the relevant policy area (or areas). Also, empirically, the shape and dynamics of a political feasibility domain are in part determined by the political leverages of the actors active in respect to the involved policy area.

Focusing attention on political feasibility prediction in respect to policy alternatives, let me point out that this is a probabilistic (predictive) concept and should be expressed as a probability distribution in respect to each policy alternative. Similarly, a political feasibility domain is constructed in layers, according to the different probabilities of the policies falling into those layers receiving sufficient political push and support to be approved and politically implemented. Also, political feasibility is highly time-sensitive; that is, the probability that a given policy will receive sufficient political push and support

---

[4]Compare Yehezkel Dror, *Design for Policy Sciences* (New York: American Elsevier, 1971), chapter 9.

to be approved and politically implemented varies over the time range during which that push and support are to be achieved.

The relationship between time and political feasibility is not only nonlinear, but not fixed in directions nor continuous. Sometimes feasibility will increase (possibly in jumps) for a larger time span; sometimes it will decrease (possibly in jumps), such as when political opportunities are lost. Therefore, the political feasibility of a policy alternative is a probability-distribution trajectory, moving in different directions and often noncontinuous. Similarly, political feasibility domains change, possible noncontinuously, when various time spans are considered.

Additional complexities are the absence of a reliable theory of political feasibility and the dependence of political feasibility on a large number of dynamic variables, in respect to many of which, reliable predictions are, in the foreseeable future, impossible. Hence, empirical data needed to estimate with reasonable confidence political feasibility domains beyond a short-time horizon is conceptually difficult to specify. Furthermore, even if theory-grounded and empirically supportable approximations can be made, they may be too complex to be of much use other than better to sensitize some policymakers to the problems and facets of political feasibility.

Nevertheless, progress is possible in the direction of better predicting of political feasibility; even short-range predictions and the sensitizing of more policymaking are, after all, radical improvements in comparison with the usual states of present policy analysis. But some understanding of the main feasibility-changing variables is required for that purpose.

Variables Shaping Political Feasibility

Not enough is known about political feasibility to permit its modeling, even qualitatively. Nevertheless, it is possible to identify some of the variables which influence political feasibility and the directions of their impact, at least in Western political culture.

I propose that political feasibility be viewed in terms of the following variables:

1. *The main actors,[5] their capacities, and their intentions.* These actors will include, among others, the relevant government agencies, producers, employees, and other organized interests. For purposes of the present analysis I regard the capacities of these actors (their political leverage) as given. But actors' intentions interact with policy alternatives: the more a policy alterna-

---

[5]To improve readability, I am using the common term "actor," but the fallacy of regarding an organization or other social unit as comparable to an individual should be guarded against. Therefore, it may be preferable to use a new term, such as "multi-actor."

tive is regarded by an actor as promising utilities and/or as belonging to his sphere of legitimate activity and/or as meeting his emotional tastes, habits, and predispositions, the more the actor will tend to develop strong intentions and convert his capacities into action. The image of potential utilities depends in part on the goals of each actor and his prediction of the results of the various alternatives. But, as a rational model does not adequately represent organizational behavior, an actor's behavior will be strongly influenced by historic attitudes, personal relations, internal processes, and other socio-psychological factors. The image of an issue belonging to an actor's legitimate sphere of activity depends mainly on the structure of the field (constitutional laws, conventions, rules of the game) and on historic attitudes and patterns of behavior.

2. *Inputs into the policy area, both actual and potential.* These include public opinions, availability of resources, political climate, pressures, technological innovation, and other political-system exogenous variables. Some assumptions concerning the impact of these variables on political feasibility are supportable: for instance, in an expanding economy with no expensive war, more money has a higher probability of becoming available and thus increases the political feasibility of expensive alternatives. Or, the more large groups and strong actors get intensely dissatisfied with the present situations, the more support may be available for more than incremental innovative alternatives. Or, the more a radically new alternative becomes technologically feasible and glamorous, the higher are its probabilities of becoming politically feasible. Concerning other developments, such as changes in taste and culture, the prediction of impacts on political feasibility is very unreliable.

3. *The actor interactions and aggregated political leverages.* Here, one basic notion is "required coalition."[6] Political feasibility requires actor cooperation sufficient to achieve the political leverage to provide the desired probability, within the stipulated time span, of approving and implementing an alternative. In part, actor interaction will depend on the same variables as 1 above; in part, it depends on interaction-history and interaction-shaping phenomena involving the same actors in other areas. Also, every policy area has its formal laws and informal rules of the game, which channelize many of the actor interactions.

4. *The critical leverage mass needed for political feasibility.* This depends in turn on the rules of the field, such as the required majority to approve a

[6] The concept of "minimum-winning coalition" is developed in Theodore Riker, *The Theory of Political Coalitions* (New Haven: Yale University Press, 1962). Care must be taken to avoid neglect of the political in the construction of economic or theory-of-games models for social phenomena. For instance, in many political situations, much broader coalitions than needed to "win" are required—to demonstrate support, strengthen cohesion, and build up power for the future. Therefore, I prefer the broader term *required coalition.*

party decision, the required push to get a bill through Parliament, etc. The critical leverage mass itself may change, depending, for instance, on the mood of Parliament and its timetable.

To sum up, I have compiled the following illustrative list of political feasibility variables:

1. *The main actors:* capacities and intentions. Capacities are shaped by many variables external to our analysis. Intentions depend on the image of potential utilities and disutilities, which depend on the actor's goals and his prediction of policy-alternative results, and on the image of the sphere of legitimate action. Intentions also depend on various actors' propensities and habits.
2. *Inputs into the policy area:* public opinion, resources, pressures, political climate, etc.
3. *Actor interaction:* as in 1, plus interaction-history, rules of the game, spill-over effects from other areas.
4. *Critical leverage mass.* Rules of the field, subjected to change by variables external to our analysis.

This list serves as a basis for one of the two main approaches to political feasibility estimation, to be discussed soon.

The Prediction of Political Feasibility

The method I propose for predicting political feasibility is a trip-facet Delphi,[7] in which persons with tacit knowledge in political feasibility ("experts") fill in three different types of prediction schemes, so as to increase reliability through convergence and consistency testing.

The prediction panels are to be composed of persons knowledgeable in political feasibility, that is, politicians, senior executives, and politics-observing persons. While politicians are the ideal panel members for political feasibility prediction studies, their use may be politically and personally nonfeasible, especially if such studies become widespread. Therefore, main reliance may have to be put on politics-observing persons, such as personal aides, political correspondents, political science scholars, senior civil servants, and the like. In this case, the few feasible studies in which politicians can be involved should be utilized to identify those groups of politics-observing persons whose responses best correspond with those of the politicians and who can, therefore, serve as the best surrogate for the latter in the study of political feasibility.

The prediction schemes deal with (1) direct political feasibility estimation, where the predictors express their straightforward opinion on the political feasibility of different alternatives, broken down by explicit time dimensions

---

[7]The Delphi method, as developed at Rand, is described by its main inventor Olaf Helmer in *Social Technology* (New York: Basic Books, 1966).

(see table 8-1 page 90); (2) conditional predictions, where the predictors identify various conditions which will make a given policy alternative politically feasible (see table 8-2 page 90); and (3) variable predictions, where predictors deal separately with the different variables of political feasibility, permitting derivation of political feasibility through processing of the variable predictions (see table 8-3 page 91).

In filling in the tables, the following rules, among others, should be observed:

1. Detailed questionnaires (which can also be filled in through structured interviews) should try to elicit as elaborate estimates—in terms of probabilities, time dimension, and assumptions—as the sophistication of the panel members permits, but without forcing them to "invent" in order to fill in the questionnaires.

2. The questionnaires are to be processed through the Delphi Method, with one or two iterations.

3. Different panels—selected by randomization of the stratified total panel membership—should fill in the three tables, so as to permit comparison and convergence testing. At a second and third stage, each group should fill in the other schemes, to permit consistency testing.

The results provide (*a*) a political feasibility estimate in respect to each policy alternative; and (*b*) by putting together all political feasibility estimates, a part of the political feasibility domain (but there may be many additional highly politically feasible alternatives waiting to be discovered).

The results should be regarded as of limited validity and as depending *inter alia* on the absence of unexpected occurrences (which often are probable). Nevertheless, the results should be of help to the main policymakers in better making their own estimates of political feasibility. Another important benefit is the education of prediction experts, and policy analysts in general, in politics and the explicit treatment of politics in predictions—important steps in developing capacities better to deal with more complex issues.

Some Caveats

Having proposed a method for predicting political feasibility, I should like to conclude this chapter too with a word of warning. This warning does not relate to the obvious unreliabilities of the proposed methods or the uncertainty of all predictions based on them. What really worries me is a much more fundamental danger, namely, the danger that every political feasibility prediction tends to ignore the capacities of human devotion and human efforts to overcome apparently insurmountable barriers and to achieve not only the improbable but the apparently impossible. A good policy may be worth

Table 8-1

Direct Political Feasibility Estimation

	Political Feasibility Estimate			
Policy Alternatives	Next X Years	Next Y Years	. . .	Next N Years
Alternative One				
Alternative Two				
. . . .				
Alternative N				

Each cell is to be filled in with a probability, or a probability distribution, or alternative probabilities with explicit assumptions—depending on the capacities of the predictor.

Table 8-2

Political Feasibility Conditions

Policy Alternatives	Is It Politically Feasible During Next X Years?	If Not, What Changes in Conditions Are Required to Make It Politically Feasible?
Alternative One		
Alternative Two		
. . . .		
Alternative N		

Depending on interest and on capacities of the predictor, the table can deal with various time spans, different feasibility probabilities and probability changes, and various combinations of conditions and assumptions.

Table 8-3
Variable Political Feasibility Estimation
Alternative X

Main Relevant Actors	Leverage	INTENTION			Input Image	Probable Action	Actor Combinations
		Alternative Image, in Terms of Actors' Goals and Sphere of Legitimate Activity	Relevant Propensities, Tastes, and Historic Habits	. . . . .			
Central Government Units							
. . .							
Local Government Units							
. . .							
Employees							
. . .							
Producers							
. . .							
Consumers							
. . .							
Interest Groups							
. . .							

This matrix is to be prepared in respect to each policy alternative. Every cell should include a concise statement of the relevant images and variables—in quantitative and qualitative terms, with alternative predictions, probabilities, time dimension, and explicit assumptions—depending on the capacities of the predictors.

Support Balance

Critical Leverage Mass

Political Feasibility Estimation

fighting for, even if its political feasibility seems to be nil, as devotion and skillful efforts may well overcome political barriers and snatch victory out of the mouth of political unfeasibility.

Any political feasibility estimate, however carefully derived and however correct at its time, must, therefore, be regarded as provisional, sometimes to be taken up as a challenge rather than accepted as an absolute constraint. In this respect, political feasibility fits well into the basic orientation of policy sciences, to serve as a heuristic aid in high-level policymaking, but not as a decision-determining algorithm or a set of self-fulfilling predictions.

Planning is at present the most structured and professionalized mode of policymaking. Distinguished by a medium-range time perspective and by explicit attention to internal consistency, planning constitutes a main effort to apply structured rationality and some knowledge to societal self-direction. The few successes and many failures of planning throughout the world are, therefore, a source of experience and knowledge which is most important for policy sciences. Planning theory in its several versions and disciplines also has significant contributions to make to policy sciences. At the same time, the absence of a broad policy sciences' approach may well be a main reason for the many failures of planning in practice and for the many inadequacies of planning theory. A new view of planning as a component of policy sciences is, therefore, required. The reconstruction of planning theory and the planning profession as a part of policy sciences, or at least in close affiliation with policy sciences and in much overlap with it, is an urgent task—but one which goes beyond the confines of this volume. All that I can do here is to examine some selected planning issues which are essential for a policy sciences view of planning, but are only a small part of the latter. In particular, this part discusses some issues of planning during rapid societal transformation, presents a facet analysis for planning as a concept package for planning theory, examines some issues of comprehensive planning, and presents an applied study on the improvement of decisionmaking and administrative planning in Israel.

PART III

A Policy Sciences View of Planning

CHAPTER 9

Planning and Rapid Societal Transformation[1]

COMMENTS

The accelerated rate of societal change throughout the world makes a radical difference for policymaking in general, and planning in particular, both in the problems that are faced and—even more so—in the preferable modes for dealing with those problems. Therefore, a main danger facing planning and policy sciences is scientific and professional conservatism, which fails to adjust to rapidly changing conditions. Some features of planning and policymaking are less sensitive to the rate of societal change; but many are very sensitive. In particular, preferable megapolicies and related aspects of metapolicy seem quite different for conditions of rapid societal change.

The dependence of actual and preferable policymaking on the rates of societal change requires much attention by policy sciences. In this short chapter, some of the problems of planning, as a mode of policymaking, under conditions of rapid societal transformation are indicated in a preliminary way.

Introduction

"Planning" is a multimeaning term, but at the very least, it implies efforts to shape the future with the help of structured rationality, systematic knowledge, and organized creativity. It constitutes one mode of policymaking distinguished by *(a)* a medium-to-long time perspective and *(b)* much attention to internal consistency within a range of subdecisions.

Beyond these generalized characteristics, planning can deal with different types of units, various levels of action, a range of subject matters, and a variety of goals and time perspectives. There are many possible planning styles, and the number of available planning modes, methodologies, methods, and tools is very large.

Whatever type of planning one has in mind, the context within which planning takes place is critical for its characteristics. In particular, planning under conditions of rapid societal transformation is basically different from planning under conditions of stability.

The one most important difference between planning under conditions of

[1]An earlier version of this chapter is being published in *Public Administration Review,* (1971), in press.

95

rapid societal transformation and planning under conditions of stability is that when society is passing through rapid transformations, much less can be taken for granted. Goals, resources, cultural infrastructure, institutional settings, implementation technologies—these and all other planning-relevant variables become less predictable, thus inhibiting present policymaking for the future.

Four main implications for planning of rapid societal transformation deserve special attention:

1. Because goals and values are changing, it is difficult to identify criteria for deciding between alternatives. Only if *(a)* values in the period of plan realization are expected to be the same as now and *(b)* this is regarded as a satisfactory state of affairs, should present values and goals serve as planning criteria. This is not the situation in rapidly changing societies, including the United States. Values and goals of societal action are changing, even if the labels (democracy, equality, freedom, etc.) are the same. As we do not know how to predict future goals and values, the answer that planning should be oriented towards the future goals and values is quite useless. Hedging, sensitivity testing, and similar uncertainty-handling techniques are better than nothing, but cannot handle primary uncertainty (when not only probabilities are unknown, but the basic dimensions of the future are unknown). Therefore, a main megapolicy for planning must be to maximize options and multiuse resources that can meet unforeseen goals and values, rather than to direct planning at operational targets. To illustrate, investments in research and development, land reserves, educated population, elastic transportation modes—these are resources (rather than goals) for the future to be aimed at by planning under conditions of rapid social transformation.

2. Suboptimization is more dangerous than ever. When main systems features can be taken for granted, careful suboptimization through incremental change is useful. But, when the social system as a whole goes through rapid transformations, the always present danger of doing more efficiently the wrong things becomes a near certainty for suboptimizing approaches. Therefore, planning of specific programs, planning for individual cities, planning of single areas—all such suboptimized efforts are doubtful, unless they are tied in with broad all-societal policymaking.

3. Available alternatives are insufficient. When society is changing slowly, incremental innovation may often be sufficient. But under conditions of rapid social transformation any efforts to direct, or at least influence, the main transformation vectors require very innovative alternatives, reaching up to new designs for main institutions and basic social policies. This necessitates social inventions. Such social inventions are made all the more possible and necessary by rapid transformations in technology. But, at present, planning

is not oriented towards far-reaching innovations in alternatives.

4.Different megapolicies become preferable under conditions of rapid societal transformation. In particular, as already indicated, incremental change becomes less attractive, and highly innovative policies are required (see chapter 24). Also, higher risks are unavoidable, permitting high-risks policies to be adopted, together with efforts at risk-producing approaches such as sequential policymaking. Under conditions of rapid societal transformation, predictability is so reduced and social regularity, even on the ultrastability level (i.e., the level of the rules of change), is so doubtful that comprehensive approaches are most difficult and shock alternatives become sometimes the only reasonable choice.

Such specifications for planning under conditions of rapid societal transformation are faced by very strong barriers which inhibit planning (and policymaking) from moving in the necessary directions. The two most important barriers are:

1. *Involvement in immediate crises.* Under conditions of rapid societal transformation, crisis and turmoil are widespread and pressures for immediate action to solve "burning issues" (both figuratively and physically) are tremendous. Politically and morally, it is hard for planning (and policymaking) to preserve its perspective and indeed most planners (and policymakers) do not.

2. *Absence of relevant knowledge.* Present planning theory does not provide knowledge that is useful for planning under conditions of rapid societal transformation. Instead, accepted concepts such as "comprehensive planning" are often counterproductive.

Caught in between immediate crises and long-range uncertainty, between an explosion in knowledge and the absence of planning-relevant knowledge, between the dangers of suboptimization and the incapacity to engage in overall policymaking improvement, and between strong value clashes and the probability that these value clashes will be outdated before they are resolved —planning faces fundamental dilemmas. Whether we look at planning as a social process, as an institutional activity, as an area of knowledge, or as a professional occupation, these are among the more difficult dilemmas which planning (and policymaking) face.

Much heart-searching is going on in the community of planners (in the broad sense of this term) in the United States and in other countries. But much of it is misdirected and suffers from overconfidence in narrow techniques on one hand, and extreme self-doubts about rationality and higher mental processes on the other hand. Internal and external pressures to give up thinking while "the city is burning" play their role in hindering planners from gearing themselves to undertake the urgently needed functions of contributing to societal self-direction with the help of structured rationality, systematic knowledge, and organized creativity.

In their problems, planners are not alone. All over the world the questions "How can we increase human capacities for conscious self-direction?" and "What are the roles of policy professionals in doing so?" are urgent and difficult. What is needed on a global scale is a transformation in the planning disciplines themselves—their basic paradigms, their methods and methodologies, their tools, their institutions, their professional traditions, their teaching, and their self-perceptions. This involves transformation of the planning disciplines into policy sciences and transformation of the planning profession into a policy profession. In order to fulfill its functions under conditions of rapid transformation, planning itself must be transformed.

CHAPTER 10

The Planning Process: A Facet Design[1]

COMMENTS

Policy sciences needs research methods fitting its interests and orientations. Especially pressing is the need for methods which permit focused and clear treatment of complex phenomena that cannot be quantified with conventional tools and for which purely "qualitative" prose is an inadequate investigatory instrument.

This chapter combines discussion of planning with illustration of one research method that may well be very important for policy sciences, namely, nonmetric measurement as developed by Louis Guttman. The reader is invited to consider the relations between facet design, as illustrated here in respect to planning, and "concept packages," and to ponder on the potentials of facet design and more advanced nonmetric methods for policy sciences, both in behavioral and in prescriptive studies.

Introduction

A close perusal of the large and growing literature dealing with different kinds of planning shows a transfer of the focus of attention from ideological discourses on the desirability of planning to examination of substantive problems associated with the planning process, such as its nature, the phases of planning, conditions for successful planning, planning techniques, etc. This change of emphasis in discussions on planning goes hand-in-hand with recognition of the basic nature of planning as a methodology of rational thought and action, rather than a blueprint for one or another definite course of action.

Emancipation of the concept of "planning" from any ideological annotations or connotations other than a belief in the ability of *homo sapiens* to engage to some extent in the shaping of his future and a belief in the desirability of his doing so is an essential prerequisite for scientific examina-

[1]This chapter is based on a paper first published in the *International Review of Administrative Sciences* 29, no. 1 (1963): 46-58.

tion of planning as a basic social-administrative process; but in order to be able to approach the study of planning in a really scientific and systematic way, we need first of all a much closer and more refined examination of its components and elements than is generally found in the literature dealing with it. In fact, it is very interesting to note that, despite the growing number of articles and books dealing with planning on one level or another, only a few efforts have been made to develop a systematic approach to the study of planning as an administrative process. Even authors well known for their original contributions to the administrative sciences have often failed to deal adequately with the planning phase of institutional action. A more systematic approach to the study of planning, utilizing more refined concepts and more advanced research designs and methods, is urgently needed, if we want our knowledge of this basic and often crucial phase of organizational action to be in line with the progress being made in other areas of administrative science; if we want to advance the study of planning as a part of policy sciences; and if we want knowledge to contribute to the improvement of the rapidly spreading practice of planning.

In this chapter an effort is made to deal with one of the first phases of a systematic study of planning, namely, a preliminary concept analysis—or, to use a more technical term, facet design—trying to identify the main factors and variables composing and shaping the planning process. We will first explain and justify the methodological rationale and objective of this paper and discuss briefly its significance for the study of planning as a part of policy sciences; then we will define our subject matter and proceed to the presentation of the various primary and secondary facets of planning; finally, we will point out some lines for empirical research, based on the facet design and directed at various problems of planning identified with the help of the facet design.

Methodology[2]

The concept of facet design, as first developed by Louis Guttman[3] and as applied to the study of various phenomena,[4] is based on R. A. Fisher's

[2]I am indebted to Professor Louis Guttman for his important help and suggestions concerning the methodological aspects of this paper.

[3]Louis Guttman, "An Outline of Some New Methodology for Social Research," *Public Opinion Quarterly* 18 (1954): 395-404; Louis Guttman, "What Lies Ahead For Factor Analysis," *Educational and Psychological Measurement* 18 (1958): 497-515; Louis Guttman, "Introduction to Facet Design and Analysis," *Proceedings of the Fifteenth International Congress of Psychology,* Brussels, 1957 (1959): 130-132; Louis Guttman, "A Structural Theory for Intergroup Beliefs and Action," *American Sociological Review* 25, no. 3 (June 1959): 318-28. Currently, Professor Guttman is working on more sophisticated methods of nonmetric measurement, which may provide more advanced designs for the study of planning.

approach to the design of experiments and tries to systematize the construction of a semantic structure which identifies the different elements and variables of which the phenomenon to be studied is composed and by which it is shaped.

A short citation from the paper by Louis Guttman in which the concept of "facet" was first proposed will serve to clarify the general methodological significance of this concept:

Perhaps the most practical way of defining the concept is in most general terms. Consider a set of A of any elements a_1, a_2 ..., and a set B of any elements b_1, b_2 ... Let C be the *direct product*[5] of A and B: $C = A \times B$. That is, a typical element of C, say c, is a pair of elements $c = (a_j, b_k)$, one coming from A and the other from B. If A has m elements and B has n elements, then C has mn elements. We shall say that C is a two-faceted set, and that A and B are facets of C. A facet, then, is a *set* of elements. In general, C may be the direct product of any number of facets, not just two.

Facet theory is useful for designing the *universes of content* of research projects. This aspect of the theory is part of *facet design*. Facet design may also refer to the population, P, being studied. The facet formula for a project can always be written in the general form: $P \times C = R$, where R is the set of possible responses of results.[6]

Application of the methodology of facet design to the study of the planning process is not easy because of the very complexity of the planning process, which results in a complex and multifaceted set, in which each facet in turn is the product of a large number of secondary facets, which in turn are the product of various tertiary facets which can be analyzed in terms of different subsets, and so on. Nevertheless, if the study of planning is to progress beyond impressionistic images or generalizations based on limited experience, it is essential that an effort be made to identify the main elements of planning, that is, that a preliminary facet design of planning should be constructed.

Construction of a facet design is but a first, though very important, step which should, if possible, be followed by construction of a statistical or quasi-statistical structure designed for empirical research. While some of the primary and secondary facets to be presented in this paper form a

[4]Uriel G. Foa, "The Foreman-Worker Interaction: A Research Design," *Sociometry* 18, no. 3 (August 1955): 226-44; Uriel G. Foa and Louis Guttman, *Facet Design and Analysis of Data on Personality and Attitudes Related to Human Organization* (Jerusalem: Israel Institute of Applied Social Research, 1960).

[5]Not to be confused with the "logical" product or the "intersection" of two sets.

[6]Guttman, "An Outline of New Methodology," op. cit. [in footnote 3], p. 399.

simplex[7]—the primary facets being ordered in a simple order pattern from more external to more internal ones and the secondary facets being partly ordered from more simple ones to more complex and comprehensive ones— it may be necessary at a later stage to try to construct more complex structures for empiric research of planning.

In its present, rather amorphous form, the facet design of planning to be presented in this chapter is intended to serve more as stimuli for directing thought toward basic problems than as a ready-made apparatus which can be directly applied to empiric investigations.[8] Nevertheless, even in its present form, the facet design should be of help for comparative study of planning instances, and should serve as a checklist of factors to be considered and dealt with in any investigation of planning and in any attempt to set up, improve, or analyze planning processes.

An additional remark must be made here on the relation between our facet design of planning and various "models of planning" and other discussions of some of the issues involved in the planning process found in modern literature on decisionmaking, statistical decisions, theory of games, etc. Nearly all these models and discussions, insofar as they are relevant to our subject, deal with the sequential phases of rational action, providing various schemes or sequences which are designed to lead to rational outputs. If for some purposes some of these models can be regarded as parts of blueprints of an ideal flowchart for the planning process, then our facet design should be viewed as dealing with the environment and structure, or, to use a technical term, *space* within which the planning process takes place. Thus, we are dealing here with one part of a general theory of the planning process from the point of view of policy sciences.

The Concept of Planning

Any effort to deal in a methodologically sound way with so elusive a phenomenon as planning must be anteceded by a more or less exact delimitation of the area of investigation, that is, a definition of planning. While the validity of the definition is by its very nature limited to our world of discourse and adjusted to the purposes we have in mind, the definition should be in line with the more commonly accepted uses and meanings of the verbal referent *planning*, to avoid unnecessary communication difficulties. Simultaneously, our definition must be wide enough to include planning processes taking place in

[7]Louis Guttman, "A New Approach to Factor Analysis: The Radex," in Paul F. Lazarsfeld, ed., *Mathematical Thinking in the Social Sciences* (New York: Free Press, 1954), pp. 258-348.

[8]This paper can also be regarded as trying to apply the "facet" concept to a decision process as an experiment designed to test the usefulness of this methodological tool for policy sciences in general.

different contexts and sharp enough to distinguish between planning and other related processes.

A short examination of some commonly used definitions will facilitate preparation of our own definition. Even leaving out of consideration definitions explicitly dealing with a limited area of planning—such as physical planning, economic planning, regional planning, etc.—we are faced with a wealth of definitions, only a few of which can be quoted here. We will select our quotations so as to illustrate the main basic approaches to the definition of the concept "planning."

One school of thought emphasizes the nature of planning as decisions concerning future action, as illustrated by the following definitions:

Planung ist die geistige Vor-Formung eines Organismus, Organs oder eines Funktionsablaufs.[9] (Planning is the mental preformation of an organism, an organ, or a process-flow.)

Speaking generally, planning is deciding in advance what is to be done; that is, a plan is a projected course of action.[10]

Planning . . . is the working out in broad outline the things that need to be done and the methods for doing them to accomplish the purpose set for the enterprise.[11]

Another school of thought regards rationality and the utilization of knowledge as characterizing planning:

Planning is an organized effort to utilize social intelligence in the determination of national policies. It is based upon fundamental facts regarding resources, carefully assembled and thoroughly analyzed; upon a look around at the various factors which must be brought together in order to avoid clashing of policies or lack of unity in general direction; upon a look forward and a look backward. Considering our resources and trends as carefully as possible, planners look forward to the determination of the long-time policies.[12]

Planning consists in the systematic, continuous, forward-looking applica-

---

[9]Karl Stefanie-Allmayer, *Allgemeine Organisationslehre* (Vienna: Humboldt Verlag 1950), p. 136.

[10]William H. Newman, *Administrative Action* (New York: Pitman Publishing Corp., 1958), p. 15.

[11]Luther Gulick, *Notes on the Theory of Organization, Papers on the Science of Administration* (New York: Institute of Public Administration, 1937), p. 13.

[12]Charles E. Merriam, "The National Resources Planning Board," in G. B. Galloway, ed., *Planning for America* (New York: Henry Holt & Co., 1941), p. 486.

tion of the best intelligence available to programmes of common affairs in the public field....Planning is a continuous process, and necessitates the constant reexamination of trends, tendencies, policies, in order to adapt and adjust governmental policies with the least possible friction and loss.... Planning is not an end, but a means, a means for better use for what we have, a means for emancipation of millions of personalities now fettered, for enrichment of human life....[13]

Planning is one of the functions of the manager, and, as such, involves the selection, from among alternatives, of enterprise objectives, policies, procedures, and programmes. It is thus decisionmaking affecting the future course of an enterprise....Planning is thus an intellectual process, the conscious determination of courses of action, the basing of decisions on purpose, facts, and considered estimates.[14]

. . . Planning is more and more regarded as equivalent to rational social action, that is, as a social process for reaching a rational decision.[15]

Of special interest in this connection may be a similar definition by a Soviet economist:

By "Planning" we mean the fullest and most rational utilization of all work and of all the material resources of the community, in the light of a scientific forecast of the trends of economic development and with strict observance of the laws of social development.[16]

Some of the quoted definitions already include the evaluative element of being directed at the "social good." This element becomes predominant in some other definitions of planning:

Planning is the means by which the discipline of Science applied to human affairs will enable man to incarnate his purposes. It is the inevitable link between means and ends. Moreover, it is in itself an inspiring ideal. For once it is realized that there is no natural harmony of nature, no Divine or other purpose hidden beneath the flux and chaos of present planlessness, it becomes immoral to let poverty, ignorance, pestilence, and war continue if they can be obliterated by a plan. Although there is some disagreement

[13]National Resources Planning Board, *A Report on National Planning and Public Works,* 1934, pp. 83–84.

[14]Harold Koontz and Cyril O'Donnel, "The Nature and Purpose of Planning," in David W. Ewing, *Long-Range Planning for Management* (New York: Harper and Row, revised edition, 1964, pp. 21, 22.

[15]Robert A. Dahl, "The Policies of Planning," *International Social Science Journal* 11, no. 3, 1 (1959): 340.

[16]Ch. Touretzki, "Regional Planning of the National Economy in the U.S.S.R. and Its Bearing on Regionalism," *International Social Science Journal,* 11, on. 3, (1959): 380.

as to the nature and desirable limits of planning, students of administration are all "planners."[17]

Planning is an activity by which man in society endeavours to gain mastery over himself and to shape his collective future by power of his reason. . . . Planning is nothing more than a certain manner of arriving at decisions and action, the intention of which is to promote the social good of a society undergoing rapid changes.[18]

Some modern students of public administration have tried to present more elaborate definitions of planning, composed of various elements:

Planning . . . is that activity that concerns itself with proposals for the future, with the evaluation of alternative proposals, and with the methods by which these processes may be achieved. Planning is rational, adaptive thought applied to the future and to matters over which the planners or the administrative organizations with which they are associated have some degree of control.[19]

Planning is essentially a means of improving decisions and is therefore a prerequisite to action. It seeks to answer two vital questions: What is the purpose of an agency or a program, and what are the best means of achieving that purpose? However, policy, organization, and the social environment are in a constant state of flux. This means that planning must be continuous and dynamic; it must anticipate change. Very broadly, administrative planning must consider political ends and the appropriate ways of achieving them. It must design effective operating procedures and provide supervisory techniques which will ensure that what has been planned is in fact being achieved. In the process, planning touches upon every aspect of management, including decisionmaking, budgeting, coordination, communications, and problems of structure. Planning, in a word, is management.[20]

Taking into account this variety of definitions, it is not surprising that some authors get weary of the whole business and despair of any attempt at formulating a generally valid definition of planning:

Planning is a word of many meanings. To some it means a blueprint for

[17]Dwight Waldo, *The Administrative State* (New York: Ronald Press Co., 1948), p. 67.

[18]John Friedmann, "Introduction" (to series of articles on The Study and Practice of Planning), *International Social Science Journal*, 11, no. 3, (1959): 327-28, 329.

[19]Herbert A. Simon, Donald W. Smithburg, and Victor A. Thompson, *Public Administration* (New York: Alfred A. Knopf, Inc., 1950), pp. 423-24.

[20]John M. Pfiffner and R. Vance Presthus, *Public Administration* (New York: Ronald Press Co., 1953), p. 83.

the future; to others it means only foresight, and action with the forward policies of the government for regulation of the economy as a whole. To some it means government responsibility to take whatever action is necessary to ensure that the economic system operates efficiently, to others it means only that the government should correlate whatever functions it undertakes toward desired overall objectives.[21]

We could go on and quote a large number of additional and more recent definitions of planning; or we could choose to subject the various definitions to critical examination, showing that most of them are of limited validity, include irrelevant elements, or are unsatisfactory in some other respect. But it seems that there is a better way to achieve our objective of clarifying the concept of planning as used in our paper, namely, presentation of our own definition of planning. As will be easily discerned, our definition relies on some of the quoted ones, covers most of the elements included in them, but is constructed in a different way designed to meet the needs of the study of planning within the framework of policy sciences.

It seems to me that for the purposes of policy sciences,[22] planning can usefully be defined as follows:

Planning is the process of preparing a set of decisions for action in the future, directed at achieving goals by preferable means.

This definition includes seven different elements. A short discussion of each of these elements in turn will clarify the meanings and implications of the proposed definitions and will introduce some of the concepts of which the facet design of planning is to be composed.

1. *Planning is the process*

Planning is a process, that is, a continuous activity taking place within a unit and requiring some input of resources and energy in order to be sustained. Planning as a process must be distinguished from a "plan." A plan can be defined as "a set of decisions for action in the future" and can be arrived at either through planning, or through some other—rational or irrational—methods of decisionmaking.

2. *Of preparing*

Planning is substantially—and, in most cases, also formally and legally— a process of *preparing* a set of decisions to be approved and executed by some other organs. Even if the same unit combines planning functions with authority to approve and execute, these are distinct, though interdependent, processes which must be kept analytically separate.

---

[21]Emmette S. Redford, *Administration of National Economic Control* (New York: Macmillan Co., 1952), p. 18.

[22]The dependence of the definition's validity and utility on the world of discourse within which it is to be used must be borne in mind.

3. *A set*

It is very important to emphasize the difference between planning and decisionmaking and policymaking in general. While planning is a kind of decisionmaking and policymaking, its specific characteristic in this respect is its dealing with a set of decisions, that is a matrix of interdependent and sequential series of systematically related decisions.

4. *Of decisions for action*

Planning is primarily directed at action and not at other objectives, such as pure knowledge, development of the planners, and so on. Planning does in fact have various secondary results, such as executive development, better decisionmaking on other issues, training in teamwork, etc., but as long as those results are only secondary objectives, the planning function is not impaired. It is true that often a planning activity is engaged in as a device to mobilize support, improve public relations, and so on. If this is the case, the process is not "planning" in its full sense and the actual process in such cases will deviate in most respects from the characteristics and phases of the "pure-type" planning process as defined by us, which is essentially *action* or *execution*-oriented.

5. *In the future*

Nearly all definitions recognize that planning is directed toward the future. This is perhaps the most important characteristic of planning, introducing the elements of prediction and uncertainty and conditioning all aspects, problems, and features of planning.[23]

6. *Directed at achieving goals*

The planning process cannot operate unless it has more or less defined goals to the achievement of which its recommendations for action in the future are directed. This does not mean that the planning process begins to operate with clearly defined objectives. Rather, in most cases, the first phase of the planning process consists in the formulation of operational planning objectives on the basis of rather ambiguous and undefined goals set before the planning process by some other, in most cases "policy," processes.

---

[23]Friedmann, op. cit. [in footnote 18], p. 334, gives an interesting list of planning characteristics resulting from the futuristic orientation of planning: "(1) It places a limit upon the time period over which projections into the future can be made without loss of practical significance for present decisions. (2) It establishes the necessity for continuing planning analysis and assessment throughout the planning period and the constant reevaluation and adjustment of means to ends. (3) It suggests the use of expectational calculus in connection with statements about the future. (4) It argues for adoption of a system of framework or structural planning. (5) It forces the careful consideration of flexibility in planning where the degree of flexibility explicitly introduced into a solution must be proportionate to the degree of uncertainty about future events. It is through an approach such as this that reason can come to terms with uncertainty."

7. By preferable means

The very nature of planning, as a process for rational shaping of the future according to our desires, depends on the means-ends relationship, which is basic to the planning process. The planning process is directed at suggesting the preferable means for achieving our goals, that is, at selecting on the basis of rational processes—including, for example, collection of information, utilization of knowledge, and systematic and integrative data processing,— the preferable means for achieving the desired goals. The basic problem of planning methods, procedures, and techniques is the provision of ways for identification of these preferable means with a feasible input of resources.

It is on these elements of the definition our facet design of planning is based.

The Facets of Planning

Following the concept of facet, as developed by Louis Guttman, we will now present the primary facets and secondary facets of planning.

The four primary facets of planning appear to be the following:

Primary facet A: The general environment of the planning process.
Primary facet B: The subject matter of the planning process.
Primary facet C: The planning unit.
Primary facet D: The form of the plan to be arrived at.

Each primary facet is the product of a number of secondary facets, which in turn are the product of a series of tertiary facets, and so on. We will now proceed to an examination of these various facets and secondary facets and some of their subsets. To concretize our presentation, a few observations on the relative significance of the various elements of the facet design and some of their characteristics will be introduced from time to time, which will point out some examples of possible lines for empiric investigation utilizing the tools provided by the facet design.

Primary Facet A: The General Environment of the Planning Process

One of the more interesting characteristics of planning is its bi-directional relation with its environment. On the one hand, the planning activity is shaped and conditioned by various environmental factors; on the other hand, planning is in many cases directed at that environment, trying to shape it to a greater or lesser extent. While, therefore, the environment is not a fully independent variable, it nevertheless is at any point in time relatively fixed and is one of the primary facets shaping the planning process.

The main secondary facets of the general environment are these:

A_1. The basic environmental factors which constitute the physical, demographic, ecologic, social, cultural, geophysical, geoeconomic, etc., phenomena which are the general background against which the planning process takes place.

A₂. The resources in manpower, knowledge, capital, etc., which are potentially available for the planning process and for eventual plan execution.

A₃. Various values, power groups, and ideologies which limit the alternatives to be considered by the planning processes, in terms of methods that can be used for plan execution (e.g., force), of conditions that are required for recruiting the necessary support for the planning process, of the actual resources that will be put at the disposal of plan execution, and the like. Neglect by the planners of these limitations results in utopian, non-realistic planning.

A₄. The terms of reference within which the planning process is to take place, including general goals set for the planning process; contextual goals, that is, values and institutions which should not be impaired;[24] basic directives concerning some aspects of the working methods to be used during the planning process, such as giving an opportunity to interested persons to have a hearing; and so on.

It is these environmental elements which constitute the basic framework within which the planning process takes place and which also determine, or at least influence, directly and indirectly, the form of most of the other facets.

Primary Facet B: The Subject Matter of the Planning Process

The subject matter of the planning process is the product of at least nine different secondary facets:

B₁. The structural relation between the subject matter and the planning unit.

B₂. The degree to which the subject matter is predetermined or elastic.

B₃. The degree of penetration.

B₄. The significance of the subject matter of the planning process.

B₅. The orientation of the subject matter toward the planning process.

B₆. The extent to which the subject matter has already been subjected to planning.

B₇. The scope of the activity subjected to planning.

B₈. The demographic territorial area related with the subject matter of the planning process.

B₉. The time span.

---

[24]"Contextual ends are represented by social values and traditions that do not, in themselves, constitute the immediate objectives of planning, but are sufficiently vital to make their preservation socially worth while." Friedmann, op. cit. [in footnote 18], p. 330.

Let us examine these secondary facets more closely, one by one:[25]

B₁. *The structural relation between the subject matter and the planning unit.*

The structural relation between the subject matter of the planning process and the planning unit can take either of three forms, which constitute the subset of this secondary facet:

a. The subject matter is structurally identical with the planning unit or a part of it, for example, planning the future staffing of the planning unit or planning the work program of the planning unit.

b. The subject matter belongs to an organizational structure of which the planning unit is itself a part, for instance, the personnel department planning the executive development scheme for the enterprise.

c. The subject matter does not belong to an organizational structure of which the planning is itself a part, for example, a central planning agency preparing a master plan for a town or an economic development plan for a region or state.

While these distinctions are, at least partly, relative ones, depending on the strictness or looseness of the organizational structure which serves as a frame of reference for the analysis (e.g., one can regard a whole society as a kind of loose organizational structure), they help in pointing out the basic difference between so-called organizational planning, which is more "inner directed," and various kinds of "outer directed" planning.

B₂. *The degree to which the subject matter is predetermined or elastic.* There is a big difference between various planning instances in the extent to which the subject matter of the planning process is clearly delimited and defined when submitted to the planning unit or is left for the planning unit to determine and to change from time to time. In general, it seems that planning units—driven by their bona fide sense of mission, their belief in their own expert knowledge, and their empire-building drives—have a tendency to try to overcome even rigorously predetermined definitions of their subject matter, and to enlarge the scope of activities subjected to their planning.

B₃. *The degree of penetration.* Planning can penetrate more or less into its subject matter, trying to deal with all the elements and aspects of the subject matter or aiming only at its main directions and central factors. This is an important dimension for comparative study of planning, because even

---

[25]Compare this list with the "dimensions of planning" suggested by LeBreton and Henning: complexity, significance, comprehensiveness, time, specificity, completeness, flexibility, frequency, confidential nature, formality, authorization, ease of implementation, ease of control. See Preston P. LeBreton and D. A. Henning, *Planning Theory* (Englewood Cliffs, N.J.: Prentice-Hall, 1961), pp. 22-56.

if identical activities are subjected to planning, entirely different degrees of penetration may be aimed at.

B_4. *The significance of the subject matter of the planning process.* Depending on the subject matter of the planning process, the (public or private) character of the planning unit and of the organization to which it belongs, and the socio-political-ideological environment, the significance of the subject matter of a certain planning process will be viewed mainly from the angle of the organization engaging in the planning activity, from the angle of various political-economic-social interests, from a "public interest" angle, or from the angle of various combinations of these different points of view.

From these different points of view, the subject matter of a planning process can be of high or low significance, either objectively (in the sense of the impact of the subject matter of the planning process on other areas of activity) or subjectively (in the sense of the importance of the subject matter of the planning process according to various cognitions, values, or ideologies).

B_5. *The orientation of the subject matter toward the planning process.* Depending on various tertiary facets, the persons and institutions related with different subject matters can have a more passive or active and more positive or negative orientation toward the planning process (and the planning unit— these two are closely related in the public image). A moot point, in urgent need of research, is what orientation of the subject matter toward the planning process provides better results in terms of the quality of the planning process; it seems that often the planning process and, even more so, the plan execution process need a lot of active, positive support to be successfully maintained.

B_6. *The extent to which the subject matter has already been subjected to planning.* Prior subjection of the subject matter to planning does not only influence its orientation toward the present planning process, but creates various expectations, traditions, and factors which are of much importance in shaping the future planning processes. In this respect, there are significant differences between various planning instances dealing with subject matters (or even an identical subject matter) subjected to more or less prior planning.

B_7. *The scope of the activity subjected to planning.* Planning always deals with a delimited subject matter, which is defined in terms of functions, territorial units, or some other characteristics. Total planning, that is, planning including within its subject matter all extrapersonal and interpersonal (and perhaps even intrapersonal) activities, is unimaginable outside of a fantastic counter-Utopia. The limitations of the human mind, the limitations of resources and the many competing alternative uses for them, the limits on the maximum integrating capacity of organizations, and the existence of strong opposition to planning of certain subject matters—all these limit planning at any given time to a selected, relatively small number of subject matters. On the other hand, recognition of the interdependence of various aspects of activity, especially under conditions of rapid change (e.g., rapidly developing societies, rapidly growing enterprises), is one of the more important reasons for enlarging the scope of activities subjected to planning, leading in the direction of a comprehensive planning approach. (But see chapters 9 and 11 on the difficulties of comprehensive planning, especially under conditions of rapid social transformation.)

B_8. *The demographic territorial area related with the subject matter of the planning process.* The relation between planning and demographic territorial area is a rather complex one, which has at least three distinct, though closely interrelated, possible aspects. Since all human activity takes place in space time, by its very nature planning must, and does, take into account this fact, and delimits its scope within these dimensions. Even in the few cases where the subject matter of planning is not defined in demographic territorial terms (e.g., *all economic activities*), the fact that all material phenomena are distributed in space will make it convenient, and even inevitable, to use some demographic-territorial subdivision as units for delegated planning purposes.

To this general consideration on the inherent role of space in human thought and activity, a second aspect of the relation between area and planning must be added—the specific importance of demographic territorial units in social affairs. Beginning with the nearly instinctive, emotional attachment of an individual to his place of birth, and going through all levels of social institutions, the special role of territory in social life is always apparent (though, in the future, it may decrease very much).

A third aspect of the relation between demographic territorial area and planning has its roots in the fact that one of the most important functions of every society is adjustment to its territory. Such adjustment is brought about to some extent by changing the physical environment and making the territory fit the needs of the society. In the field of planning this aim is reflected in the many planning activities having as their subject matter certain aspects of what we call territory. Such "earthbound" fields include landscaping, resources conservation, flood control, urban redevelopment, and many more. The present pollution and environmental concerns belong to this aspect.

In all these cases, the relation between demographic territorial area and planning poses two problems, the solutions of which have to be reconciled somehow. First, the *technical-optimum* area for dealing with the subject matter of the planning activity must be defined; and second, this technical-optimum area must be reconciled with the existing demographic territorial units of social action and the limited freedom of the planning unit.

The best possible compromise between the two sets of areas will yield the *social-technical-preferable* demographic territorial areas for the designed planning activity.[26]

B_9. *The time span.* Each planning process deals with a certain, though not necessarily exactly predetermined, time span. The selection of the preferable time span for each planning activity depends on various factors, including, for example, the natural cycle of the subject matter of planning, the acute need for interference to change an unbearable situation, limitations on our ability to predict the future, our evaluation of present versus future needs, and the desire that planning should serve as a guide to present actions.

We shall now proceed to the two remaining primary facets of planning, which are of a somewhat more limited nature but exert a tremendous influence on the planning process.

Primary Facet C: The Planning Unit

The characteristics of the planning unit are the product of seven secondary facets:

C_1. *The basic nature of the planning unit.* Planning, as defined by us, can take place on the level of individuals and on the level of various institutions, such as a family, a tribal council, and the like. A special case of institutional planning which is of highest contemporary importance and which includes most socially significant planning processes, is planning in and by bureaucratic structures. It is this kind of planning, which is particularly related to policymaking, at which our facet design is mainly directed.

Because of the underdeveloped state of neurology and individual psychology, we know nearly nothing on the factors conditioning and shaping planning on the individual level. This is all the more regrettable because, after all, organizational planning is also done by individuals, and more knowledge on planning on the individual level may well contribute much to the understanding and improvement of the organizational planning process.

C_2. *Primary or delegated planning units.* Delegated planning is planning which constitutes plan execution from the point of view of another planning unit; primary planning is planning not as part of any higher-level plan. In

---

[26]It is incorrect to regard the technical-optimal area as the "desirable" area of action which is "distorted" by the "unfortunate" existence of nations, states, local units, etc. We have already mentioned the psychological importance for human happiness of emotional attachment to territories and the inevitability, till basic social institutions change, of territorial units of social action and their role in planning. Here it should be emphasized that these existing demographic territorial units of social action have to play a significant role in planning: the most important initiators are those who can mobilize loyalty, resources, and support. The planner cannot and must not neglect these human and moral facts in favor of a quasi-mechanical "social engineering" approach.

general, delegated planning will be more detailed, will be for a shorter time span, and will deal with a smaller subject matter.

The importance of this distinction can be illustrated by applying it to a concrete issue, for example, the preferable subject matter of city planning. Some authors[27] relied on the precedent of large-scope city planning in the United States during the big depression, including economic and social spheres of social activity, to justify a similar large subject matter for city planning at later periods. But it seems that much of the enlarged scope of city planning at that period was delegated planning, part of a national plan to relieve unemployment and rehabilitate the economy. Therefore, what happened then is not directly relevant to the problem whether, in the absence of national planning of some subject matters, cities should deal with them through primary planning.

C_3. *Status.* The status of the planning unit (including the status of the institution and of the planners as individual role bearers) influences the resources which can be mobilized for the planning process, the extent to which limitations on alternatives and similar externally determined limits imposed on the planning process can be overcome, and so on. In other words, the status of the planning unit is closely correlated, though not identical, with its power, which is an important factor in the implementation strategy of planning.[28]

C_4. *Values, information, and character of the planning unit.* The planning process in all its phases entails constant judgments involving the value systems, the information, and the character of the decisionmakers—the planning unit as a collection of individuals and the planning unit as an institution. This is a factor of tremendous importance, having significant implications for the selection of planners, their education and their control, and for the design of planning units.

C_5. *Resources and means.* The resources in manpower, knowledge, equipment, time, etc., at the disposal of the planning unit and the planners are other important factors which have a definite influence on the planning process and must therefore be carefully considered.

C_6. *Work systems, procedures, and methods.* The systems, methods, and procedures of work in the planning unit determine the detailed form of the planning process. The more important systems, procedures, and methods deal with information gathering, data processing, and decisionmaking. The

[27]E.g., cf. Robert A. Walker, *The Planning Function in Urban Government* (Chicago: University of Chicago Press, 1950).

[28]The policy of planning is still a sadly neglected subject. With the exception of single case studies on concrete planning instances and planning institutions and a few general studies dealing with some relationships between macro-planning and political regimes, only very little is known on this critically important subject.

introduction of electronic data-processing equipment, while much increasing the possibilities of planning, introduces serious complexities into work systems, work methods, and procedures and makes even more essential careful attention to consciously and rationally established explicit systems, procedures, and methods through which the planning process is channelized. Even more important is the emergence of policy sciences, which provides novel designs for planning—designs which require radical changes in contemporary planning patterns.

C_7. *Organizational structure.* Last, but not least, the organizational structure of the planning unit (already mentioned in a different context) raises difficult problems, especially concerning the distribution of functions between specialized overhead planning function and the ordinary line units in charge of day-to-day operations in regard to specific subject matters. In both small- and large-scale, inner- and outer-directed planning, the organizational issues are most complex and the solutions adopted determine to a considerable degree the form taken by the planning process, and its success or failure in fulfilling its tasks. As yet, despite some recent literature on the subject, the organizational problems of planning are among the most neglected subjects— in the study of planning, in organization theory, and in policy sciences as a whole.

Primary Facet D: The Form of the Plan to Be Arrived at

D_1. *The realism of the plan.* We have already mentioned cases of planning directed at political advantages, public relations, training objectives, and the like. In these cases, it is not always necessary to arrive at the final phase of the planning process, that is, preparation of a plan; and even if a plan is prepared, it is often on purpose utopian in nature. Leaving such cases of "quasi-planning" aside, there is a legitimate span of more or less realism aimed at in the preparation of a plan. Indeed, a certain utopian element may be essential for gaining the necessary support and may be fully compatible with a realistic approach to planning and with successful plan realization. In any case, the degree of realism of the plan to be arrived at is an important subfacet influencing the entire tone of the planning process.

D_2. *The form of the plan.* The subset of this secondary facet includes various forms of plans: fixed-time plans, such as five-year or seven-year plans; contingency plans, to be executed at a given occurrence which might or might not happen at an unknown point in the future, such as most military operation plans; master plans, showing a blueprint of a desired state of affairs without setting down a fixed timetable for its achievement, such as many town plans; budgetary plans, constructed in terms of monetary units; work plans, constructed in terms of technical specification, drawings, etc.; and more.

The modern tendency seems to be in the direction of composite plans, including long-range and short-range timetables, financial and physical breakdown, contingency and predetermined elements, and so on. It seems that the more complex and large-scale the subject matter of the planning process is, the more multiform and complex the plan has to be.

D_3. *Degree of details.* The plan to be arrived at can be more or less detailed. In general, the larger the time span to be covered by the plan, the more the plan will include general frameworks and directions, leaving details for later or delegated planning.

A related element of the subset is, will the plan be single-alternative, providing one direction of action, or multialternative, providing different directions, for later selection (in the light of developments) of the preferable one?

Conclusions

Returning to the concept of facet as used in this paper, we can regard planning (P) as the product (in the mathematical sense of *cartesian product*)[29] of primary facets A, B, C, and D.

In other words, generally speaking,

Planning = (general environment) $\times$ (subject matter) $\times$ (planning unit) $\times$ (form of plan), or $P = A \times B \times C \times D$.

Each primary facet in turn is the product of a number of secondary facets, namely:

$A = A_1 \times A_2 \times A_3 \times A_4$
$B = B_1 \times B_2 \times B_3 \times B_4 \times B_5 \times B_6 \times B_7 \times B_8 \times B_9$
$C = C_1 \times C_2 \times C_3 \times C_4 \times C_5 \times C_6 \times C_7$
$D = D_1 \times D_2 \times D_3 \times D_4$

We have thus 24 secondary facets of planning, each one of which—even if not regarded as the product of a series of tertiary facets—can take different forms. Thus, we have:

$A_{1a}, A_{1b}, A_{1c} \ldots D_{4a}, D_{4b}, D_{4c}, \ldots D_{4n}$.

The forms of some of the secondary facets (e.g., the time span) can be expressed in metric units; others can be expressed in transitive but not fully comparable units (e.g., the secondary facet "significance"); still others can only be expressed by rough qualitative terms (e.g., most of the secondary facets related to the form of the plan to be arrived at). Following further elaboration of various classifications of the form of the various secondary facets, the basic problems are reached: Which combinations of forms do in fact appear in real planning instances? What combinations give, under various conditions, the best results? Why?

---

[29]Guttman, "An Outline of New Methodology," op. cit. [in footnote 3], p. 1.

In other words we would like to know for which values of a_{11}, a_{2j}, ... d_{4n}, planning ($p = a \times b \times c \times d$) can exist in reality, and given the values of some of the secondary facets—which values for the non-predetermined secondary facets will maximize the quality[30] of the planning process (qp).

Available experience and impressionistic data provide some guidelines to these problems. Thus, we would not expect long-range planning of a large-scope subject matter to go with very detailed plans and a high degree of penetration; we would not expect planning to succeed if the planners lack certain qualifications; and so on. But available material, based as it is on limited experience and subjectivistic impressions, does not permit many conclusions beyond such rather obvious and partly semantic ones. Only systematic empirical study, utilizing the best available research designs and methodologies, can perhaps provide us with valid and reliable answers to these and other problems and provide a sound basis for the study of the planning process and its improvement as part of policy sciences.

[30]On the problem of evaluation of quality, see Yehezkel Dror, *Public Policymaking Reexamined* (San Francisco: Chandler, 1968), part 2.

CHAPTER 11

Comprehensive Planning:
Common Fallacies versus Preferred Features[1]

COMMENTS

The idea of comprehensive planning is the most ambitious effort to direct human fate through conscious decisionmaking. Therefore, comprehensive planning is of intense interest to policy sciences. In this chapter, six main fallacies of comprehensive planning theory are contrasted with eight features required for preferable comprehensive planning. Much of this analysis also applies, with suitable changes, to policymaking in general.

Introduction

In order to clarify some basic problems relating to the nature and preferable characteristics of comprehensive planning, it is necessary to engage first in some unlearning and then in some positive analysis. We must get rid of some of the proverbs and images accepted, explicitly or implicitly, by many of the advocates of comprehensive planning, and we must identify some of the specifications of useful comprehensive planning. In this chapter, I try to take some exploratory and tentative steps in these directions, by first discussing widespread fallacies of thinking on comprehensive planning and then presenting nine main preferred features of desirable comprehensive planning.

The Main Fallacies of Comprehensive Planning

The main fallacies in respect to comprehensive planning can be summarized conveniently under six headings: (1) the fallacy of universal usefulness; (2) the fallacy of maximization of comprehensiveness; (3) the fallacy of free inputs; (4) the fallacy of desired balance; (5) the fallacy of plans as output; and (6) the fallacy of finity.

1. The Fallacy of Universal Usefulness

Many of the proponents of comprehensive planning seem to assume, explicitly or implicitly, that comprehensive planning is an ideal mode of direction for all types of systems and should therefore be encouraged as much

[1]An earlier version of this paper was first published in F. Van Schlagen, ed., *Essays in Honour of Professor Jac. P. Thijsse* (The Hague: Mouton Co., 1967), pp. 85-99.

as possible. This opinion stems from lack of familiarity with other types of system direction which often are not only more efficient (that is, provide more *net* benefits in terms of output minus input, or, in less sophisticated terms, provide a more favorable output-input ratio), but are also more effective (that is, provide more desirable *gross* outputs, with inputs not being taken into account). In other words, preferable direction of systems is often achieved by other modes than comprehensive planning. In particular, various forms of mutual control by the components of the involved system can sometimes be more effective and more efficient than direction through comprehensive planning. This is the case not only in respect to the classical free-market mechanism, but also in respect to many interaction processes by small numbers of partisan interest groups, which under some conditions achieve better results than any form of comprehensive planning.[2] Therefore, even when we face a system in which no such self-directive mechanisms operate, our first choice may often be to introduce changes in the system, to encourage and facilitate such mechanisms; our second choice may often be to engage in compensatory planning designed to redress distortions in the working of the system. In many cases, comprehensive planning is the third best choice when the first and second alternatives are not feasible.[3]

2. The Fallacy of Maximization of Comprehensiveness

Another widespread fallacy among proponents of comprehensive planning is that the more "comprehensive" planning is, the better. This opinion ignores the tremendous difficulties of comprehensive planning. These difficulties seem often to increase in an exponential ratio to the degree of comprehensiveness, making much comprehensiveness very soon impossible and, even sooner, counterproductive.

It follows, that the degree of optimal comprehensiveness of comprehensive planning is itself a dependent variable, the optima of which depend on a number of systems characteristics (such as the complexity of the system and the cost of necessary resources), on some information variables (e.g., human knowledge), and on some institutional constraints (e.g., limitations of the human mind and the nature of political struggle).

[2]The best systematic expositions of different modes of social direction are Robert A. Dahl and Charles E. Lindblom, *Politics, Economics and Welfare: Planning and Politico-Economic Systems Resolved into Basic Social Processes* (New York: Harper, 1953); and Charles E. Lindblom, *The Intelligence of Democracy: Decision Making Through Mutual Adjustment* (New York: Free Press, 1965).

[3]Western economists are not prone to the fallacy of universal usefulness of comprehensive planning, being well familiar with the advantages of market-type modes of systems-management. Instead, many of them tend to the fallacy of universal usefulness of market-type mechanisms, supplemented by some aggregative economic policies, ignoring the very important cases in which comprehensive planning is preferable.

3. The Fallacy of Free Inputs

Closely related to the other fallacies is the tendency to neglect the costs of comprehensive planning. True, when measured in money, the costs of comprehensive planning are so small in comparison to the costs of the planned actions that they can be neglected. But when measured in opportunity costs, the price of two of the main specific resources needed in comprehensive planning—qualified manpower and time—becomes often prohibitive. Especially in modernizing countries these two resources are very expensive in terms of opportunity costs: qualified personnel is very scarce and can provide big net marginal outputs when used for other purposes, such as improvement of national policymaking or improvement of operations management; and time is very expensive, in terms of missed options and irreversible facts created while comprehensive planning proceeds. Therefore, when we apply, as we should, cost-effectiveness analysis to the comprehensive planning activity itself, comprehensive planning emerges often as nonpreferable under the very conditions for which it is many times most strongly advocated.

4. The Fallacy of Desired Balance

An argument basic to the ideas of comprehensive planning is the desirability of avoiding distortion and assuring balanced growth. This is often a fallacy. Balanced systems have often a tendency to preserve equilibrium and to evolve by incremental change. This is frequently preferable, but when such is the case, there is little need for comprehensive planning. Comprehensive planning is most often proposed as a method for achieving directed and accelerated social change (as in regional development planning) or for radically changing extrapolated tendencies (as in comprehensive city and urban renewal planning). In these circumstances, comprehensive planning tries to bring about states-of-the-future different in many respects from the present. Here, comprehensive planning is faced both by very high degrees of uncertainty and by the inertia of the present situation. These two reduce the inherent possibilities of comprehensive planning and its chances of exerting a real impact on reality. Therefore, under these circumstances, it may often be better to concentrate on achieving controlled imbalance, which will start movement of the system in the desired direction, leaving more detailed planning of the various facets of the new emerging reality for later on, when uncertainty is reduced and the inertia-reinforcing balance has been broken.[4]

[4]Compare Albert Hirschman, *The Strategy of Economic Development* (New Haven: Yale University Press, 1958), where the desirability of deliberately unbalancing the economy as a preferable way to achieve economic development under some conditions is forcefully presented.

5. The Fallacy of Plans as Output

In a large majority of cases, comprehensive planning is regarded as a method for preparing comprehensive plans. This is an insidious fallacy which ignores both the real outputs of any planning activities, including comprehensive planning, namely, the objective expectation of impact on reality, and the importance of other types of nominal outputs of comprehensive planning,[5] such as policy-directives (as set down, for instance, by the Dutch Physical Planning Act, 1962, in respect to national physical planning, which is of a rather comprehensive nature). The danger of this fallacy lies in its self-fulfilling influence: because of the belief in comprehensive plans as a reliable indicator of good comprehensive planning, the latter is often directed at producing comprehensive plans rather than at achieving multidimensional desirable impacts on future reality by whatever tools are most useful.

6. The Fallacy of Finity

Closely related to the image of plans as the main product of planning is the tendency—implied in much planning behavior and planning literature, even though rejected on the level of verbal pronouncements—that planning is a finite process. The very often used distinction between *planning* and *replanning* itself implies a break in the continuous character of the process, which can be quite misleading. In contrast to the policymaking and megapolicy decisions on one hand and operational planning on the other hand, comprehensive planning does not deal with cyclic phenomena, but with the continuous direction of a system.[6] Comprehensive planning, therefore, should be an iterative continuous process. It is permissible and necessary to divide the comprehensive planning activity into convenient phases and subprocesses, the useful delineation and interconnection of which depends on the characteristics of the involved target system and planning system. But such subdivisions should not be mistaken for any real break in the comprehensive planning process and provide no justification for viewing comprehensive planning as a finite process.

The Main Features of Preferable Comprehensive Planning

Exploration of the six main fallacies in thinking on comprehensive planning has provided us with an opportunity to identify some preferred features of desirable comprehensive planning. Turning around the six fallacies we can, through mirror-effect, identify six positive characteristics of good com-

[5]See Bertram M. Gross, "When Is a Plan Not a Plan?" *Challenge,* December 1961.
[6]For a similar distinction between strategic planning, systems planning, and operational planning, see Robert N. Anthony, *Planning and Control Systems: A Framework for Analysis* (Boston: Graduate School of Business Administration, Harvard University, 1965).

prehensive planning: (1) good comprehensive planning deals with system problems which cannot be better treated by other methods of systems direction, and especially systems auto-direction; (2) good comprehensive planning limits the degree of comprehensiveness within the boundaries of manageability; (3) good comprehensive planning is itself subjected to cost-effectiveness analysis with special attention to the opportunity costs of highly qualified personnel and time; (4) good comprehensive planning regards both balance and imbalance as often useful intermediate stages of system-development and limits balance-aiming comprehensive planning to appropriate situations identified after careful scrutiny; (5) good comprehensive planning aims at maximizing the objective expectation of desirable impact on future reality, using whatever nominal tools are most useful for that purpose; and (6) good comprehensive planning is continuous and iterative, regarding all subphasing as instrumental.

These six characteristics are important, but do not exhaust the positive features of desirable comprehensive planning. To advance our analysis and to gain a better understanding of the nature of good comprehensive planning, a number of additional preferred features must be examined. It seems to me that eight additional preferred features which characterize good comprehensive planning warrant some detailed attention: (a) an intermediate position between policymaking and megapolicy decisions on one hand and operational planning on the other hand; (b) a multidimensional, but manageable, system as the target for planning; (c) an interdisciplinary approach; (d) high development of rationality components and extrarationality components; (e) much sensitivity to value judgments and value assumptions; (f) much political sophistication; (g) orientation of idealistic realism; and (h) self-consciousness, self-evaluation, and continuous self-development.

a. An intermediate position between policymaking and megapolicy decisions on one hand and operational planning on the other hand. Comprehensive planning deals neither with policymaking and megapolicy decisions nor with operational planning, but occupies a position in between—on the level of system planning.

In general, the very existence of comprehensive planning will be the result of policymaking and depends on policymaking for basic directives. But, from the point of view of policymaking, comprehensive planning constitutes in most cases an "execution" activity, closely interconnected by feedback loops with policymaking, but essentially distinct from it.

This does not imply that comprehensive planning does not contribute to aggregate policymaking; but policymaking in the main proceeds actually, and should proceed preferably, by different modes than comprehensive planning. Thus, for instance, policymaking is an aggregate process in which many relatively autonomous units (including comprehensive planning units) participate, while comprehensive planning requires a well-integrated organizational structure. Also, policymaking is more cyclic, taking up a variety of issues at different points in the time-streams, which are dealt with in relative independence from one another, while comprehensive planning deals simultaneously with a set of interdependent components which form a distinguishable system.

Similarly, operation planning takes place one step below comprehensive planning, dealing with detailed planning of specific projects and activities—either as independent operations or as execution activities of comprehensive planning.[7]

b. A multidimensional, but manageable, system as the target for planning. The noun *comprehensiveness* refers to two interrelated characteristics of comprehensive planning, namely, attention to multiple dimensions of a system and an interdisciplinary approach.

I am leaving for the next characteristic a discussion of the interdisciplinary approach. Now I want to emphasize the critical importance for understanding the nature of comprehensive planning, of multidimensional, but manageable, systems serving as its target.

Comprehensive planning deals with a system, that is, with an entity composed of a number of interrelated components (or subsystems).[8] These components are multidimensional; that is, they belong to different facets or types of structures or processes. For instance, comprehensive planning can deal with a region, including a physical subsystem, a population subsystem, an economic subsystem, and a cultural subsystem. But in order for comprehensive planning to be feasible and worthwhile, the complexity of the system must be limited—as already pointed out when discussing fallacy 2—so as to be susceptible to a meaningful planning. Thus, comprehensive planning on a national scale may be possible only in respect to relatively underdeveloped societies, and even there the number of facets to be planned simultaneously must be strictly limited—depending on available knowledge and techniques.

Here the relative nature of the comprehensiveness of comprehensive planning becomes visible. Even the simplest planning activity deals with

[7]Both policymaking and operational planning can be more or less comprehensive. Comprehensive policymaking and comprehensive operational planning do share many characteristics with comprehensive planning in the meaning suggested by me, but are nevertheless distinct activities. Any broader use of the term *comprehensive planning* puts into it so many heterogeneous activities, as to make the term useless for most theoretical and applied purposes alike. When, for some analyses, we want to discuss together all these types of "comprehensive" activities, I suggest we use the term *comprehensive institutional decisionmaking,* or—when we want to include also comprehensive individual decisionmaking—just simply *comprehensive decisionmaking.*

[8]This is very important, because it points out the affinity between comprehensive planning and systems management.

more than one type of variable and is therefore to some degree multidimensional. And, even the most comprehensive planning activity deals only with a few facets of reality, and is therefore neither all-inclusive nor complete. It follows that any dichotomous distinction between *non-comprehensive* and *comprehensive* planning is quite misleading: we have *"less* comprehensive" and *"more* comprehensive" planning, dispersed on a continuum between the non-existing polar "pure types" of single-dimensional and all-comprehending planning. For the sake of convenience, I will continue to use the term *comprehensive planning* when I have in mind the range from *quite* comprehensive to *highly* comprehensive; but the *relative* nature of the concept and its heterogenous contents should be kept in mind.

   c. *An interdisciplinary approach.* Not every interdisciplinary planning activity is comprehensive. For instance, good economic planning in a modernizing society must take into account socio-psychological variables influencing economic phenomena, such as levels of aspiration and propensity to change. Therefore, under such conditions, good, but not very comprehensive, economic planning will adopt some elements of an interdisciplinary approach. But every good comprehensive planning has to be highly interdisciplinary.

   This desirable feature follows from the multidimensional nature of the target of comprehensive planning and the soon to be discussed preferable feature of highly developed rationality components. In order to deal well with a multidimensional system, all relevant knowledge must be utilized, including also the various disciplines dealing with the different dimensions of the planning system and the variables shaping them. Most instances of comprehensive planning will require, at least, high-grade knowledge in economics, sociology and social psychology, political science, social geography, agronomy, and some areas of engineering life and physical sciences. In addition, knowledge is required in the various disciplines and techniques of policy sciences, such as policy analysis, systems management, systems analysis, decision theory, operations research, mathematical statistics, futures studies, and information processing.

   Comprehensive planning requires more than eclectic aggregation of such different disciplines. What is needed is the integration of different disciplines, approaches, and techniques into a really interdisciplinary—as distinguished from multidisciplinary—approach. This is a very difficult task requiring long periods of running-in of the planning staff. More important, quite radical changes may be needed in the academic and in-service training of planners, both in order to prepare single-disciplinary professionals to operate in a comprehensive planning setup, and in order to educate and develop highly qualified persons with a multidisciplinary background and an interdisciplinary approach to serve as the heads of teams in comprehensive planning units. These are the persons who may form a new profession of "comprehensive planners," as a subspecialization of policy sciences.

d. High development of both rationality and extrarationality components.
I am discussing together the need for high development of rationality components with high development of extrarationality components in order to emphasize the mixed nature of preferable comprehensive planning. Comprehensive planning requires much creativity and originality in inventing new alternatives and adjusting old ones to new conditions and tasks; comprehensive planning requires full utilization of modern knowledge to reduce uncertainty and to deal simultaneously with a large number of variables; comprehensive planning needs highly developed tacit knowledge and intuition to provide a feeling for the *Gestalt* or "configuration" of the involved situations and to supply good subjective probabilities, based on a combination between guess and estimate, for the many situations in which uncertainty cannot be otherwise reduced or contained. In order to make specific these general remarks, let me mention three more concrete propositions:

1. At present, many of the newer developments in knowledge of how to deal with uncertainty and how to identify preferred system designs are not utilized in most planning activities. These developments in knowledge include, for instance, systems and policy analysis, welfare theory, and decision theory. Many planners seem to lack even the background knowledge necessary for understanding such knowledge and for adjusting it to the contexts of comprehensive planning.
2. Most planning units familiar to the author or discussed in literature conspicuously lack staff development and career planning schemes, designed to provide the professional staff with opportunities to develop their intuition and tacit capacities through suitable systematic rotation, planning games, organizational development activities, and the like.
3. Most planning units familiar to the author or discussed in literature seem to neglect, and often ignore, the possibilities for encouraging innovating and imaginative thinking by methods such as brainstorming, counterfactual thinking and scenario writing.

These three propositions are only a few examples of the operations involved in upgrading the rationality components and extrarationality components of comprehensive planning—as urgently required for better comprehensive planning.

e. Much sensitivity to value judgments and value assumptions. Planners are very prone to mix up their scientific knowledge with their value convictions and value assumptions. Economic planners quickly accept, for instance, increasing per capita income as an axiomatic goal of economic activity; city planners regard a garden city, a house machine, or some other type of human habitation as an obvious ideal environment for human beings; regional planners regard green belts, recreation areas of defined function, etc. as a must of good life; and so on. Even comprehensive planning soon becomes a self-evident value by itself, instead of an instrumental activity with a significant but limited domain of usefulness.

Such naivety concerning the role of values and knowledge in planning, ill befits planners. Especially in comprehensive planning, explicit examination of value assumptions is essential, because of the multipurpose nature of comprehensive planning and the complex possible trade-offs between the various goals and alternatives. In comprehensive planning, careful value sensitivity analysis of the various main alternatives is essential, in order both to encourage search for alternatives which are less sensitive to different value judgments and to permit the political bodies to guide the planners by explicit value judgments made in operational terms.

f. Much political sophistication. Clear confrontation of the implied value issues involved in all planning activities is also one step in the direction of another desideratum of good comprehensive planning, namely, much political sophistication. Comprehensive planning presumes to deal with the future of social systems through organized social action. As such, it is essentially a highly political activity taking place in the political arena. Though planners as such are not politicians, they are—whether they like it or not—partners of politicians, and junior partners at that. Often, lack of emotional readiness to accept this position goes hand-in-hand with ignorance about the political contexts of comprehensive planning, with one weakness reinforcing the other and the unavoidable end result being futile planning and frustrated planners.[9] Much political sophistication, on the emotional as well as on the intellectual levels, must therefore be added to the features of good comprehensive planning.

g. Orientation of idealistic realism. Political sophistication is also essential to avoid cynicism resulting from naivety meeting reality—which is a sure poison for good comprehensive planning. Comprehensive planning is a most difficult activity with limited probability of clear-cut successes and high probability of starkly visible failures at best. One possible and quite widespread defensive reaction by comprehensive planners is to retire into a closed world of their own, which produces plans for consumption by other planners, but without any significant impact on reality. Another possible reaction is to accommodate oneself to a surrealistic view of reality and to become a servant of power, instead of a proinnovations force. What comprehensive planners need is a balanced mix of realism and idealism, in which idealism is conditioned by a hard view of reality and in which realism is tempered by a strong feeling of the missions of planners as professional reformers of reality.

---

[9]A study well illustrating these and related phenomena is Alan A. Altshuller, *The City Planning Process: A Political Analysis* (Ithaca, N.Y.: Cornell University Press, 1965).

h. Self-consciousness, self-evaluation, and continuous self-development. Beyond the various discrete features of good comprehensive planning, and underlying all of them, is the requirement that good comprehensive planning must be self-conscious, self-evaluative, and continuously self-developing. Good comprehensive planning does not come naturally. The opposite is true: in most respects the features of good comprehensive planning contradict the usual tendencies of organizational behavior. Constant self-awareness and efforts for self-improvement are therefore essential.

This requirement has a number of different implications. For instance, comprehensive planning bodies, as all organizations, need special units in charge of self-analysis and self-improvement, dealing with management analysis, staff development, feedback processing, etc. Comprehensive planning units also have to program carefully their own activities, realizing that planning must be planned, with special attention, *inter alia,* to delimiting the preferable scope and detailedness of planning, to selecting suitable nominal output forms, and to utilizing the best existing tools and techniques. Most important of all, persons engaged in comprehensive planning must preserve and increase their readiness and capacity for continuous learning and development, and must always be ready to give up cherished opinions and dearly held convictions whenever there is sufficient reason to regard the wisdom and knowledge of the past as the conventional wisdom and blind spots of the future.

This chapter has presented only some of the main features of good comprehensive planning. But this short and incomplete list is demanding enough to raise the question to what extent comprehensive planning is at all feasible. Available evidence provides little ground for undue assumptions and an arrogant attitude in this respect. Would-be comprehensive planners have good reason for an attitude of humility and careful hope, rather than a self-confident posture. The number of cases in which comprehensive planning has successfully dealt with multidimensional systems is limited at best. Even on the relatively small scale of city planning, comprehensive planning has not yet provided any convincing solutions for basic problems of transportation, air pollution, and recreation (not to mention more difficult problems of youth culture, community relations, etc.).

Those of us who nevertheless think that comprehensive planning does hold forth significant promise as one of the methods for better shaping of the future must assume the burden of proof. Only through significant progress in the theory and practice of comprehensive planning as part of policy sciences as a whole, can some elements of this promise be realized. Identification of progress-retarding fallacies and clarification of the features of good comprehensive planning are a necessary part in any such endeavor.

CHAPTER 12

Improvement of Decisionmaking and Administrative Planning in Israel[1]

COMMENTS

This chapter is based on a memorandum prepared in 1965 for the Israeli government on the improvement of decisionmaking and administrative planning. Its main recommendations are to introduce a multiple-year planning system combined with PPBS and to establish policy analysis and planning units in all ministries. The memorandum emphasizes the need to train professional personnel for those functions, with the curriculum of the courses held, after approval of the recommendations, included in Appendixes A and B. Thus, this chapter illustrates an effort to realize some recommendations based on policy sciences. It deals specifically with Israel, but in its present version it applies in general also to other countries.

Introduction

1. This chapter presents the preliminary results of a study on ways and means for improving administrative planning and decisionmaking in Israel's government ministries; the study was commissioned in 1965 from the Central School of Administration by the Budget Division of the Ministry of Finance and the Inter-Ministerial Efficiency Committee.

2. The investigation comprised four stages:

   a. An overall survey of administrative planning in most ministries.

   b. A more intense examination of planning in three selected units.

   c. Examination of relevant literature on planning theory, systems analysis, and decision theory.

   d. Construction of a preferable model for administrative planning in ministries and its translation into operational directives.

Stages *a* and *b* were carried out by a research team of graduates of the Central School under the supervision of Mr. Hillel Ashkenazi, Dr. Moshe Shani, and the author. Stages *c* and *d* were carried out by the author, with the assistance of Dr. Shani. An earlier version of the present chapter formed a basic component of stage *d*, being based on the findings of stages *a* to *c*.

[1] An earlier version of this chapter was published in *Public Administration in Israel and Abroad, 1966* (Jerusalem: Israel Institute of Public Administration, 1967), pp. 121–131.

3. The investigation was carried out under the direction of a committee of senior civil servants, presided over by Mr. Ariel Amiad, Director-General of the Ministry of Agriculture; this committee made a substantial contribution towards its progress. During the first stage, Mr. Jacob Salman was in charge of the investigation and, in that capacity, laid the foundations for continuation of the study.

4. The ideas and summary topics presented here were intended to be a basis for preliminary discussions with a view to determining the principles for an administrative planning scheme and for identifying the preconditions for its implementation. The object of this chapter was to present basic ideas requiring discussion and decision in as precise, concise, and clear a manner as possible.

Central Assumptions

5. Since the establishment of the State of Israel, much progress has been made in improving and systematizing administrative operations. The Budget Division played a vital part in the attainment of this progress. Nevertheless, the survey of administrative planning in 1966 pinpointed serious deficiencies in the modes of operation and degree of rationality in several government units. Particularly striking were the following:

a. Lack of clarification of desired medium-term outputs.

b. Lack of institutionalized evaluation and of systematic follow-up after operations and of reexamination of goals set down or crystallized in the past.

c. Lack of proper benefit-cost analysis and of the data and personnel required for such an analysis.

d. Lack of sufficient efforts to measure outputs, to establish evaluation criteria, and to develop costing, as more rational bases for the future allocation of resources.

e. As a necessary consequence of the above: lack of well-founded medium-term plans, laid down after consideration of alternatives, and, frequently also, lack of short-term plans. Therefore, also absence of an adequate basis for budget planning.

6. These shortcomings are not specific to Israel's governmental administration. Indeed, until about 1955, only few planning methods and decisionmaking patterns were available anywhere for the introduction of any effective improvements in the existing state of affairs. Isolated ideas, such as performance budgeting, were introduced in Israel, but these devices were not enough to exert a decisive influence over usual organizational phenomena. Methods through which decisionmaking may be systematized and rationalized had been devised only after 1955—as developed, for instance, by The Rand Corporation in the United States. Some of these methods were introduced into

the Pentagon by Robert McNamara and, by special administrative order of President Johnson, they were to be adopted by the whole federal adminstration of the United States.

7. It is necessary to avoid the erroneous impression that some kind of panacea or philosopher's stone had been discovered by means of which a decisive revolution might be wrought in the administrative decisionmaking process. Decisionmaking in public administration involves political considerations and value judgments and deals with largely intangible outputs. It takes place under conditions of considerable uncertainty and is confined by a large number of constraints, both general and specific. Nevertheless, through new methods—many of which are part of systems analysis and include benefit-cost analysis and planning-programming-budgeting—it has become possible to make a real stride ahead toward systematization and rationalization of administration decisionmaking.

Even if these advances are unlikely to modify existing patterns of activity by more than, say, 10 percent, the marginal benefits of the modification are highly important and undoubtedly justify the far-reaching efforts required.

8. Systems analysis and planning-programing-budgeting methods, as chiefly developed in the United States, constituted a major, but not the only, source for the construction of a preferable model for improved administrative planning in Israel Ministries. No less important were the planning patterns pragmatically evolved in Israel, especially the overlapping planning system of the Israel Army for periods of one year, three years, five years and, later on, for ten years and more. The proposed model in some respects also took into account the experiences acquired by public enterprises and institutions in other countries, to the extent that this experience was available in literature or from other sources, as well as actual conditions prevailing in Israeli Government offices and public administration generally. Furthermore, some elements of the proposed model were based on theoretical work on the improvement of policymaking by the author.

Principal Objectives

9. The main objective of the present proposal was to strengthen the degree of rationality of government decisions.

10. More specifically, the intention was to strengthen the following elements of administrative decisionmaking:

  a. Goal-setting with a more developed order of priorities for a medium-time-range based on a consistency analysis of different goals, some examination of marginal rates of exchange, and some clarification of operational values.

b. Increasing the time span considered in the determination of administrative operations, together with a systematic effort to foresee problems and reduce uncertainty by evolving appropriate prediction methods.

c. Expanding the range of alternatives by encouraging the search for new alternatives and periodically reexamines current activity patterns.

d. Stimulating output measurements and estimates based on explicit criteria, and improving both current feedback and learning feedback, based on a systematic follow-up after current operations.

e. Achieving more reliable estimates of expected benefits-costs in respect to medium-time-range alternatives, to serve as a basis for more rational allocation of resources.

f. Achieving greater consistency of administrative operations and a more systematic approach to the attainment of medium-time-range goals, combined with more attention to long-term goals.

11. These elements are to be developed at the level both of the ministries and of their subunits, as well as at the level of different superunits and interministerial units. It should be stressed that, while in individual ministries some improvements may be usefully introduced without changes in the overall governmental planning patterns, it is doubtful whether it is feasible in Israel significantly to improve the overall administrative planning process (as distinct from policymaking and strategic planning, which may be improved by direct means and which are not dealt with in the present chapter) without an improvement in the corresponding operations at the level of individual ministries. In order to move the entire governmental administration in the preferable direction, all the relevant elements must be improved—on the ministerial, subministerial, and supraministerial levels. Some preliminary ideas on the interconnection between the proposed micro-planning improvements and macro-planning were presented separately. (See chapters 26 and 27.[2])

Main Tools

12. Two main tools for achieving the objectives indicated above are—

a. the introduction of an overlapping administrative planning system, for one year, a small number of years (e.g., three years), and a medium number of years (e.g., five years);

b. the development of planning and policy analysis units in all ministries, and better planning and policy analysis in overhead units, especially the Budget Division.

[2]An analysis of macro-planning in Israel and the variables shaping its characteristics at that time is provided in Benjamin Akzin and Yehezkel Dror, *Israel: High-pressure Planning* (Syracuse: National Planning Series, Syracuse University Press, 1966).

13. I want to stress the relations between these two tools. On one hand, it is impossible to introduce better administrative planning without at the same time developing policy analysis units, since any useful planning requires units capable of good analysis. On the other hand, it is useful to set up policy analysis units even in the absence of an overall administrative planning system, since such units may contribute to improved operations even without a highly developed planning system. What should be emphasized is that a planning procedure by itself is likely to contribute but little, and may become a mere ritual, doing little good and perhaps much harm.

14. Regarding the proposed administrative planning system, I suggest the following:

a. That an explicit administrative planning system be introduced in all ministries.

b. That the system should be uniform in general, but sufficiently elastic in detail to be adapted to the specific characteristics of each minstry.

c. That every ministry should prepare a general operations plan for a period of three years and a detailed work program for one year. Each ministry should elaborate a series of goals to be attained within five years and perhaps also preliminary ideas for a longer range. These plans, programs, and goals are to be regularly and systematically revised: the three-year plan every two years; the annual program every year; and the series of goals every three or four years. In addition to these overlapping administrative plans dealing with all organized operations, plans are to be prepared, dealing with specific projects and different facets of society handled by the respective ministries. The time span, degree of details, etc., of these plans depend on the characteristics of their subject matters.

d. That the annual work program should constitute a one-year projection of the three-year plan. It should include at least an operations plan, a manpower utilization plan, and a budget plan.

e. That a planning and policy analysis unit should be established in each ministry, at the highest level. These units should be staffed by trained professionals.

f. That the preparation of the plan components should be a joint operation by the proposed staff unit and the regular line units of the ministry, the latter making most of the substantive decisions, while the planning analysis units supply the tools, develop the decisionmaking methods, and deal with interunit integration, in addition to helping the heads of the ministry in overall policymaking for, and management of, the system.

g. That an interlinked follow-up system be introduced, whose findings, among others, should form the basis for changes in operations and for replanning, as the need may arise.

h. That a central governmental overhead unit, preferably related to the Budget Department, should be responsible for consultation and guidance to the ministries in implementing the proposed planning system and providing the trained manpower required for the planning and policy analysis units. (The need for additional planning and policy analysis units close to the Cabinet, the Budget Department, and other central policymaking units is dealt with in chapters 20 and 24).

15. With regard to the professional manpower required for staffing the planning and policy analysis units, I want to stress the need for directing to these posts persons of high intellectual ability, as well as a capacity for maintaining good interpersonal relations even in situations fraught with a considerable amount of tension. Candidates having the necessary personal qualifications and a university degree in the appropriate disciplines (mainly the decision and behavioral sciences), as well as, if possible, some previous experience in organizational work, should be required to undergo a very intense planning and policy analysis course. This must be at least a seven-month course, whose preparation requires much effort. To my mind, the staffing of the planning and policy analysis units with suitable, properly trained manpower is an essential prerequisite for the attainment of progress in the directions outlined.

16. One of the conclusions from the foregoing is that the improvement of administrative planning in Israel Government offices is no easy task, and that considerable efforts and resources are required to achieve that end. Above all, it is, to my mind, essential to avoid any short cuts in the training of the personnel required to provide formal planning with a meaningful content. At the same time, I have little doubt that any improvements of the elements mentioned in paragraph 10 above, with the aid of the means proposed, will lead to a rise in the quality of administrative decisionmaking and operations.

17. Once the proposal outlined has been approved in principle, it will be necessary to work out a detailed program, dealing with the following items:

a. Fixing a timetable and outlining specific transition stages.

b. Laying down a program for recruiting the personnel required for the planning and policy analysis units, and preparing the appropriate training for this personnel (See Appendix A).

c. Preparing the ground by a program which should, in particular, provide for appropriate information, instruction, and involvement for the senior civil servants (see Appendix B).

d. Adopting the working methods of the Budget Division to the new pattern.

e. Determining the detailed structure, staff, and organization of the planning and policy analysis units.

f. Determining the division of labor between the line units and the planning and policy analysis units in the Ministries, and with the corresponding overhead units.

g. Synchronizing activities for mutual reinforcement.

APPENDIX A

A Course for Planning and Policy Analysis Officers[1]

One of the unique features of Israel's endeavors to improve governmental decisionmaking was a special, very intense residential course for planning and policy analysis staff officers held in 1966-1968 at the Government Staff School.[2] The main features of this course are described in this appendix. Following the success of the course, initiation of a graduate program in planning and policy analysis is being considered at one of the universities in Israel.

1. *Preparatory period* (November 27 to December 18, 1966)

The preparatory period was designed for about ten of the course candidates who lacked necessary background knowledge in basic subject matters. Additional course candidates audited some of the courses given during the preparatory period, as a refresher.

The curriculum of the preparatory period was as follows:

Subject	Number of Hours
Introduction to Statistics	20
Introduction to Economics	32
Theory of Prices	27
Introduction to Mathematics	22
Tutorship in Mathematics	30
TOTAL	131

2. *First stage of the course* (December 18, 1966, to April 17, 1967)

The first stage of the course was conducted on a residential basis in the Central Staff School of the Government. The students engaged in very intense studies for five days a week, with additional individual tutorship available in the evenings. Most of the students did spend the sixth day in their Ministries, to update themselves on current activities.

[1]The course was headed by a small staff, including the Director, Mr. Yaacob Salman; two Chief Training Officers, Mr. D. Felsenthal and Mr. E. Fucks; and the author, who served as Academic Director. Dr. Henry Rowen and Mr. Peter Szanton served as senior consultants during the planning of the course. Dr. Edward Quade served as consultant during the course.

[2]The lecturers included experts from the Rand Corporation and the Bureau of the Budget from the United States; university teachers; senior military staff officers; and senior civil servants.

The curriculum of the first stage was as follows:

Subject	Number of Hours
I. Policymaking and Policy Analysis	*32*
II. Advanced Administrative Theory	*26*
(1) Administrative Theory	6
(2) Administrative Reform	13
(3) Problems of Israeli Public Administration	7
III. Systems Analysis, Operations Research and Management Sciences	*96*
(1) Systems Analysis	23
(2) Theory and Practice of Systems Analysis	23
(3) Operations Research and Systems Analysis (Cases)	17
(4) Introduction to Operations Research	17
(5) Integrated Data Processing	12
(6) Psychology of Decisionmaking Processes	4
IV. Mathematics and Statistics	*104*
(1) Differential and Integral Calculus	38
(2) Linear Algebra	30
(3) Probability Theory and Methods in Mathematical Statistics	36
V. Economics and Welfare Theory	*55*
(1) Macro Economics and Economic Policy	12
(2) Welfare Economics	24
(3) Capital Budgeting	11
(4) Problems in Welfare Theory	8
VI. Advanced Budgeting	*54*
(1) Budgeting	26
(2) Costing	24
(3) Governmental Accounting	4
VII. Administrative Planning and Control	*33*
(1) Methods of Administrative Planning and Control	9
(2) Administrative Planning in Israel (Cases)	24
VIII. Projects	*104*
(1) Master-Plan for Civil Aviation—Lod Airport	23
(2) A Model Framework for Multi-Year Planning in the Revenue Service	31
(3) Decisionmaking in the Welfare Service (two selected problems)	8
(4) Desalination of Sea Water	17
(5) Decisionmaking in Education (two selected problems)	7

(6) Force Composition (one selected problem)   18
Total number of hours in first stage of course   *504*

3. *Second stage of the course* (April 1967 to March 1968)

During this period the participants returned to their Ministries to work in newly created positions as planning and policy analysis staff officers. The students were provided with professional guidance and individual support by the central unit in charge of introducing PPBS and policy analysis. Also, about once every six weeks a study day took place at which the experiences of the various participants in their Ministries were discussed and relevant guest lectures were delivered. Literature on PPBS, planning, and policy analysis was distributed regularly to the participants.

4. *Third stage of the course* (April 21 to May 30, 1968)

During the third stage of the course, additional intensive studies took place during six weeks of residence, on the same pattern as the first stage (see section 2 above).

The curriculum of the third stage was as follows:

Subject	Numbers of Hours
I. Policy Analysis and Systems Analysis	*75*
(1) Advanced Policy Analysis	20
(2) Applied Policy Analysis: Higher Education Policy	10
(3) Policy Analysis and Systems Analysis in Action: Experience in the Ministries	30
(4) Cases in Systems Analysis	15
II. Mathematics	*44*
(1) Probability Theory	30
(2) Theory of Games	14
III. Economic and Welfare Theory	*55*
(1) Benefit-Cost Analysis	20
(2) Utility Theory	25
(3) Problems of Welfare Theory	10
IV. Operations Research and Management Sciences	*50*
(1) Linear Programming	15
(2) Nonlinear Programming	15
(3) Prediction Methods	10
(4) Simulation	10
Total number of hours in third stage of course	*224*

5. *Details about participants*

In the first and second stages of the course thirty students took part.
The academic qualifications of the participants were as follows:
B.A. (Economics, Statistics, Political Science, Social Work): 21 students.

B.Sc. (Electrical Engineering, Civil Engineering, Mechanical Engineering, Production Engineering, Agricultural Engineering): 6 students.
M.D.: 1 student.
M.A. (Humanities): 1 student.
M.B.A. (Business Administration): 1 student.
Most of the participants with a B.A. degree were pursuing graduate studies in administration at The Hebrew University.

In the third stage of the course about twenty students took part, with others auditing parts of the course. This group included a few students who had not participated in the first two stages.

APPENDIX B

The Program for a First Short "Eye-opener" Course for Senior Officials
Duration of course: Two weeks, five days a week, eight hours a day, eighty hours in all.

	Hours
Policymaking and decisionmaking	12
Planning, analysis and managerial economics	15
Planning and budgeting	8
Planning-programing-budgeting systems	20
Organizational and human problems of planning	5
Work planning in Israel's Army	5
Work planning in the Ministry of Agriculture	5
Exercise I: Evaluation of ministerial decisionmaking	5 (apart from independent work)
Exercise II: Overlapping multiple-year planning	5 (apart from independent work)
TOTAL	80

Behavioral sciences are one of the foundations for policy sciences. Furthermore, the contribution of behavioral sciences in their normal form to better policymaking constitutes a main subject for study and improvement by policy sciences. Therefore, this part deals with a set of very important problems of policy sciences. The first chapter introduces parts of the subject through empirical material, namely, some case studies on the uses of sociology in policymaking in Israel and the Netherlands. The second chapter takes a much broader and deductive view, using a general systems approach to consider the uses of behavioral sciences for better policymaking, with conclusions in respect to required changes in the behavioral sciences, in the policy-making system, and in the intertransport between them. The third chapter examines some implications for behavioral sciences meta-megapolicies of postulating for them the goal of contributing to the advancement of policy sciences.
In addition to the relevance of the various chapters to a policy sciences view of behavioral sciences, each chapter also illustrates some methods or concepts of policy sciences through application to behavioral sciences issues: the first chapter illustrates the utilization of short case studies as stimulants for hypotheses; the second chapter illustrates the application of a general systems model to an issue; and the third chapter exercises the concepts of metapolicy and megapolicy and some of their dimensions.

PART IV

A Policy Sciences View of Behavioral Sciences

CHAPTER 13

The Uses of Sociology in Policymaking:
Four Cases from Israel and The Netherlands[1]

COMMENTS

Case studies are an important research method of policy sciences, essential for understanding policymaking reality. For reliable findings, large numbers of case studies which permit inductive conclusions are necessary. But even single cases can provide important insights and understandings and can serve, through deduction, as a basis for generalization. Thus, the intense studies of the Cuban missile crisis in the United States provided important knowledge on top-level crisis policymaking, thanks to the availability of rich material on this single case, on one hand, and its critical nature, on the other hand. This is true despite the uniqueness of this case (as of every other top-level policymaking instance).

This chapter illustrates the utilization of short case studies as stimulants for hypotheses on one of the basic issues of policy sciences, namely, the uses of professional experts—in this study, sociologists—in policymaking. This chapter is based on cases collected in Israel and in the Netherlands, thus also illustrating the international domain of the problems faced by policy sciences.

Introduction

Two approaches to the problem of how to make preferable use of sociologists in policymaking are most fruitful: (1) abstract analysis and (2) empirical case studies. Abstract analysis involves deductive construction of a preferable model of the utilization of sociologists in policymaking, based on organization theory and decision sciences, on one hand, and analysis of sociological knowledge, on the other hand; evaluation of the actual situation in policymaking agencies in terms of the preferable model; identification of the main barriers hindering approximation of preferability; and suggestions designed to overcome those barriers—so as to move reality toward the preferable model. Empirical case studies begin with real cases of sociologists in policymaking; derive insights from the cases into the variables shaping the role of sociologists; and, if possible, proceed to statistically reliable generalizations, preferably in the form of a quantitative behavioral model.

[1]This chapter is based on an earlier version called "Public Administration: Four Cases from Israel and The Netherlands," first published in Paul F. Lazarsfeld, William H. Sewell, and Harold L. Wilensky, ed., *The Uses of Sociology* (New York: Basic Books, 1967), pp. 418-26. Copyright, Basic Books.

Using the second approach, I shall outline four cases of sociologists in action in policymaking, two from the Netherlands and two from Israel. The cases are based on interviews with participants. Each is accompanied by a short interpretation, an attempt to derive insights from the facts. The chapter concludes with some tentative hypotheses. My limited purpose is to illustrate some problems facing sociologists and other behavioral scientists in policymaking organizations.

Case 1. The Community Health Center[2]

Facts

In 1952 the Israeli Ministry of Health considered establishing a community health center in an Arab village in the coastal plain of Israel. A preliminary decision was taken to build the center in Taiba, and a social anthropologist was invited to prepare an anthropological and social study of relevant habits and attitudes of the local population. His study, paid for by United States aid funds, dealt mainly with the local power structure and with local health habits. The main recommendation was that steps should be taken to mobilize the support of the local power elite for the proposed center.

The report was distributed in writing to the members of a ministerial committee in charge of planning the health center. The anthropologist never appeared in person before that committee. For reasons of military security and geography, the center was finally built in another, similar village. The study was totally ignored in the work of the committee. When interviewed, most members of the committee did not even remember having heard about it.

After the center was built, serious difficulties in running it were encountered, mainly because of lack of support by the local power elite and differences between local health habits and the medical treatment patterns followed in the center.

Interpretation

In this case, the social scientist was not a member of the organization, but an outsider. He was given a rather ill-defined task, not clearly related to the problems as perceived by the main decisionmakers, and not paid by them. He did not participate in the on-going decisionmaking process, and no effective communication channels existed between him and the decisionmakers. His survey did include relevant data, but he was unable to educate the decisionmakers to appreciate that data and to see its significance for their problems.

[2]This description is based on a case study prepared by Rachel Elboim-Dror and published in Hebrew.

Case 2. The Sociological Advisor of an Israeli Revenue-Collecting Agency

Facts

In 1962 the director of an Israeli revenue-collecting agency decided to appoint a sociologist as a member of his personal staff. After some search, a highly qualified sociologist who had studied in Israel and the United States was engaged.

Neither the director nor the sociologist had any clear role expectations. Both agreed to let things work themselves out on an experimental basis. The director was, at the beginning, mainly eager to utilize the sociologist for improving relations with the clientele; then he asked the sociologist to examine some problems of internal administration and staff training. In general, the sociologist was left to his own resources. He participated in the regular meetings of the director with his senior staff advisors, commenting on the subjects under discussion.

The sociologist did a number of small field studies. For instance, he investigated the reasons for delays in tax payments due to one of the divisions of the agency; his main finding was that officials were often unwilling to impair their continuous working relations with the clientele by imposing a monetary penalty for overdue tax payments, though entitled by law to do so. As a result of this study, administrative instructions were issued to be more strict in imposition of sanctions for delays in tax payments.

The various divisions of the agency, which enjoyed considerable autonomy, resented the intrusions of the sociologist, who was regarded as an agent of the director. The director became increasingly disappointed in that his rather undefined expectations were not being met. The sociologist became progressively frustrated and uneasy and looked around for an academic position.

In 1964, when an opening at one of the higher institutes of education occurred, the sociologist left the agency. The director made little effort to prevent his resignation. Shortly thereafter a new director was appointed, who had served before as head of one of the divisions and had had in that capacity some contact with the sociologist. The new director decided to delay appointment of another sociological advisor.

During interviews, the former director admitted that the sociologist had made some useful contributions. Especially interesting was the admission by a senior subdirector that the sociologist had perhaps been right in an important public-relations strategy recommendation which at that time had been rejected. Being very anxious to improve its public image and to increase cooperation by the clientele in assessing and collecting the respective taxes, the agency had adopted an active public-relations policy directed at convincing the clientele that the taxes were urgently needed for important national activities. The sociological advisor had opposed that policy, expressing the opinion that it is natural for people to dislike paying taxes; he thought that the less people heard about taxes and the agency, the better relations with the public would be. Therefore, the agency should avoid visibility rather than attract attention through public-relations activities.

But, in general, all interviewed officials professed disappointment. The sociologist also regarded his term of office in some respects as a failure, claiming that he was expected to do undefined things and blamed for not doing them. The director and his interviewed staff agreed with that formulation and blamed themselves for not arriving at a clearer job definition, but claimed that the sociologist did not show enough initiative and did not "sell" himself.

Interpretation

The sociological advisor entered an agency which had had no experience with such positions; therefore, the situation was nonstructured and his role definition, very loose. He did not succeed in building up a realistic image of his position, either for himself or for the organization. Perhaps he engaged prematurely in hostility-generating specific studies without adequate prior educational activities. He apparently did not show sufficient initiative and salesmanship. There are some indications, however, that had he stayed on, many of the difficulties would have resolved themselves.

**Case 3. The Research Division of a Physical Planning
Unit in The Netherlands**

Facts

The Physical Planning unit studied in The Netherlands is in charge of preparing physical planning studies and physical planning policies. It has a research division staffed by three sociologists and a number of social geographers. This research division tackles a variety of problems defined by the physical planners and designers in charge of the service. A typical study dealing with recreation patterns found that people do not travel far on Sundays. As a result of this finding, the policy was adopted to locate recreation areas near the population centers.

Highly regarded in the service, well staffed, and supplied with an adequate budget, the research division makes both detailed intelligence contributions and general educational contributions to the agency. The head of the research division participates in all senior staff meetings and has full opportunity to participate in decisionmaking as a member of the higher management team.

Despite these favorable conditions, the interviews uncovered some mutual disappointments of the sociologists and the physical planners, and some substantial frustrations. The main difficulties mentioned in the interviews were as follows:

1. There are differences in outlook between the sociologists, on one side, and the physical planners and physical designers, on the other side. The sociologists tend to stick to facts, while the physical planners and designers—in the opinion of the interviewed sociologists—are trained to use imagination and prize creativity.

2. Trained in physical planning disciplines, the physical planners demand from the sociologists definite, quantitative answers to clear questions; with respect to their concrete and detailed planning work (in contrast to the more imaginative aspects), they have a very low tolerance of ambiguity. Thus, the sociologists were asked to predict the number of sailing boats the population will own in 1980 and to determine the amount of land which should be allocated for gardens in a town of a given size. The sociologists explained that they were unable to provide such data and could give only general answers, such as that the number of sailing boats tends to increase and that a town with inhabitants having an agricultural background needs more land for gardens than a town with inhabitants having an urban background. These answers did not meet the needs of the planners, who had to prepare a detailed master plan and as a consequence were irritated with the sociologists.

3. Another difficulty mentioned was the problem of lead time. The sociologists demanded a substantial lead time before answering queries, in order to be able to do the necessary studies. The physical planners often wanted an answer from one day to another, blaming the sociologists for seeking scientific certainty instead of making, when necessary, a good guess. The sociologists reported that they developed a strategy of stockpiling answers by trying to anticipate the probable questions and doing the necessary studies in advance. But this did not always work out.

Although these conflicts were mentioned, both sides plainly regarded the partnership as a permanent one and evaluated the benefits highly.

Interpretation

The interviews in this case show a rather sophisticated awareness of the problems, thus making detailed interpretation redundant. By all signs, we have here an instance of quite successful symbiosis between sociologists and physical planners and designers within an organizational setting. There is some conflict, but working relationships appear to be smooth on the personal level. In this instance sociological knowledge achieved visible and recognized impact on decisions.

Case 4. The Sociological Advisor in a Social Affairs Department in The Netherlands

Facts

The department has a senior sociological advisor, who is in charge of a group of sociologists dispersed throughout the organization. The head of the department is himself a trained sociologist, but achieved his position because of personal qualities, not specific academic training.

The senior sociological advisor serves as a policy analyst. All major proposals and memoranda pass his office for comments, and he participates in the policymaking senior staff meetings. He enjoys the personal confidence of the head of the department and is apparently highly regarded personally throughout the department. His contributions include educational effects, policy recommendations, and specific data. In particular, he emphasizes the social dimensions of the various problems dealt with by the department, regarding himself, to use his phrase, as a "social critic" of departmental operations. For example, he emphasized the need to preserve a role for small shops when planning a new community center.

In the interviews, the advisor clearly differentiated between three distinct sociological roles in the organizational setup: the director of the department, the sociological advisor (himself), and the research sociologists (the other sociologists). The advisor described his role as including two mutually reinforcing functions: (1) a policy analyst, contributing a specific point of view and type of knowledge to decisionmaking, and (2) a liaison officer between the executives and the research sociologists. He felt frustration at not engaging himself in research and expressed a desire to do so.

The head of the department held very favorable opinions of the sociological advisor and his contributions to departmental policies. In respect to the other sociologists, the department head complained about lack of political sophistication, oscillation between overdetailed comments and meaningless generalities, high turnover (50 percent, or 4 out of 8, in one year), ignorance of organizational behavior, and neglect in their thinking of the cost element. Incidentally, the sociological advisor expressed essentially similar views about research sociologists, but more fully recognized their difficulties in working without sufficient basic data on which to base their recommendations.

Interpretation

This case is distinguished by the bifurcation between the sociological advisor and the research sociologists. The sociological academic training of the senior executive is unusual. It is a pity that circumstances prevented interviewing some of the research sociologists, although the view from the top provides some insight. When they heard about my interest in sociologists in policymaking, a number of persons in other departments in the Netherlands told me to study this department because, in their opinion, here sociologists achieved unusual influence on the policy level. Interviews in the agency confirm that view.

Some Tentative Hypotheses

Inferences from these cases must be taken as shaky, for the following reasons: the cases have been presented in bare outline, the number of cases is insignificant, and critical environmental variables are ignored (such as the relatively high propensity in the Netherlands to rely on experts and the tendency in Israel to discount the usefulness of behavioral sciences in government).

For instance, it would be incorrect to conclude that sociological advisors always succeed in the Netherlands and fail in Israel: there are other cases of clear failure of sociological advisors and resistance to their introduction in the Netherlands (for instance, in the Central Economic Planning Office, which is staffed by professional economists and statisticians) and of their success in Israel (for instance, the highly developed sociological advisory service in the Settlement Department of the Jewish Agency, which had some real influence on agricultural settlement planning and development).

With these reservations, I conclude by presenting a number of preliminary and tentative hypotheses formulated on the basis of the four cases:

1. Sociologists can make significant contributions to policymaking. These possible contributions can be of three main types: (*a*) general educational contributions, by sensitizing the policymakers to social aspects of their operations; (*b*) policy contributions, by helping the policymakers to choose major guidelines for operations; (*c*) tactics contributions, by providing specific intelligence and ideas applicable to concrete and detailed issues.

These different levels of contribution are interdependent and reinforce one another. General educational activities seem essential for gaining acceptability for policy and tactics contributions; specific contributions having an obvious pay-off for agency operations seem necessary for legitimizing the position of sociologists in administrative agencies and creating the favorable climate needed for educational impact.

2. In order to make significant contributions to policymaking, some conditions are necessary and helpful. The necessary conditions seem to include (*a*) availability of sociological knowledge directly applicable to the substantive activities of the agency; (*b*) close communication between the sociologists and the main executives; (*c*) a capacity by the sociologists as persons to operate in nonacademic organizations, to adjust themselves to an "action-oriented" environment, and to "sell" themselves and their professional knowledge; (*d*) some involvement and interest by the executives in the activities of the sociological advisors (at least by paying for them from the agency's budget).

Helpful conditions seem to include (*a*) familiarity by the senior executives with sociology; and (*b*) a minimum "critical number" of sociologists, who support one another, strengthen each other's morale, and can engage in research which provides significant findings relevant for agency operations. A single sociologist can—if highly qualified professionally and very strong personally—make significant educational and strategic contributions as a policy analyst. But the availability of several sociologists in an agency seems helpful for all types of contributions and is, perhaps, essential for tactical contributions.

3. The role of sociologists in policymaking involves a number of role conflicts. Especially acute are the pressures for identification with the organization and adjustment of patterns of work to organizational needs, on one hand, and professional norms and scientific criteria, on the other hand. A partial solution of this role conflict is to differentiate between a sociological policy analyst and a research sociologist.

4. Sociologists in public organizations come into conflict with administrators and other groups. These conflicts are the result, *inter alia,* of different time perspectives, different tolerances of ambiguity, different professional self-images and norms, and different locations in the organizational structure (*line* versus *staff*).

5. The introduction of sociological advisor as a new role into an established organization involves many difficulties, mainly because of the unstructured role definition and the noncomplementary expectations. Even under optimal conditions, time is needed for these problems to be worked out. (During that time, much depends on the personality of the sociological advisor and his human-relations capacities.) Therefore, study and evaluation of the actual contributions of sociology to the operations of an administrative agency are significant only if allowance is made for a considerable lead time, needed for mutual adjustment and situation structuring.

CHAPTER 14

A General Systems Approach to Uses of Behavioral Sciences for Better Policymaking[1]

COMMENTS

This chapter is devoted to an examination of the uses of behavioral sciences for better policymaking. It is prescriptive in orientation, trying to utilize a general systems theory framework of the relations between public policymaking and behavioral sciences in order to identify changes required for improved utilization of behavioral sciences for better policymaking. (Improved and better are used in the instrumental-normative sense of increasing the expected net outputs of whatever goals are stipulated after goal analysis. Such goals can also include changes—incremental or radical—in the policymaking system itself and in the social system as a whole.)

The chapter proceeds from a short characterization of the relevance of contemporary behavioral sciences to policymaking, to a simple general systems model of relations between behavioral sciences and policymaking, leading to a set of redesign specifications for improved use of behavioral sciences for better policymaking. This chapter is exploratory in nature and tentative in content, being aimed at presenting an approach to the problems of utilizing behavioral sciences for better policymaking, rather than providing a definite treatment. In particular, this paper proposes that general systems theory can provide an essential framework for transforming parts of behavioral sciences into a main component of policy sciences.

Contemporary Behavioral Sciences and Policymaking

Since the early history of mankind, policymakers have been looking to pre-science for aid in the arduous tasks of trying to control the future by choices in the face of uncertainty. Consultations with seers, astrologers, and magicians represent early efforts to utilize experts in pre-science as aids in policymaking. However, we lack reliable information to evaluate the impacts of such pre-science advisors on policymaking.[2] Often, thanks to the native in-

[1]This chapter is based on a paper presented at the Sesquicentennial Anniversary Symposium of the University of Virginia on "Global Systems Dynamics," Charlottesville. June 17-19, 1969. An earlier version was published in Ernest O. Attinger, ed., *Global Systems* (New York: S. Karger, 1970), pp. 81-91.

[2]There are available some histories of the uses of pre-science as a decision-making aid, e.g., F. N. David, *Games, Gods, and Gambling* (New York: Hafner, 1962), and Richard Lewinsohn, *Science, Prophecy and Prediction* (New York: Harper, 1961). But no systematic studies of the history of high-level policymaking systems, in which pre-science was only one, and probably a minor, component, are available. Such studies just do not seem to fit the foci of interests of contemporary historic and social science research.

149

telligence of some such pre-science advisors, they may have been quite helpful—at least by reducing subjective uncertainty and aiding policymakers in crystallizing their own intents and recruiting support. On the other hand, they may often have encouraged recklessness and repressed more intelligent considerations. Certainly, we hope that modern science can do better to aid growing desires for social self-direction.[3]

But I am afraid that a frank examination of the utility of modern behavioral sciences for better policymaking gives little ground to regard them at present as much superior to pre-science in this respect. Certainly, methods are, by definition, more "scientific;" knowledge is more comprehensive and reliable; and concepts are much more sophisticated. But as an aid to policymaking, the possible help that can be received from contemporary psychology, sociology, anthropology and political sciences—that is, from contemporary behavioral sciences—[4] is most limited. Some contributions to better understanding of social issues are available. But the widespread combination of conceptual sophistication with some factual knowledge and weak comprehensive theories, on one hand, and with fuzzy thinking, on the other hand, does not help provide many contributions to complex problem treatment.[5] Behavioral sciences do provide some relevant facts and, more important, may help sensitize policymakers to some dimensions of complex problems; but they also increase subjective uncertainty and feed multiplicity of opinions. The latter, however preferable intellectually, again do little to help existing policymaking systems in better directing social change.

There is a growing literature on the problems of applying behavioral sci-

[3]On this trend, see Amitai Etzioni, *The Active Society: A Theory of Societal and Political Processes* (New York: Free Press, 1968).

[4]Following widespread practice, I am not including economics among the behavioral sciences. In orientations, methodology, methods, and tools, economics is quite different from the behavioral sciences and it is those differences which explain its successful use in highly developed societies for some policymaking. In many of its characteristics, economic theory is, in essence, a theory of efficient resources allocation, belonging more to decision theory and indeed policy sciences than to behavioral sciences.

[5]Let me illustrate, though not prove, my point by mentioning three of the better collections of papers trying to apply behavioral sciences to policy problems, which bring out their inadequacy as policy knowledge: Arthur B. Shostak, *Sociology in Action* (Homewood, Ill.: Dorsey, 1966); Paul F. Lazarsfeld, William H. Sewell, and Harold L. Wilensky, eds., *The Uses of Sociology* (New York: Basic Books, 1967); and Quincy Wright, William M. Evan, and Morton Deutsch, eds., *Preventing World War III: Some Proposals* (New York: Simon and Schuster, 1962).

A comparison of the papers based on behavioral sciences with those based on economics or strategic analysis in Kermit Gordon, ed., *Agenda for the Nation* (Washington, D.C.: Brookings Institution, 1968) also supports, I think, my claims on the weaknesses of behavioral sciences in policy-relevance.

ences to public policy, including Congressional Committee reports,[6] public and semipublic committee reports,[7] and many articles.[8] But one does not find in them a broad framework for redesigning behavioral sciences to make them more useful for better policymaking. The available material is rich in ideas and insights and stimulating in many respects, but no signs of the needed breakthrough can be discerned in it.

Accepting the risks of overgeneralization, unfairness to particular studies, and a somewhat dogmatic appearance, let me point out in over-sharp language some of my impressions on the inadequacies of contemporary approaches to the uses of behavioral sciences for policymaking:

1. There is a far-reaching mixup between reliable factual knowledge, axiomatic assumptions, provisional theories, conceptual taxonomies, doubtful hypotheses, and various types of value judgments—on substantial goals, on willingness to take risks, and on evaluation of time.

2. No effort is made to approach fusion with, or at least build bridges to,

[6]Two very extensive collections of hearings and studies are the four volumes on *The Use of Social Research in Federal Domestic Programs*, a Staff Study for the Research and Technical Programs Subcommittee of the Committee on Government Operations, House of Representatives, April 1967 (Washington, D.C.: U.S. Government Printing Office, 1967); and the three volumes of hearings before the Subcommittee on Government Research of the Committee on Government Operations, United States Senate, on S. 836, *A Bill to Provide for the Establishment of the National Foundation for the Social Sciences*, February and June 1967 (Washington, D.C.: U.S. Government Printing Office, 1967).

[7]E.g., National Academy of Sciences, Advisory Committee on Government Programs in the Behavioral Sciences, National Research Council, *The Behavioral Sciences and The Federal Government* (Washington, D.C.: National Academy of Sciences, 1968); Special Commission on the Social Sciences of the National Sciences Board, *Knowledge into Action: Improving the Nation's Use of the Social Sciences* (Washington: Superintendent of Documents, 1969); and Behavioral and Social Sciences Survey Committee under the auspices of the Committee on Science and Public Policy, National Academy of Sciences, and the Committee on Problems and Policy, Social Sciences Research Council; *The Behavioral and Social Sciences: Outlook and Needs* (Englewood Cliffs, N.J.: Prentice Hall, 1969).

Similar interests in other countries are illustrated by the *Report of the Committee on Social Studies* (Chairman: Lord Heyworth, England: Cmnd. 2660, HMSO, 1965) and *The Social Sciences and the Policies of Government* (Paris: OECD, 1966). Some problems of bringing social sciences into government are also discussed in a, for England, revolutionary report, namely, *Committee on the Civil Service* (Chairman: Lord Fulton, England: Cmnd. 3638, HMSO, 1968), especially vol. I (Report of the Committee) and vol. II (Report of a Management Consultancy Group).

[8]Part III of the staff study on *The Use of Social Research in Federal Domestic Programs* includes a collection of relevant articles. Another representative collection is Elizabeth T. Crawford and Albert D. Biderman eds., *Social Scientists and International Affairs* (New York: John Wiley, 1969). Very relevant also is Irving L. Horowitz, ed., *The Rise and Fall of Project Camelot: Studies in the Relationship between Social Science and Practical Politics* (Cambridge, Mass.: MIT Press, 1967).

instrumental-normative decision theory. Especially striking is the lack of attention to on-going progress in applied decision theory, such as in systems analysis[9] and in planning-programing-budgeting (PPB).[10] The problems of tying in behavioral sciences to such highly important policy-improvement endeavors are nearly completely ignored.

3. Discourse on the contributions of behavioral sciences to policymaking proceeds without serious efforts to understand the characteristics of policy-making and tends to oscillate between naivety and cynicism. While there is important work going on in respect to the study of policymaking reality,[11] this work tends to be ignored by most of the discussions on behavioral sciences' contributions to policymaking.

4. The systems changes needed to better utilize behavioral sciences in policymaking are nearly completely ignored. This includes such obvious needs as adjusting graduate training in behavioral sciences so as to prepare behavioral sciences professionals for policy-related roles. Also neglected are the problems of organizational location of behavioral sciences advisors, required interaction arrangements between them and senior policymakers, problems of

---

[9]Care must be taken not to mix up *systems analysis* and *general systems theory*. Both share a desire to look at phenomena in terms of broad interrelated sets, called *systems*. Otherwise, despite the similarities in names, there is amazingly little common ground between systems analysis and general systems theory, though there is much potential scope for mutual stimulation and perhaps even some integration.

The best recent presentations of systems analysis are E. S. Quade and W. I. Boucher, eds., *Systems Analysis and Policy Planning: Applications in Defense* (New York: American Elsevier, 1968); and C. West Churchman, *The Systems Approach* (New York: Delacorte Press, 1968).

Van Court Hare, Jr., *Systems Analysis: A Diagnostic Approach* (New York: Harcourt, Brace & World, 1967) illustrates a different approach, based more on general systems theory and systems engineering.

Some of the problems of applying systems analysis to broad policy issues are discussed in C. West Churchman, *Challenge to Reason* (New York: McGraw-Hill, 1968); and Robert Boguslaw, *The New Utopians: A Study of System Design and Social Change* (Englewood Cliffs, N.J.: Prentice-Hall, 1965).

[10]An already classic presentation of PPB is David Novick, ed., *Program Budgeting: Program Analysis and the Federal Budget* (Cambridge, Mass.: Harvard University Press, 1965). A good collection of relevant papers and material is Fremont J. Lyden and Ernest G. Miller, eds., *Planning Programming Budgeting: A Systems Approach to Management* (Chicago: Markham, 1967).

[11]Recent work on the policymaking system is represented by the following books: Raymond A. Bauer and Kenneth Gergen, eds., *The Study of Policy Formation* (New York: The Free Press, 1968); Charles E. Lindblom, *The Policymaking Process* (Englewood Cliffs, N.J. Prentice-Hall, 1968); Joyce M. Mitchell and William C. Mitchell, *Political Analysis and Public Policy* (Chicago: Rand McNally, 1969); Austin Ranney, ed., *Political Science and Public Policy* (Chicago: Markham, 1968); and Francis E. Rourke, *Bureaucracy, Politics and Public Policy* (Boston: Little, Brown, 1969).

training of senior policymakers to enable them to utilize behavioral sciences, the novel roles of Rand-type policy research organizations,[12] and so on.

5. The special characteristics and requirements of policy-oriented research receive insufficient attention. Some of the involved value-problems are recognized, though I think badly treated. But the special problems of time-scarcity, search for leverage points, need for social invention, recognition of political feasibility constraints, need for experimentation, and so on, are only beginning to be perceived.[13]

6. Idiographic and nomothetic studies and—to be more extreme—collections of many facts and comprehensive theory constructions,[14] are still going on without too much interrelation, even though the need for theories of the middle range, to use Robert K. Merton's concept,[15] was recognized long ago. Similarly, behavioral sciences tend to be a-historic, thus ignoring a dimension essential for understanding problems and treating them.[16]

[12]As a non-American, may I be permitted to express my amazement that one of the unique United States inventions in government, which may have far-reaching implications for the future—namely, the nonprofit advisory corporation, in both The Brookings Institution form and the Rand form—is nearly completely ignored in books on American government.

[13]Somewhat to balance my criticism, let me mention two recent books moving in the right direction: Herman D. Stein, ed., *Social Theory and Social Invention* (Cleveland: Case Western Reserve University Press, 1968) and George Fairweather, *Methods for Experimental Social Innovation* (New York: John Wily, 1968).

[14]This problem is well illustrated by one of the more interesting contemporary efforts to relate behavioral sciences knowledge to policy problems, namely, the attempts to develop significant sets of social indicators. The lack of relation between proposed sets of facts and any significant theory is clearly reflected (and recognized) in the basic books on social indicators, namely, Raymond Bauer, ed., *Social Indicators* (Cambridge, Mass.: MIT Press, 1966), and Eleanor Bernert Sheldon and Wilbert E. Moore, eds., *Indicators of Social Change: Concepts and Measurements* (New York: Russel Sage Foundation, 1968). The difficulties of constructing a significant social state of the nations without relevant theories are, I think, the main reasons for the unavoidable weakness of the recent attempt to prepare such a draft document, namely, U.S. Department of Health, Education, and Welfare, *Toward a Social Report* (Washington, D.C.: U.S. Government Printing Office, 1969).

Here, also, a general systems approach may be of much help, as illustrated by the work of Bertram M. Gross, *The State of the Nation: Social Systems Accounting* (London: Tavistock Publications, 1966. Earlier version in Bauer, op. cit. above).

[15]In Robert K. Merton, *Social Theory and Social Structure* (Glencoe, Ill.: Free Press, 1949; rev. ed., 1968), chapter 2.

An outstanding examination of relevant problems of theory building in behavioral sciences is Robert Dubin, *Theory Building* (New York: Free Press, 1969). But more attention is needed to the special needs and problems of policy-relevant theories.

[16]For a stimulating discussion of social sciences in these terms, see Johan Galtung, "The Social Sciences: An Essay on Polarization and Integration," in Klaus Knorr and James N. Rosenau, eds., *Contending Approaches to International Politics* (Princeton, N.J.: Princeton University Press, 1969), pp. 243-89.

I do not mean to imply that no progress in policy-relevant directions goes on. But that progress is incremental at best, while I think that much more than that is needed. Also, there are some disturbing indications that some of the more innovative parts of modern behavioral sciences are moving in a direction reducing their relevance to policymaking.[17]

Many reasons for this state of affairs in the behavioral sciences can be identified, such as[18] the complexity of subject matter; tendencies to imitate methods of the physical sciences; the personal alienation of behavioral scientists from policymaking; the misplaced seeking for certainty; propensities to prefer incremental change; the fallacy of contradiction between pure versus applied knowledge; the rigidity of university organization; the lack of resources; external restraints on subject matter, research methods, and permitted findings; and the "youth" of behavioral sciences. But my impression is that something more fundamental is at fault; that the main internal structure and inner logic of the behavioral sciences, as now constituted, prevent relevance to policymaking. What is needed, therefore, is a scientific revolution in the sense of radical innovation in basic concepts, methods, and paradigms. (See chapter 1.)

A Systems View of Behavioral Sciences and Policymaking

I doubt whether general systems theory deserves being called a scientific revolution, in the full sense of that term. But I regard general systems theory at least as a quantum jump in our framework of appreciation, and one that may be particularly helpful in improving the uses of behavioral sciences for better policymaking, as I hope to show.

Using a very simple version of systems theory, I regard public policy as an output of the public policymaking system[19] and an input into various "target systems," such as health, education, transportation, public order, and the

[17]This, for instance, is true in respect to some of the newer approaches to international relations, as clearly recognized by one of their pioneers, Morton A. Kaplan; e.g., see Morton A. Kaplan, ed., *New Approaches to International Relations* (New York: St. Martin's Press, 1968), pp. vi-vii.

Kaplan, himself, approaches international relations with a general systems model; see his *System and Process in International Politics* (New York: John Wiley, 1957), and his paper "The Systems Approach to International Politics," in *New Approaches*, op. cit. above, pp. 381-404. This illustrates quite different uses of general systems models: by Kaplan, to explain; by me, to prescribe. Quite different versions of general systems models may be needed for such different purposes, posing a number of problems not yet dealt with by general systems theory and research.

[18]These barriers are explored at greater length in Yehezkel Dror, *Public Policymaking Reexamined* (San Francisco: Chandler, 1968), pp. 225-35.

[19]For convenience, I will focus my comments on public policy; but the analysis and prescriptions apply, in principle, also to corporate and other nonpublic types of policymaking.

international system. There are strong interactions between the public policy-making system and the various target systems at which its policy outputs are directed. Thus, many values, resources, and stimuli are being supplied by the latter to the former, while the former tries to influence the operations of the latter.

Similarly, behavioral sciences are a system, the components of which include, for instance, personnel, structures, information storages, rules of behavior, and patterns of adjustive dynamics. This system interacts intensely with other systems, especially the scientific establishment, various social subsystems, and also the public policymaking system.

In the future it may, for our purposes, become useful to regard the public policymaking system and the various target systems as components of the social system, or the even broader socio-ecological system, and to analyze the relations between these subsystems in terms of compartment theory, with transport processes going on in a mammillary structure (i.e., a central compartment interacting with a number of peripheral ones). Similarly, the direct and indirect (through intervening subsystems) relations between the behavioral sciences system and the public policymaking system may, in the future, be analyzable in terms of transport processes in a catenary structure (i.e., a chain of interacting compartments).[20]

But available knowledge is still far too underdeveloped to permit worthwhile use of such advanced models in respect to social phenomena. Rather, we must as yet rely on a much simpler general systems model, which permits us the following characterizations:[21]

All three—the public policymaking system, the target systems, and the behavioral sciences system—are dynamic, open, non-steady-state; include a large variety of different and changing multirole components interconnected in different degrees and through a multiplicity of channels; are closely interwoven and overlapping with one another and with other social macro-systems (e.g., the productive system, the demographic-ecological system, the techno-

[20]For compartment theory, see A. Rescigno, "Synthesis for Multicompartment Biological Models," *Biochem. Biophys. Acta.* 37 (1960): 463-68, and A. Rescigno and G. Serge, *Drug and Tracer Kinetics* (Waltham, Mass.: Blaisdell, 1966).

[21]For the purposes of my analysis, and for policy sciences in general, general systems theory is best presented in the following texts and collections: Kenneth F. Berrien, *General and Social Systems* (New Brunswick, N.J.: Rutgers University Press, 1968); Ludwig von Bertalanffy, *General Systems Theory: Foundations, Development, Application* (New York: George Braziller, 1968); Walter Buckley, ed., *Modern Systems Research for the Behavioral Scientists* (Chicago: Aldine, 1968); Walter Buckley, *Sociology and Modern Systems Theory* (Englewood Cliffs, N.J.: Prentice-Hall, 1967); E. J. Miller and A. K. Rice, *Systems of Organization: The Control of Task and Sentient Boundaries* (London: Tavistock Publications, 1967); and J. A. Miller, "Living Systems: Basic Concepts," *Behavioral Science* 10 (1965): 193-237, 380-411.

logical and knowledge system, and the cultural system); and behave in ways which defy detailed modeling.

Using this simple model, a few main, tentative implications can be derived, of which two seem to be of overriding importance:

1. Every system being a complex set of interacting components, desirable similar changes in any system (or similar "equifinal states") can, in principle, be achieved through many alternative variations in the components. This means, for our purposes, that different mixes of changes may often be equally useful in achieving desired changes, though often some specific changes may be necessary to achieve desired results. This is a very helpful conclusion, because it permits us to pick out of a large repertoire of potentially effective changes those which are more feasible under dynamic internal and external conditions. This view also emphasizes the open-ended (or, to be more exact, open-sided) nature of any search for improvements: there is, in principle, unlimited scope for adventurous thinking and invention. Therefore, any list of proposals should be regarded as illustrative and not definitive.

2. A less optimistic implication of our systems model is that changes must reach a critical mass in order to influence the overall operations of the system. Changes which do not reach the relevant impact thresholds will, at best, be neutralized by countervailing adjustments of other components or, at worst, may result in undesired results.

These general conclusions apply, in principle, to all directed system changes. Thus, they apply to the problems of preferable policy-mixes in respect to specific desired changes in designated target systems; to overall improvement of the public policymaking system; and to advancement of the scientific endeavors in respect to specific disciplines and in stipulated directions. In this chapter, we are interested in changes of those features of the public policymaking system and of the behavioral sciences system and of their modes of intertransport which will improve the utilization of behavioral sciences for better policymaking.

Behavioral Sciences and Policymaking Improvement:
Some Redesign Specifications

My views on the contemporary weaknesses of behavioral sciences as an aid to policymaking also indicate some of the changes required in order to increase their salience to policymaking. But it is our general systems view of public policymaking, of behavioral sciences, and of the relations between them, which leads to a major conclusion: a broad set of changes in the public policymaking system and in the behavioral sciences, and in their mutual transport channels and mechanisms, is essential for massive improvements in the uses of behavioral sciences for better policymaking. What is required is not some incremental change here or there, but far-reaching redesign in the two relevant systems and their interchanges.

It is this point of view, orientation, and frame of evaluation which constitutes the main contribution of general systems theory to improving the uses of behavioral sciences for better policymaking. And it is this point of view, orientation, and frame of evaluation which I want to stress. Despite its simplicity and, in retrospect, obvious character, the need for systems redesigns in respect to all three—the public policymaking system, the behavioral sciences system, and their intertransport processes—is not recognized by contemporary discourse on the uses of behavioral sciences in policymaking. And the need for such systems redesign, broad and intense enough to achieve a critical mass and have significant impacts on the target realities, contradicts the conservative incremental-change propensities of both the public policymaking system (including its organizational, political, personal, and value components) and the behavioral sciences system (again including its organizational, peer-control, personal, and value components). Therefore, the general redesign specification (derived from a general systems approach) concerning the need for broad and intense system changes as essential and—if successful—sufficient for significant improvements in the uses of behavioral sciences for better policymaking, does constitute an innovation in respect to contemporary opinions and actions alike.

The required next stage of our endeavors is elaboration of detailed redesign specifications in respect to the two involved systems and their intertransport modes, with due attention to the distinctions between essential, helpful, and sufficient change specifications, in alternative combinations and with efficiency comparisons. But such an endeavor requires unavailable knowledge of the working of the two systems and their intertransport, in addition to much innovative invention of new systems design ideas. Therefore, instead of undertaking this endeavor, I will have to limit myself to pointing out the need for it and the necessity to engage in relevant research, study, and creative invention.

Nevertheless, I want to take at least a step in the required direction, by presenting an illustrative set of redesign specifications. I do so to concretize somewhat the idea of required systems redesign and also to follow, myself, one of the precepts of policy sciences—to present, after suitable hedging, analysis-based applied proposals without waiting for exhaustive study and complete understanding.

Let me present, therefore, some illustrative redesign specifications relevant to improving the uses of behavioral sciences for better public policymaking, in regard to the public policymaking system, the behavioral sciences systems, and the intertransport between them. In respect to these specifications, we must keep in mind (1) the need to realize a number of the proposed specifications simultaneously or in programed order, to achieve critical mass and synergetically combined effects; and (2) the need sometimes to realize some of the proposed specifications in sets together with specifications of other improvements in the target systems, again for critical mass achievement and synergism.[22]

A. Some Redesign Specifications for the Public Policymaking System

1. Specific organizational roles of "behavioral sciences advisors" (some other name, such as "social science advisor," can of course be used) should be established throughout the public policymaking system. These roles should satisfy the following conditions: (*a*) dispersal throughout the main components of the societal direction system, including executive and legislative; (*b*) organizational location near the decision centers; (*c*) in part, at least, close integration with analysis and planning units; and (*d*) careful staffing of these roles with specially trained professionals (see specification B1).

2. Budgeting arrangements should be made to permit multiple-year funding of policy-oriented behavioral sciences research in policy research organizations, on a stable contractual basis.

3. Special programs should be initiated to familiarize junior and senior behavioral scientists with the problems and realities of policymaking. Such a program should include, for instance, (*a*) one-year appointments to fulltime positions; (*b*) fellowship and internship arrangements; (*c*) part-time consultantships; and (*d*) special summer training institutes.

4. The realities of policy problems as seen by the policy system components should be opened up for study, by providing easier access, with due safeguards to protect privileged and sensitive information (see also specification B2).

5. Basic understanding of the potential contributions of behavioral sciences to better policymaking should be disseminated through the higher levels of the executive branch, and also, as far as possible, in the legislature. This can be done, for instance, by the inclusion of new courses and material in the various senior executive training and development programs; and in special workshops, in which emphasis is on realistic cases and projects.

B. Some Redesign Specifications for the Behavioral Sciences System

1. New graduate teaching programs should be established, directed at preparing behavioral sciences advisors for policy contributing roles and, especially, advisory roles in the public policymaking system. This involves *inter alia* (*a*) a broad, interdisciplinary, problem-oriented approach; (*b*) strong attention to analytical methods and prescriptive decision theory, in combination with behavioral sciences knowledge, and within a broad policy sciences framework; (*c*) new teaching methods, with emphasis on cases and projects; (*d*) internship programs as an integral part of the teaching program; (*e*) new types of doctorate theses, in the form of applied behavioral sciences policy studies.

[22]For instance, these proposed changes in the public policymaking system may have to be combined with other and broader changes in that system.

2. A new professional concept of "behavioral sciences policy advisor" should be developed. This involves, in addition to new teaching programs, professional activities such as conferences and publication of a periodical. Special attention must be devoted to the ethical problems of such a profession, such as how to combine intellectual and scientific honesty with acknowledgment of organizational demands for the protection of privileged and sensitive information and for at least ad hoc acceptance of basic organizational values. Also, the distinction between the basically clinical role of a policy advisor and more "change agents" and "action-involved" advocacy roles must be emphasized. The professional concept of "behavioral sciences policy advisor" is distinct from the more decision-methodology-oriented concept of "policy analyst" and from the much broader concept of "policy scientist"—though there is much overlapping.

3. Research orientations, methods, and subjects must be changed to meet the needs of behavioral sciences contributions to better policymaking. Thus, for instance, the following changes are needed: (*a*) broad historic and cross-cultural studies of policy problems (e.g., addiction to narcotics, cigarette smoking, leisure-time use); (*b*) methods for social experimentation, and longitudinal evaluative follow-up; (*c*) time-compressing research methods to meet strict time constraints; (d) main attention to methods for identifying leverage points for directed change, without need to wait for full understanding of the involved target system; (*e*) acceptance of the encouragement of social invention as a main goal of study and research; (*f*) the evolvement of methods to recognize potentially difficult problems, while still latent.

C. Some Redesign Specifications for the Intertransport between the Public Policymaking System and the Behavioral Sciences System

Many of the redesign specifications in respect to the public policymaking system and the behavioral sciences system already relate to the intertransport between items. These include, for instance, the proposals for behavioral sciences advisory roles in the public policymaking system (specification A1) and for dissemination of knowledge regarding the uses of behavioral sciences in this system (specification A5), and the proposals in respect to the training of behavioral sciences advisors as a main change in the behavioral sciences system (specification B1).

But additional changes are required, such as the following two:

1. Policy-relevant behavioral sciences material must be presented in a language understandable to policymakers and in easily accessible communication media (e.g., new types of behavioral sciences texts directed at policymakers).

2. The social distance between behavioral scientists and policymakers must be reduced, for instance, by mixed workshops and informal mixed clubs.

CHAPTER 15

Behavioral Sciences Meta-Megapolicies:
Concepts and Applications[1]

COMMENTS

This chapter combines demonstration of the metapolicy and megapolicy concepts through application to a policy issue, with examination of the implications of policy sciences for behavioral sciences policy. Following a short redefinition of terms, some dimensions of metapolicy and megapolicy are applied to issues of behavioral sciences policy. This chapter concludes wiht some illustrations of the implications for behavioral sciences meta-megapolicy of contributions to the advancement of policy sciences as a postulated goal for behavioral sciences policy.

1. I use the term *meta-megapolicies* to cover both *metapolicies* and *megapolicies*. *Metapolicy* refers to policies on how to make policies. Metapolicies deal with the characteristics of the policymaking system, including structure, process patterns, personnel, inputs, and stipulated outputs. The term *megapolicy* refers to master policies which deal with overall goals, basic assumptions, conceptual frameworks, policy instruments, implementation strategies, and similar interpolicy directives.

The concepts of meta-megapolicy can be used behaviorally, to describe and explain actual (past, present, and expected future) phenomena. A meta-megapolicy behavioral analysis can improve our knowledge concerning actual policymaking by providing better frameworks for identifying and ordering data, and improved models for interrelating policy variables. The concepts of meta-megapolicy can also be used normatively, to indicate arrangements needed for better policymaking. These two main uses of a meta-megapolicy framework are interrelated, in the sense that all normative recommendations must be based, in part, on behavioral knowledge, and that collection of behavioral information depends, in part, on the uses of that information in which we are interested. Therefore, meaningful and reliable application of the meta-megapolicy concepts to behavioral sciences requires comprehensive knowledge of actual behavioral sciences meta-megapolicies, of the relations between behavioral sciences meta-megapolicies and behavioral sciences outputs, and of the values which we want behavioral sciences to advance (includ-

[1]This chapter is based on a paper prepared as background material for the International Social Science Council Conference on Social Science Policy, Paris, April 13-17, 1971. The paper was first published in Albert B. Cherns et al, eds., *Social Science Policy* (London: Tavistock Publications, 1971), in press.

160

ing knowledge for its own sake). One of the main utilities of the concepts of behavioral sciences meta-megapolicy shǫuld be to stimulate research, study, contemplation, design, and analysis focusing explicitly on the meta-megapolicy level.

2. To illustrate the applications of the meta-megapolicy concept to behavioral sciences policy, I will take up a few main meta-megapolicy issues, explain them briefly, and transform the general meta-megapolicy issues into behavioral sciences meta-megapolicy issues. I will use normative language, but the same issues can easily be transformed into behavioral ones:

Metapolicy Issue	Short Explanation of Issue	Transformation into Behavioral Sciences Metapolicy Issue
A. Basic *modus operandi* of policymaking systems	Mix between market, polycentric, and hierarchic structures in policymaking systems, with spontaneous evolution of policy as one extreme.	To what extent should there be behavioral sciences policy involving explicit policymaking and a formalized policymaking system? What should be the basic *modus operandi* of that system, varying from control by overlapping peer groups to central decisionmaking?
B. Main components of the policymaking system, especially (*a*) organizations and (*b*) personnel	What should be the main components of the policymaking system, with special attention to (*a*) organizational components and (*b*) policymaking personnel? In addition to the usual components, the possibilities of new types of organizations (such as policy research organizations) and new types of professionals (e.g., policy analysts) raise novel opportunities and issues.	What special organizations for behavioral sciences policymaking should be developed? With what functions, power, and resources? For instance, what about permanent behavioral sciences policy analysis units? What should the behavioral sciences policymaking personnel be? What about the participation of politicians, administrators, and community representatives in various behavioral sciences policymaking roles? What about the training of professionals who specialize in issues of behavioral sciences policy?

Metapolicy Issue	Short Explanation of Issue	Transformation into Behavioral Sciences Megapolicy Issue
C. Information inputs into policymaking	What types of information are needed for good policymaking? Which parts of that information are cost-effective? What arrangements are needed to collect and process that information and to introduce it into actual policymaking?	The general problems of information for better policymaking apply directly to behavioral sciences policy. Specific information needs include, for instance, data on current studies and manpower, predictions of studies and manpower, data on the image of behavioral sciences held by various relevant groups, and feedback on the results of study—both theoretic and applied. Criteria to ascertain results and standards for appraising them are also needed.
D. Main policymaking methods	Patterning of policymaking, phasing in time stream (e.g., by sequential decision-making), and developing of methods and techniques for explicit analysis (e.g., policy analysis, benefit-cost estimation, multiple-year planning, etc.).	Development of methods for behavioral sciences policymaking, on different macro-levels (international, cross-national, national) and micro-levels (e.g., universities, institutes, etc.). Policy analysis and sequential decisionmaking seem especially applicable, but research explicitly directed at developing methods for behavioral sciences policymaking seems urgently needed.

Megapolicy Issue	Short Explanation of Issue	Transformation into Behavioral Sciences Megapolicy Issue
E. Values and cutting-off horizons (including the question, to what extent should values	Master policies guiding policymaking on specific issues, in particular: (*a*) the main values at	Master policies guiding policymaking on behavioral sciences policy, in particular:

Megapolicy Issue	Short Explanation of Issue	Transformation into Behavioral Sciences Megapolicy Issue
and cutting-off horizons be explicated?)	which policymaking should aim, with explicit determination of considered impact-space and of borders of alternative sets to be considered. The costs (political, psychological, moral, etc.) of classifying values and cutting-off horizons must be considered to decide how far to proceed with this megapolicy.	(a) the values at which behavioral sciences policy should be oriented, such as (1) pure knowledge and (2) social goals (specific and/or as set down by legitimate policymakers). The borders of behavioral sciences policy. What are behavioral sciences, and to what exent should behavioral sciences policy be considered as a component of broader issues (e.g., science policy as a whole)? What are the limits of values and issues to be considered as subjects for behavioral sciences policy? What are the costs of establishing this megapolicy and what are its benefits (including sensitivity analysis)? Does this megapolicy really make much difference?
F. The nature of operational goals	Should policies be mainly directed at achieving specific goals at providing options, or at building up resources for the future?	Should behavioral sciences policies be directed at solving defined theoretic or applied questions? And/or providing knowledge which can be used to deal with various questions? And/or building up the resources to develop knowledge in the future (for example, through training of academic and applied scientists, longitudinal data collection, refinement of methodology)?

Megapolicy Issue	Short Explanation of Issue	Transformation into Behavioral Sciences Megapolicy Issue
G. Degrees of innovation	Incremental change versus radical change: how to encourage, and to what exent, heresy and far-reaching innovations?	To what extent should behavioral sciences policy aim at incremental progress and/or at radical breakthroughs—up to "scientific revolutions"? How encourage/control far-reaching innovation? What about incentives, resources allocation, and peer support for unconventional approaches?
H. Attitudes to risks (closely related to point C above)	Mix between maximax, minimax, etc.	To what extent should behavioral sciences policy become adventurous, follow risky research possibilities (e.g., on altered states of consciousness), take up taboo issues (e.g., as tried in the Chicago jury studies), and provide low reliability recommendations?
I. Time preferences	Preferences between outputs located on different points of the time stream.	Should behavioral sciences policy be more oriented to immediate issues and problems (as expressed, for instance, by the social advocacy approach) or adopt longer (how long?) time preferences?

3. As already indicated, this is too analytic a presention, the obvious preference being for some mix between various policymaking-system alternatives and megapolicy alternatives. But the concept *mix*—however in accord with our a priori preferences for some "Golden Mean"—is of little help. The question is, What mix? Explicit considerations of behavioral sciences meta-megapolicy issues hopefully can help in at least formulating relevant questions, and thereby taking one step in the direction of identification of preferable meta-megapolicy mixes.

4. To illustrate further the uses of the meta-megapolicy concepts, let me indicate briefly the implications for behavioral sciences meta-megapolicy of one view of a desired direction for the development of behavioral sciences,

namely, the view that behavioral sciences, should, in part, fuse with analytical decision approaches and serve as a foundation for policy sciences. Let me emphasize (*a*) that this proposal is used here only as an illustration to "exercise" the meta-megapolicy concept and (*b*) that the proposal aims to add an approach to behavioral sciences policy, without in any way degrading the importance of other approaches.

5. I will proceed by referring to the various meta-megapolicy issues by the letters used in paragraph 4 above, and indicate the respective meta-megapolicy implications of the proposed approach (which, strictly speaking, belongs itself to behavioral sciences meta-megapolicy):

A. Explicit behavioral sciences policymaking is needed, in order to advance efforts in the policy sciences direction. Much of this policymaking can proceed in "invisible colleges," but some formalization seems to be required. This is especially necessary in order to get cooperation between the interested scholars and institutions and to assure at least minimum support by the behavioral sciences community as a whole.

B(a). Special organizations which critically consider behavioral sciences policy may be needed to perceive the need for change in the direction of policy sciences. Ad hoc committees can (and do) fulfill important functions in this direction. Specific behavioral sciences policy units are also necessary to support the efforts, supervise them (to avoid the fate, for instance, of futures studies which get ruined through overpopularization), and advance them.

B(b). The special characteristics of policy sciences require more heterogeneous policymaking personnel than normal behavioral sciences policymaking. In particular, an interdisciplinary composition is needed, with some participation also of policy practitioners—politicians, as well as senior executives.

C. Information is needed on persons able and willing to participate in a policy sciences development effort, on relevant studies, and on relevant experience. As much of the relevant personnel, material, and experience is located outside the normal behavioral sciences community (e.g., at policy research organizations, legislative and governmental research units, and private consultant), a suitable new information network must be built up.

D. Sequential decisionmaking on an international scale seems a preferable method.

E. The goals of policy sciences are mainly instrumental-normative policymaking improvement, within the boundaries of morally acceptable values. The boundaries of policymaking here are much broader than in normal behavioral sciences policy, including other disciplines and some aspects of politics as well.

F. A necessary main initial operational goal is to start to build up the infrastructure of policy sciences, including (1) the establishment and reinforcement of policy sciences research organizations; (2) the establishment and reinforcement of policy sciences teaching; (3) the initiation of suitable professional activities, such as periodicals, conferences, and the like; and (4) the recruitment of financial support. In other words, a main meta-megapolicy should be to develop resources for building up policy sciences.

G. Policy sciences directed behavioral sciences policy should be very innovative-oriented, with the presumption of designing a "scientific revolution"

H. There should be a significant propensity to accept risks.

I. The policy sciences directed behavioral sciences policy should show preference for the intermediate future, about five years and more ahead, with the main results to take longer.

6. My overall main conclusion and recommendation are that every concern with behavioral sciences policy should devote considerable attention to explicit consideration of behavioral sciences metapolicy and megapolicy issues.

Law is seldom considered a policy sciences-related discipline and social institution. This, I think, is a mistake. As early recognized by Lasswell and McDougal, law is a policy discipline par excellence, even though of limited scope and underdeveloped in explicit policy-oriented contents. A main function of lawyers is to render policy advice to their clients; this advice is confined to a specific and, sometimes, narrow area—but is policy advice nevertheless. When the legal background of most politicians in many countries is added to the picture, then the importance of law as a training ground for policymaking becomes even more pronounced.

To move on from law as a discipline and as a profession to law as a social institution, again reality is different from the image conveyed by literature. Even though law is seldom viewed as a policy instrument, law is, in reality, of utmost importance in societal management and societal direction.

My conclusion is that law—as a discipline, as a profession, and as a social institution— must be closely considered within policy sciences. This part presents some initial efforts

PART V

A Policy Sciences View of Law

in that direction. The first chapter uses a policy analysis frame to discuss law as a policy instrument. The second chapter provides some theoretical underpinnings for the uses of law as a policy instrument, through examination of relations between social change and law. The third chapter takes up a different subject, namely, interaction between administrative agencies and courts. Through analyzing these interactions as an interorganizational conflict-cooperation decision process, another area important for policy sciences is opened up, namely, interorganizational processes—which constitute a main mode of policymaking. Also, some additional considerations relevant to the use of law as a policy instrument are brought out in this chapter, in particular, the dependence of the effectiveness of law as a policy instrument on complex decision processes in various interacting law-enforcement agencies.

CHAPTER 16

Law as an Instrument of Directed Social Change: A Framework for Policymaking[1]

COMMENTS

This chapter provides an overall overview of law as an instrument of directed social change, as seen from the perspective of policy analysis. This requires consideration of the different components of the legal system within a much broader set of societal policy instruments, to be used in different combinations as appropriate. More important than the details is the general perspective—namely, treatment of law (in addition to its other social functions) as a policy instrument.

Introduction

The use of law as an instrument of directed social change is widespread in all contemporary societies whether underdeveloped or postindustrial, democratic or totalitarian. But both our systematic knowledge of how to use effectively and efficiently law, in order to achieve more of our goals, and our practical state of the art of doing so, approximate zero.

One set of reasons for this state of affairs includes various factors diverting attention from the uses of law as an instrument of directed social change. These are, for instance, metaphysical concepts of law, purely formal concepts of law, and preoccupation with other functions of law, such as stabilization, prediction-reinforcement, power restraint, and authority control. But the long list of distinguished classic and modern scholars who have devoted their efforts to the study of law and social change, and who have made important contributions to many aspects of the subject[2] (other than a comprehensive policy-oriented theory of law as an instrument of directed social change) precludes the explanation of our theoretical ignorance in terms of lack of high-quality efforts. Similarly, the use of law as an instrument of directed social

---

[1] An earlier version of this chapter was first published in *American Behavioral Scientist* 13, no. 4 (March-April 1970): 553-59.

[2] For an excellent survey and discussion, see Julius Stone, *Social Dimensions of Law and Justice* (Sydney: Maitland, 1966).

169

change in a large number of jurisdictions and many periods of history precludes the explanation of our state-of-the-art weaknesses in terms of lack of experience.

Rather, it seems that the basic difficulties of studying and improving the use of law as an instrument of directed social change result from the fact that law, by itself, is only one component of a large set of policy instruments and usually cannot be used and is not used by itself. Therefore, the focusing of exclusive attention on law as an instrument of directed social change is a case of tunnel vision, which lacks the minimum perspective necessary for making sense from the observed phenomena. Furthermore, the "frames of appreciation" of law, political science, and behavioral sciences (which today enjoy a near monopoly over the study of law and social change) are inadequate for dealing with the prescriptive and policy-oriented aspects of law as an instrument of social direction.

What is necessary is a redefinition of the subject of law as an "instrument of directed social change" in two main directions: (1) as a subcomponent of the study of social policy instruments, and (2) as a subcomponent of normative policy analysis.

Law and Other Social Policy Instruments

A first required step on the way to examination of the uses of law as an instrument of directed social change within an adequate framework of social policy instruments involves consideration of law within the legal system.

The main components of the legal system can in part be classified for our purposes as follows:

    a. Substantive law: constitutional, statutory, judge-made, administrative

    b. Procedural law: constitutional, statutory, judge-made, administrative

    c. Personnel: judges, lawyers, legislators, police, other law-enforcing and law-administrating persons

    d. Organizations: legislature, court system, police, legal firms, administrative agencies

    e. Resources: budgets, information and information-processing capacities, physical facilities

    f. Decision rules and decision habits: formal, informal, implicit

Even though this classification does not cover all aspects (e.g., distinction by jurisdictions and clientele), it is sufficient for bringing out both the richness and the complex overlappings and interdependencies in the legal system. My main point here is that each one of the components of the legal system is a potential policy instrument. Indeed, in most circumstances, utilization of any one or few of these components as tools of directed change in isolation from the others will at best be very inefficient, usually useless, and often counterproductive.

Therefore, for better use of law as an instrument of directed social change, it is essential in each case to examine carefully the interdependencies between the various components of the relevant legal systems, the interrelations between these components and the target phenomena, and the feasibility and costs (including political feasibility and costs) of changing those components of the legal system which are more salient for the target phenomena. On the basis of such an examination, a preferable set of leverage points in the legal system should be identified, to be used in combination as a policy instrument.

If this task looks formidable, the real needs are even more demanding. Consideration of the whole relevant legal system is an essential requisite for effective and efficient use of law as an instrument of directed social change, but an inadequate one. The legal system being a subsystem of society, consideration of legal policy instruments in abstraction from other social policy instruments is misleading. Instead, the uses of law as an instrument of social change must be considered within a broader series of possible policy instruments, such as economic, educational, ecologic, and technological ones.

The relevant domains of policy instruments may be quite narrow when we deal with very limited policy objectives. But even when we take a relatively narrow objective, such as reducing court congestion, the relevant policy instruments are many, and a preferable mix may well include some from outside the legal system—such as insurance schemes to take care of some issues which today reach the courts. When we take the more significant social problems (such as, in the United States, race relations, public safety, drug use, pollution, and the like), the necessity to use law as a policy instrument only within a multiple mix of carefully considered social policy instruments should be quite convincing.

Our conclusions apply not only to the policy approach to law and social change, but to the behavioral approach, too. If we want to understand the operation of law as an independent variable in social change, we must study the social impact of changes in law within the context of the other components of the legal system and of other relevant policy variables. Since in no real case the requirement of "all other policy variables being static" is met, a complex multivariable analysis seems essential for valid and reliable behavioral study of law and social change. Only such a methodology can provide the knowledge essential for supporting policy recommendations on how better to use law as a tool of directed social change.[3]

Law and Normative Policy Analysis

A broad approach to the use of law as one policy instrument in combination with many others requires not only a new perspective on the relations between

[3]See Stuart S. Nagel, *The Legal Process from a Behavioral Perspective* (Homewood, Ill.: Dorsey, 1969).

law, other legal-system policy instruments, and extra-legal social policy instruments; it requires also a new methodology for designing and identifying preferable combinations of a multiplicity of policy-instrument settings. This task is in all respects beyond the present and potential capacities of both jurisprudence and behavioral sciences. Rather, it belongs to the emerging policy sciences[4] and especially to policy analysis, which focuses on the stimulation of policy designs and identification of preferable policy alternatives.

Policy analysis constitutes an extension of systems analysis to complex policy issues which cannot be quantified and represented by exercisable models.[5] Applied to the uses of law as a tool of directed 'social change, policy analysis (combined with knowledge on the substantive phenomena of law and social change, which must be supplied by behavioral study) is designed to provide systematic heuristic aid in dealing with the following interrelated issues:[6]

a. Decisions on main megapolicies in respect to risk, degrees of innovation, main goals, feasibility domain, and time perspective. Such explicit megapolicy decisions are essential for reducing the policy design and choice tasks to meaningful and manageable dimensions.

b. The design of main policy alternatives, with different combinations of various changes in law with changes in other policy instruments.

c. A prediction of probable consequences of main policy alternatives (with fast elimination of many of them, if necessary, to make further analysis easier) through novel methods, such as social-legal experimentation and sequential decisionmaking on the uses of law.

d. An examination of remaining main policy alternatives in terms of probable first-, second-, and third-order consequences within a benefit-cost framework.

e. A comparison of probable consequences in terms of value preferences with special attention to reduction of sensitivity to unresolvable value differ-

[4]Compare H. D. Lasswell and M. S. McDougal, "Jurisprudence in Policy-Oriented Perspective," *University of Florida Law Review* 19, no. 3 (1968): 486-513.

[5]See Yehezkel Dror, *Design for Policy Sciences* (New York: American Elsevier, 1971), chapter 9.

[6]For important steps in the direction of a policy analysis approach to law and legal policy, see Stuart S. Nagel, "Optimizing Legal Policy," *University of Florida Law Review* 18 (1966): 577-90; and Louis H. Mayo and Ernest M. Jones, "Legal-Policy Decision Process: Alternative Thinking and the Predictive Function," *George Washington Law Review* 33, no. 1 (1964): 318-456.

Also very relevant in this context, though overoptimistic on the scope of "science," are F. K. Beutel, *Some Potentials of Experimental Jurisprudence as a New Branch of Social Science* (Lincoln: University of Nebraska Press, 1952); and F. K. Beutel, *Democracy or the Scientific Method in Law and Policy Making* (Rio Piedras: University of Puerto Rico, 1965).

ences and to impairment of other functions (including symbolic ones) of law.
f. The presentation of policy analysis findings in a form conducive to political and executive decisionmaking through explicated judgment.
g. The design of follow-up, evaluation, and policy-redesign methods with special attention to the impact of the law instruments and to the possibilities and costs of readjusting them.

Let me be clear; we do not yet know how to do good policy analysis, though much more is known than is used in actual policymaking. But the seven issues mentioned above must be faced in using law as an instrument of directed social change and constitute parts of the basic framework for doing so. Therefore, policy analysis must constitute one of the foundations of a policy-oriented approach to law and social change.

Applied Implications

Our findings emphasize the necessity to base the study and practice of the use of law as an instrument of directed social change on (*a*) a broad perspective of law as one of many policy instruments which must be used in combination, and (*b*) policy analysis as the methodology for identifying preferable combinations of such policy instruments. These findings have a number of applied implications, including, in particular, the following:

1. As already mentioned, behavioral studies of the use of law as an instrument of directed social change (and of law and social change in general) must be broadened to cover other relevant policy variables.

2. Prescriptive study on the use of law as an instrument of directed social change must be based on both a broad view of policy instruments and policy analysis methodology. This, in turn, requires:

    a. Mixed teams of lawyers, behavioral scientists, and policy analysts to engage in relevant studies and prepare policy recommendations.

    b. The location of such teams at various points of the societal direction system, such as the legislature, the executive, special policy research organizations, and universities.

    c. Changes in various characteristics of the policymaking system to permit utilization of the work of such teams through a broader and more systematic approach to policymaking as a whole.[7]

3. Essential for progress in the indicated directions is availability of highly qualified and motivated personnel for behavioral and prescriptive research on the uses of law as an instrument of directed social change. This, in turn, requires:

[7]In many respects, improvements in the use of law as a tool of directed social change are impossible and perhaps dangerous, unless public policymaking as a whole is significantly improved.

a. Changes in university training. In particular, law schools should become substantially policy-oriented and supply their interested students with basic knowledge in analytical approaches, in behavioral sciences, and in policy sciences as a whole.[8] Also, the increasing number of special programs in policy sciences and public policy analysis should include the use of law as a policy instrument within their research and teaching programs.

b. Efforts to convey the necessary knowledge in analytical approaches to interested jurisprudence and behavioral sciences scholars and the necessary knowledge in law and behavioral sciences to interested analysts. This may, for instance, be done through summer institutes similar to the Social Science Research Council Summer Training Institutes, which pioneered the *rapproachement* between behavioral scientists and law.

Modern societies are more and more "future-directing" societies. Law constitutes one of their sharper tools of direction—very useful when used correctly, very dangerous when utilized inappropriately. This explains the urgency of a new approach to the use of law as an instrument of directed social change within a broad policy sciences framework.

[8]This proposal was first made in modern form by H. D. Lasswell and M. S. McDougal in their article, "Legal Education and Public Policy: Professional Training in the Public Interest," *Yale Law Journal* 52 (1963): 203-95. Various attempts have been made in this direction, but with very limited success, especially because of neglect of analytical approaches. Contemporary faculty interests and student pressures seem to encourage new and promising efforts, such as the combined program in law and public policy at Harvard University and the proposed new program at Brandeis Law School. Some student pressures may undermine the intellectual foundations of a policy-oriented study of the social roles of law and should therefore be strongly resisted. See, for instance, Paul N. Savoy, "Toward a New Politics of Legal Education," *Yale Law Journal* 79, no. 3 (1970): 444-504.

CHAPTER 17

Law and Social Change[1]

COMMENTS

Correct utilization of policy instruments depends on understanding of their operations as social variables and on at least some knowledge of their interdependencies with other variables and with different social institutions and characteristics. This chapter explores the relations between law and social change, so as to provide some of the background required for utilization of law as a policy instrument. Included also are some comments on comparative cross-national research as a method for investigation of law as a policy instrument; these comments apply also to the study of other policy instruments.

Introduction

The varied aspects of the relationship between law and social change pose some challenging problems of great significance for an understanding of the role of law in modern societies and its uses as an instrument of social direction. These aspects include new modes for changing the law, the lag in the development of law behind social change, the use of law as a device to induce social change, and others.

Despite the universal recognition of the significance of social change, the great amount of research going on in this area, and the progress being made at the same time in the social study of law, these fields of investigation have been isolated from each other, and relatively little has been done to investigate their interrelationships. Among the reasons for the lack of research in this area might be the dearth of research personnel trained in both law and the behavioral sciences, the absence of research methods adjusted to investigation of the social aspects of normative systems such as law, the overconcern of behavioral scientists with the "social control" function of law, the underdevelopment of the social study of law, and the neglect of a policy sciences approach to law in general.

In exploring some central issues we will first examine some basic concepts; then we shall proceed to a brief discussion of main modes for changing the

[1]An earlier version of this paper was first published in *Tulane Law Review* 33 (1959): 787-802.

law, which will lead to a more detailed analysis of the relationship between law and social change. Finally, some implications of our investigation will be examined, especially in regard to their significance for the social study of law and the development of a policy sciences approach to law as an instrument of societal direction.

At this point, some close connection between the comparative study of law and the investigation of the relationships between law and social change should also be noted. On the one hand, the methods developed by the comparative study of law provide research methodologies essential for the study of law and social change. The difficulties of conducting controlled experimentation in this area and the inherent limitations of inductions based on the experience of any one society emphasize the necessity of utilizing comparative research methods; these enable us to gain an insight into legal and social processes by investigating comparable phenomena and problems in different societies and examining the impact of different variables and factors operating in these societies. On the other hand, the continuous development and progress of the comparative study of law, including study of its policy uses, depends, to some extent, on an understanding of the basic processes of the relationships between law and society, which must provide the essential background and perspective for the study of the various legal phenomena which are scarcely susceptible to meaningful investigation when isolated from their social contexts.

Some Basic Comments

The two basic concepts of our investigation are social change and law. Society is always undergoing processes of change; human generations follow one another and different persons fulfil various social roles. The concept *social change* does not refer to this constant change in the population of every society, but refers to changes in the society as such, including the various social institutions, roles and status definitions, accepted ideologies, value patterns, pattern variables, and value profiles. In other words, the concept of social change refers to changes in social structure or in culture, including some of the patterns of change itself or, to use cybernetic terminology, in the conditions of "ultra-stability."

Social change can be initiated by various factors, including changes in the physical environment of the society; changes in the genetic constitution of the population; contact with other societies; internal social change, such as general social movements; and new technological or social inventions. One of the characteristics of all contemporary cultures is their high rate of social change. In modern Western societies a high rate of social and cultural change, associated especially with changes in technology, has become a permanent feature of social life, while the various modernizing societies, which are already changing rapidly, aim at achieving an even higher rate of social change, so as to enable them rapidly to reach the level of technical development character-istic of Western societies. Contemporary behavioral sciences devote much attention to the study of social changes, but as yet its basic pre-conditions and processes are little understood. Very little is known of basic problems, such as whether human societies are able to exist in a state of permanent high rate of social change, and for how long, and how high-rate social change influences the mental stability of the individual.

Society consists of a large number of social institutions and components. Social change in most cases begins in some of these institutions or elements, which, in turn, influence other institutions and elements until the whole of society changes. This raises the problem of the extent to which certain com-ponents of society and culture can change without bringing about changes in other aspects of society, and the extent to which some components of society and culture can remain static despite changes in other aspects.

This problem is closely related to the more general one, that is, to what extent the various aspects of society form an intensely interacting system, every change in one part of which must bring about corresponding changes in all other parts. The more autonomous a certain area is, the more it can be studied in isolation from the other institutions of its society and the easier it is to compare it with parallel areas in other societies. But, if a certain area of culture or social activity is very closely interwoven with other aspects of the same society, it becomes difficult to study it in isolation and it becomes nearly impossible to compare it by itself and outside its social context with parallel areas in other societies.

The application of these concepts to our subject becomes clear when we take into account the character of law, which from the point of view of the behavioral sciences (and of policy sciences) constitutes a part of the culture of every society.

However we may define law, it must be regarded for our purpose as a part of the culture of every society. Applying our previous comments on social change to the relationship of social change and law, the questions arise as to how far it is independent of other parts of culture and society, how far changes in law follow changes in other aspects of society, and how far changes in law bring about changes in other aspects of society. In other words, we can define the problem as one of the relative autonomy of law vis-à-vis other components of society. Its central concerns are the processes creating a lag between law and other components of society and culture and the processes adjusting law to society and society to law.

The relationship between law and social change is further complicated by the dual social character of law. The whole of the law of a given society forms a system consistent within itself, with a whole network of internal relationships, which constitutes a subsystem of that society's total culture and is intimately linked with its lawmaking, law-applying, and law-enforcing institutions and processes. Furthermore, law is a pervasive element of every social institution and plays an important role in all of them. Thus, family law forms a part of the whole of law and cannot be understood in isolation from the legal system as a whole; but family law is also an internal and essential part of the family institution, and cannot be fully understood without consideration of it.

Processes of Change in the Law

Three main types of units bring about changes in the law: specialized legislative units, specialized law-applying units, and various law-enforcing and law-using units. The existence of differentiated and formally defined legislative bodies which are supposed to enact statutory law, courts which are supposed to apply the law, and prosecution and police agencies which are supposed to enforce it is a characteristic shared by all modern societies (though the lawmaking, law-applying, and law-enforcing activities of various administrative agencies confuse, to some extent, the social division of work in this respect). In many of the primitive societies, social differentiation of work is less developed, and some or all of the legal functions may be performed by the same body or may be left to the basic units of social action (e.g., the family); but wherever we find law (or pre-law), these basic functions are performed to some extent and serve as vehicles through which changes in the law occur.

Conscious legislation by a special legislative body constitutes today one of the most important avenues for changing the law.[2] While conscious legislation by a special unit can be found at various periods and in different kinds of societies, it is mainly in Western bureaucratic society (beginning with the period of enlightened absolutism in the seventeenth and eighteenth centuries) that conscious lawmaking by a central legislative body has become of predominant importance and constitutes the main mode for changing the law, though some similar tendencies can be discerned in Rome during the period of the empire.

Concerning the role of the central legislature vis-à-vis the other units of law-changing, two phenomena merit special attention. In a country with a rigid constitution and with an agency authorized to pronounce the validity of legislation in the light of that constitution, the possibilities of changing the law by conscious legislation are limited. Therefore, in such a country, the other units of law-changing bear a special responsibility and fulfil an impor-

[2]This development is associated wtih the evolution of the concept of public policy and the desire to use legislation as a conscious instrument to achieve the policy objectives. This approach was perhaps best expressed in the writings of Jeremy Bentham.

tant role. The United States illustrates the case: the power of Congress to legislate is limited by the Constitution; since the constitution-amending process is rather cumbersome, the courts, especially when interpreting the Constitution, change the law in important areas. In England, on the other hand, where there is no rigid constitution limiting the powers of the central legislature, all parts of the law are susceptible to change by direct legislative action and the responsibility of the courts in this respect is more limited.

Another phenomenon worthy of note is the reliance of the central legislature on secondary legislation. In all modern societies, the scope and spread of secondary legislation is growing, despite constant efforts which are made to limit it. In fact, many of the legislative changes of the law are brought about today through delegated legislation by administrative units. It may well be that one of the reasons for the universal development of delegated legislation is the inability of the central legislature to deal with all needed changes of the law. Coupled with the undesirability or impossibility of leaving the problem to the courts, the only remaining solution lies in the grant of authority to administrative bodies to change the law through secondary legislation. The apparent correlation between the high rate of social change experienced by modern societies and the large extension of the legislative authority of administrative bodies seems to bear out this hypothesis.[3]

Historically speaking, the courts and, to some extent, the administrative agencies have been the most important organs for shaping and changing the law and adjusting it to social change, especially under the Anglo-American system of law. The courts rely on various well-known mechanisms for changing the law. These vary between countries which accept the doctrine of binding precedent to various degrees and countries in which courts are not bound by previous decisions. If the courts are not bound by precedent, they may reinterpret the law, relying mainly on contemporary ideas and concepts, or change the law with the aid of legal fictions or constructions. When the courts are bound by precedent, they use, in addition to fictions, various distinguishing techniques, limiting and reinterpreting the *ratio decidendi* (i.e., binding rule) of previous decisions.

It would be interesting to consider the extent to which the courts themselves and various segments of the population are aware of the lawmaking functions of the courts. At certain periods, the function of the courts was regarded as pure law-applying and it was thought that this function did not involve the making of new law, but today legal theory both on the Continent and in Anglo-American jurisdictions tends to recognize and appreciate the creative function of the courts.

[3]This is only a partial explanation of the phenomenon of widespread delegated legislation. Additional important variables operate and shape the extent and form of delegated legislation in various societies.

Furthermore, whether law-enforcing agencies prosecute or refrain from prosecuting certain offenses affects the impact of the law on society, although the "formal" law, itself, is not changed. Still more important, from the view of changing the law, are the practices of law-users, such as trade practices, standard clauses, and agreements, which constitute a rather important mode of changing the law—one that reflects rather accurately certain aspects of social change.

The Relationship Between Law and Social Change

There is nearly always a difference between actual social behavior and the behavior demanded by the legal norm; the existence of some "tension" between actual behavior and legally demanded behavior (and between legally demanded behavior and morally demanded behavior) belongs to the characteristics of law in all societies and does not, by itself, signify the existence of a lag between law and social change. A lag appears only when there is more than *some* tension, when the law does not, in fact, answer the needs arising from major social changes or when social behavior and the sense of obligation generally felt towards legal norms significantly differs from the behavior required by law. In other words, while some difference between actual behavior and legally required behavior can be found in all societies, the concept of *lag* applies to law and social change in dynamic situations, after more than incremental social change or changes in the law occur and no parallel changes and adjustment processes take place in law or society respectively.

Some historic illustrations will clarify the concept of lag relative to law and social change. After the invention of the automobile, the totally unsuitable laws developed for horse-drawn carriages were applied. After the industrial revolution, the various laws against conspiracy were applied to workers' organizations in a way which constituted a clear lag behind the new social situation, which included both new techniques and ways of economic organization and new public sentiments and ideologies. It took the law in England and other countries a long time to catch up with these developments and provide answers to the problems raised by them. Contemporary illustrations are so abundant and visible as not to require elaboration. Drug use, sexual behavior, peaceful protest movements—these are some of the more obvious areas of lag of law behind changes in behavior in the United States in the early 70's.

All these illustrations deal with lag of the law behind social change. Though the very high rate of social change in contemporary societies confronts the agencies in charge of changing the law with difficult problems, the relative ease of legislation and other modes of changing the law provide rather simple ways of adjusting the law to social change, if the political will to do so exists.

In some jurisdictions, especially the international society and, to some extent, countries with rigid constitutions and judicial review powers over the constitutionality of legislation, the use of legislation to adjust the law to social change is somewhat limited. In all countries, difficulties are faced concerning the problem of the best way of effecting this adjustment. But, in general, the use of conscious legislation in modern societies makes the process of adjustment of the law to social change rather easy. At a time when legislative action was not accepted as readily and legislatures were composed of conservative elites generally opposed to social change and averse to corresponding changes in the law, the lag of the law behind social change was very formidable, indeed, and the primary responsibility for changing the law was imposed on the courts (themselves often composed of judges opposed to social change) and the enforcement agencies (also composed of particular personnel). But today the general orientation of broad strata and elites is in favor of change, and popular elections in democratic countries as well as support requirements in many a dictatorship assure the necessary sensitivity of the legislative organs and their willingness in general to change the law and adjust it to social change. More and more the need here becomes one of preserving social continuity and legal security, which are endangered by too rapid changes in the law, in addition to preventing the lag of law behind social needs and developments.

Not less important, both from the theoretical and the practical point of view, is the problem of the lag of society after changes in the law. How far, if at all, can changes in the law be used to bring about social change? The first question is whether it is feasible and possible to change society through changing the law. Classical Marxian theory and some modern social and economic theories answer in the negative. Regarding law as a superstructure on technology and the economy, those theories admit the possibility of the lag of law behind social change and fully conceive that it might take some time for changes in technology and economy to be reflected in the law; but it would be inconceivable, according to those theories, for law to bring about changes in the basic technology and economy of society.

A different argument against the possibility and desirability of using law to bring about social change was made by the historical school of jurisprudence and its founder, Savigny. Savigny, applying to law parts of Hegel's philosophy, regarded law as an organic growth indigenous to every society. Therefore, he opposed legislation, and especially legislation adopting foreign institutions and laws.

These arguments have been clearly overruled by the facts of reality. The growing use of law as an instrument of organized societal direction seems to be one of the characteristics of modern society. The relative novelty of the conscious, systematic, and large-scale use of law as an instrument of societal direction, and the apparent contradiction and real tension between the ideology of the rule of law—which regards law as the stable foundation of social order—and the instrumental orientation toward law associated with the utilization of law as an instrument of societal direction may provide a partial explanation for the lack of scholarly attention paid to these crucial evolutions in the role of law and lawmaking in contemporary society.

Closer analysis of the role of law vis-à-vis social change leads us to distinguish between the direct and the indirect aspects of the role of law.

Law plays an important indirect role in regard to social change by shaping various social institutions, which, in turn, have a direct impact on society. Thus, a law setting up a compulsory educational system has a very important indirect role in regard to social change, by enabling the operation of educational institutions which play a direct role in social change. On the other hand, law interacts in many cases directly with basic social institutions in a manner constituting a direct relationship between law and social change. Thus, a law designed to prohibit polygamy has a great direct influence on social change, having as its main purpose the bringing about of changes in important patterns of behavior. This distinction is not free from difficulties, caused mainly by the multiple character of most parts of the law, which are both in a direct and in an indirect relationship with social changes. The distinction is not an absolute but a relative one: in some cases the emphasis is more on the direct and less on the indirect impact of social change, while in other cases the opposite is true.

The indirect influence of law on social change is closely interwoven with the functions of the various social institutions of which, as already mentioned, parts of law are an important element. Full examination of the indirect aspect of the role of law in relation to social change requires, therefore, analysis of social institutions outside the scope of this chapter. We will therefore limit ourselves to citing illustrations designed to clarify this aspect.

To a considerable extent, law exerts an indirect influence on general social change by influencing the possibilities of change in the various social institutions. For example, the existence of a patent law, protecting the rights of inventors, encourages inventions and furthers change in the technological institutions, which in turn may bring about basic general social change. The absence of freedom to associate and disseminate ideas can prevent, or at least delay, the spread of new social ideas, and thus exert a very important basic influence on the processes of social change in society. The extent to which contact with other societies is limited or encouraged by law regulates one of the basic factors bringing about social change, and so on. Here, law as part of the various institutions (technology, political and social control, external relations) influences the probabilities of changes in these social institutions and through them the processes of social change in general.

A somewhat different indirect relationship between law and social change concerns the indirect use of law in directed social change. The legal basis of organized social action in all modern societies—associated as they are with the internal functional needs of large-scale bureaucratic societies—calls for the reliance on legal means as indirect aids for nearly all attempts to bring about directed social change. Thus, if the state desires to set up a public body the functions of which include bringing about certain social changes, it is necessary to use law to set up the body and define its powers; here, law indirectly serves social change by setting up organs which directly try to further various social developments. The act setting up the Tennessee Valley Authority in the United States and the acts dealing with new towns in England illustrate this functioning of law as an indirect factor in social change.

A slightly different illustration of the indirect use of law in organized social action involving social change is the creation of legal duties, which in turn enable direct action to bring about social change. One of the most important instruments of directed social change relied upon in many countries is education. But in order for the educational network to operate effectively, it may be necessary to create a duty to study in them. Hence, as already mentioned, compulsory education laws directly serve the operation of the educational institutions, which in turn function as a direct factor in social change.

A very interesting additional way in which law indirectly serves social change is the role of law in preserving and assuring the operation of a free market economy, which at some time served as one of the more important mechanisms of social change in many countries, especially the United States.

Further ways in which changes in the law indirectly serve or reflect social change could be enumerated, but the important fact is the distinction between direct and indirect aspects of the relationships between law and social change. While there are many marginal cases and the difference is often one of degree, this distinction is of primary importance in obtaining a comprehensive and inclusive view of the relationships between law and social change and the possible uses of law as policy instruments.

Every collection of statutes and delegated legislation is full of illustrations of the direct use of law as an instrument of directed social change. This is true for all modern societies. But the more interesting and extreme examples of the use of lawmaking as an instrument designed to bring about social change, from which we can hope to study its processes and problems, are provided by those cases where a revolutionary or intellectual minority obtains legislative power and uses it in its efforts to bring about extensive changes in social structure and culture. This was the case in Japan and Turkey, where whole parts of Western law were received with the intention thus to further the Westernization of these countries; this was also the case in Soviet Russia. To a much more limited extent, the efforts of various colonial powers, especially France, to introduce their law into various territories under their rule was also motivated by the desire to shape the social realities of those places.

Illustrations of the use of law to bring about substantial social change can also be found in modern Western countries. An interesting case illustrating an ambitious effort to shape social behavior through the use of law was the enactment of prohibition in the United States. It was also one of the most conspicuous failures, showing that there are strict limits to the effective uses of law as a policy instrument.

Consideration of the conditions for effective use of law as an instrument for directed social change and of the limits of such use is of the utmost practical and theoretical importance, as such a study provides a key to the development of a policy sciences study of legislation and to an understanding of some of the basic social processes associated with law and social behavior.

This question can be approached in two principal ways. One possible method would require an examination of the psychological and socio-psychological processes through which law operates, and a definition of the conditions under which individuals and groups adjust their behavior to new laws and, conversely, a definition of the conditions under which new laws do not significantly influence behavior. It is doubtful whether the study of psychology and social psychology has developed far enough to permit the use of this method. The role of law within the motivational system of the individual and the psychological processes by which law commands obedience under certain conditions are not understood and are not likely to be thus understood until a great deal of progress is made in the study of more elementary socio-psychological phenomena, about which too little is known. Therefore, this avenue to the investigation of the effectiveness of law is closed at present.

Fortunately, there are other ways in which this question can be dealt with, at least partially, for example, through comparative empirical investigation of the effects of attempts to use law to induce social change in various societies. While little research has been done in this direction, available material demonstrates the possibility to study the variables determining the effectiveness of the use of law to induce and influence social change. Thus, material on the impact of the reception of Western law on society in Turkey[4] clearly brings out two facts: the reception did have a significant influence on some aspects of social life, while certain other aspects were but little influenced by the new laws meant to regulate them. It seems that the aspects of social action of a mainly instrumental character, such as commercial activities, were significantly influenced by new law, while those aspects of social action involving expressive activities and basic beliefs and institutions,

[4]*E.g.*, see *International Social Science Bulletin*, Vol. 60 (1956).

such as family life and marriage habits, were very little changed despite explicit laws trying to shape them.

Intensive study is urgently needed to throw more light on the subject and to enable re-examination and elaboration of this basic hypothesis. The difficulties encountered in all countries when trying to use law as an instrument to control economic activities, evidenced by the everpresent phenomenon of the black market in periods of shortage and rationing, requires additional study which may well modify the above hypotheses in important respects. Comparative study of the experience of various countries, including, *inter alia*, the experiences of Japan, Communist China, and some of the modernizing countries, could also provide important relevant material, thus furthering the study of the direct relationship between law and social change and allowing us to grasp more fully the possibilities and limitations of the use of law as a means to induce and to direct social change.

Conclusions and Implications

Social change and changes in the law are constant and interacting processes, present to a considerable extent in all contemporary societies. From the point of view of the social study of law and the comparative study of law, the investigation of these processes can contribute much to the understanding of the various legal systems within their respective social contexts. More important for my purposes, the study of these phenomena can contribute much to our understanding of the relationships between law and society and provide a reliable basis for a policy sciences approach to law and lawmaking.

One outstanding feature of the relations between law and social change in the contemporary United States is the simultaneous lag of law behind social change and of social change behind law. In some areas law lags significantly behind new patterns of behavior and novel social institutions, while—in the same society and at the same time—in other areas, patterns of behavior and social institutions lag significantly behind new legal norms.

Such a situation calls for high-quality policymaking on behalf of all components of the legal system and of the societal direction system, to avoid transformation of the lags between law and social change into a deep cleavage—which can impair the basic social functions of law and thus endanger some aspects of social existence, in addition to reducing the usability of law as a policy instrument. To serve as a basis for such high-quality decisions, much more knowledge about law and society is needed. This knowledge should be oriented toward the uses of law, and the legal system as a whole, as instruments of societal direction—within a broad policy sciences approach.

CHAPTER 18

Administrative Agencies and Courts:
Some Patterns of Interorganizational Relations[1]

COMMENTS

Interorganizational relations are a main mode of policymaking; therefore, their study is essential for policy sciences. This chapter presents some findings of such a study, both as an illustration of the involved concepts and models and because of the direct saliency of the relationships between administrative agencies and courts for the possible uses of law as a policy instrument. In addition, this chapter constitutes a study of decisionmaking within a conflict system.[2] Even though the conflict system examined here is a limited one, it does bring out some problems of conflict systems study. This is very important for policy sciences, because so much of policymaking takes place by conflict systems, on one hand, and is oriented at adversaries with which the policymaking multiactors[3] form a conflict system, on the other hand.

Introduction

Contemporary administrative sciences are characterized by the coexistence of two distinct approaches—the judicial and the psycho-sociological. The importance of both is increasingly recognized, but, in general, they continue to be viewed as distinct points of view which cannot be integrated into a comprehensive administrative-science theory.[4] The gulf separating the judicial and the psycho-sociological approaches is deepened by their association with different research orientations, namely, behavioral empiricism and

[1]Based on a paper first printed in *International Review of Administrative Sciences* 30, no. 3 (1964): 285-96.

[2]For the concept of conflict systems and some involved issues, see Albert Wohlstetter, "Analysis and Design of Conflict Systems," in E. S. Quade, ed., *Analysis for Military Decisions* (Chicago: Rand McNally, 1964), pp. 103-48; and Albert Wohlstetter, "Theory and Opposed-Systems Design," in Morton A. Kaplan (ed.), *New Approaches to International Relations* (New York: St. Martin's Press, 1968), pp. 19-53.

[3]I am using the term multiactor whenever the involved actor consists of more than one person, so as to avoid the misleading connotation that a group, an organization, and even a nation behave as a single person. Not only do multiactors behave differently from individuals, but even analogue between the behavior of (individual) actors and multiactors is more misleading than enlightening.

[4]E.G., see André Molitor, *The University Teaching of Social Sciences: Public Administration* (Paris: UNESCO, 1959), pp. 48, 135-36.

normative-logical analysis, respectively. Further reinforced by the difference in origin between the "American" socio-psychological approach, on one hand, and the "European-Continental" juridical approach, on the other, research and teaching in administrative sciences suffer from the absence of a unified set of basic concepts, of generally accepted research methods, and of shared basic assumptions on the nature and scope of the subject matter investigated.

It seems to me that this schizophrenic structure of administrative sciences is not only very harmful, retarding as it does the emergence of a comprehensive theory of public administration which can serve as a useful input for policy sciences—but it is also inherently superfluous. On the level of general theory, utilization of the "system" concept might well provide the intellectual framework for fusion of the judicial and psycho-social approaches into a unified administrative science, but also needed are empiric investigations which cut through the barriers between the two approaches.

On the level of concrete institutional analysis, examination of the interaction between administrative agencies and courts as interorganizational relations can illustrate the possibility to aim at concepts and empiric findings in the no man's land between the judicial and the psycho-sociological approaches, thus contributing to bridging the gulf between the two.

This chapter describes some generalized findings of a study on the interorganizational relations between administrative agencies and courts, as a contribution to the integration of the judicial and psycho-sociological approaches and as an attempt to further the study of interorganizational relations in general,[5] with an emphasis on policy-oriented conflict models.

[5]Most contemporary studies in administrative sciences focus on intraorganizational processes, with very little attention to (1) the relations beween organizaions and (2) the social and political system as a whole; almost none deal systematically and meaningfully with interorganizational processes between discrete types of units. This situation can be explained by a number of barriers which hinder research on interorganizational relations, such as the complexity of relevant variables, the absence of operational models, and the dearth of comparable interaction situations which permit meaningful generalization. Since, in fact, interorganizational relations fulfill critical functions—both from the point of view of the interacting units and from the point of view of the embracing systems—more attention to the study of these relations is called for. Especially important are such relations for policy sciences, because policymaking involves intense interactions between different organizations. The study of relations between administrative agencies and courts has a number of important advantages, making it a very good test case for developing and trying out methods and concepts for dealing with interorganizational relations. These advantages include the existence of a large number of interaction bits under relatively highly standardized conditions; the availability of comparative data from different societies, which can be substituted to some extent for experimentation; ease of access to much of the relevant data, which is included in official written records; and the relative simplicity of the field of interaction, which includes a limited number of main actors and multiactors.

The methodology of the study on which the findings to be presented are based is pragmatic, adjusted to the needs of a relatively unexplored field. It included two intensive case studies, participant observation, a large number of informal interviews, analysis of official records (mainly judgments), and examination of secondary material. The study took place partly in the United States, partly in the United Nations Secretariat, and partly in Israel. It should be regarded as exploratory and suggestive, being directed toward penetrating into *terra incognita* rather than providing fully validated and detailed findings covering the area considered.

In this chapter we will, as already mentioned, present the main generalized findings without going into exhaustive details.[6] We will proceed by first considering some main channels of interaction between administrative agencies and courts.[7] Then we will examine the main phases of interaction and some of the variables shaping them, with the help of a simple interaction-decision matrix.

The Main Channels of Interaction Between Administrative Agencies and Courts

The main channels of interaction between administrative agencies and courts can be classified by two dimensions, the degree of directness of the channel and the degree of its formality. Because of the highly structured nature of the legal process, a dichotomous nominal scale of measurement is sufficient for purposes of examination of the communication channels, the cardinal distinctions being between formal and informal channels of interaction, on one hand, and between direct and indirect channels of interaction, on the other. Formal channels of interaction are those which are set down by law or explicitly recognized by the legal norms; informal channels are those not recognized by law.[8] Direct channels of interaction operate between administrative agencies and courts without any intermediary, while indirect channels of interaction operate through an intermediary. With the help of these dimensions, we arrive at a four-cell matrix of interaction channels

[6]The legal-normative material is discussed, in part, in Yehezkel Dror, "Prolegomenon to a Social Study of Law," *Journal of Legal Education* 13, no. 2 (1960); 131-56. One of the case studies is described in Yehezkel Dror, "Organizational Functions of a Domestic Tribunal: A Case Study of the Administrative Tribunal of the United Nations," *British Journal of Industrial Relations* 2 (1964): 42-56. For a preliminary statement of some findings, see Yehezkel Dror, "Administrative Agency Reaction to Court Decisions," *PROD, Political Research: Organization and Design,* November 1959, pp. 7-9.

[7]The verbal symbols *courts* and *administrative agencies* are used in this chapter to refer to both the respective organizational units and their personnel.

[8]On a more elaborate level of analysis, the nominal scale would include four points: legally established channels, formal but extralegal channels, informal and extralegal channels, and informal and illegal channels.

between administrative agencies and courts, which permits classification of the various discrete interaction bits. (See table 18-1.)

Table 18-1

Classification of Interaction Channels Between Administrative Agencies and Courts

	1. Formal	2. Informal
a. Direct	1*a. Direct-Formal* E.g., application by administrative agency to court; court order directed at administrative agency; formal hearings before the court in which the administrative agency participates	2*a. Direct-Informal* E.g., personal contact between judges and administrators at social and professional meetings; professional publications by judges or administrators mainly directed, respectively, at administrators and judges
b. Indirect	1*b. Indirect-Formal* E.g., application by administrative agency to legislature to change statute so as to overcome a court decision; court issuance of subpoena against a private person ordering him to testify before an administrative agency; appeal to the court by a private person who has been issued an order by an administrative agency; inclusion in court judgment of recommendation to change statute so as to increase authority of the court to interfere with administrative agency	2*b. Indirect-Informal* E.g., private lobbying in legislature by administrators or judges; informal agreement between administrator and private party to arrange a test-case before the court; public pronouncements, activities, and publications by judges or administrators designed to influence public or professional opinion and thus put pressure on the other side

The main findings emerging from the study in respect to the interaction can be summed up as follows:

1. The formal "rule-of-law" ideology prohibits informal interaction channels with respect to concrete cases under consideration by the courts *(sub judice),* while ignoring such channels with respect to other issues. In reality, it appears that in concrete cases under consideration by the courts, most interaction does indeed proceed through formal channels. At the same time, it is evident that there is a considerable amount of interaction that proceeds through informal channels, especially person-to-person contacts at social and professional occasions. This interaction is on a more general level, consisting of appraisal of the policies of the courts and agencies, analysis of actions and judgments, discussions of the professional validity of decisions, and so on. This informal interaction clearly has an impact on discrete cases,

both through anticipatory reaction and through direct influence. This impact of informal interaction channels, although it is acknowledged by sophisticated practitioners, is ignored in the generally expressed image of the interaction between administrative agencies and courts. The commonly accepted image seems to serve as a highly functional myth, reinforcing the legitimation of the courts and, to a lesser degree, of the administrative agencies.

2. The extent to which interaction proceeds through informal channels is determined by a number of variables, which include the degree of acceptance of the "rule-of-law" and "separation-of-functions" ideology, the social distance between judges and administrators, and the organizational distance between judges and administrators. The importance of these variables is clearly supported by comparative data. In the United States, a comparison of the differences in organizational distance between adjudicatory and administrative-policymaking units within the unitary structure of regulatory commissions, such as the NLRB and the FCC, and between the regular courts and the regular administrative agencies seems to explain the difference in intensity of interaction through informal channels.[9] Comparison of the French Conseil d'Etat—where the supreme administrative court is a part of the general administrative hierarchy and where the social distance between the judges and the administrators is very small—with the judicial structure of England and the United States and their organizational and personal relationships with administrative agencies, leads to the same conclusion.[10]

3. Most of the interaction channels are a monopoly of lawyers who serve as the main go-betweens for the courts and the administrative agencies.[11] The importance and position of the government lawyer in administrative agencies in most Anglo-American countries seem closely related to the monopoly he holds on communication with the courts; he alone is qualified by training and experience to represent the administrative agencies in their relationships with the courts, and only he can translate the action of the courts into language understood by most administrators. If this hypothesis

[9]The demand for separation of functions within the independent regulatory commissions and the use of special Trial Examiners is based largely on the recognition of the impact of informal interaction channels between prosecuting, adjudicating, and policy-determining officials within unitary organizations.

[10]See George Langrod, "The French Council of State: Its Role in the Formulation and Implementation of Administrative Law," *American Political Science Review* 49 (Spring 1955): 673-92. This article mentions some of the advantages of the existence of informal interaction channels between courts and administrative agencies.

[11]An illustration of differences among various states in this respect is the special position of the Procurator's Office in the USSR, where it seems to serve, *inter alia,* as a special communication channel between the courts, central policymaking units, and the administration. See Glenn G. Morgan, *Soviet Administrative Legality* (Stanford: Stanford University Press, 1962).

is correct, it follows that in countries where all high administrators have received a legal education, the government attorney should play a relatively minor role. Indeed, examination of the situation in Germany, Switzerland, and The Netherlands seems to support this hypothesis. Relatively few positions exist there that are comparable with those of legal officers in the American administrative agencies, and those that exist do not have comparable power or authority.

The Main Phases of Interaction

We now proceed to an examination of three main interaction phases between administrative agencies and courts, namely, action by the administrative agency, reaction by the courts, and counteraction by the administrative agencies. This "stimulus-response" model of the interaction process is admittedly too simple: it ignores the continuous character of the interaction processes, and the feedback processes between the various bits and different phases of interaction. Nevertheless, considering present knowledge about interorganizational interaction, in general, and about interaction between administrative agencies and courts, in particular,[12] I prefer presentation of the available data within a useful, though oversimplified, framework to construction of complex models which far outrun our knowledge and are therefore definitely nonoperational.[13]

Each of the three phases can be discussed with the help of a simplified decisionmaking model, composed of four elements (*a*) the alternatives,

[12]Some studies deal with this area. For example, see William M. Evan, "Due Process of Law in Military and Industrial Organizations," *Administrative Science Quarterly* 7 (September 1962): 187-207, and some studies of the Center for the Study of Law and Society, headed by Philip Selznick at the University of California, Berkeley.

An impetus in the direction of studies on relationships between judicial bodies and administrative agencies is provided by the case method in public administration. For example, see James W. Fesler, "The Case Method in Political Science," in Edwin A. Bock, ed., *Essays on the Case Method in Public Administration* (Brussels: International Institute of Administrative Sciences, 1962), pp. 66-67, which points out the need to examine administrative behavior preceding and following a court decision.

[13]Most of the efforts to utilize theory-of-games models for the study of specific interorganizational relationships failed because of the over-refined nature of these models—or, to look at the same matter from another direction, inadequate data and understanding of the interorganizational relations. Other models used for this purpose include biological ones ("symbiosis," "commensalism") or economic ones ("competition," "exchange"). See Peter M. Blau and W. Richard Scott, *Formal Organizations* (San Francisco: Chandler, 1962), pp. 214-21; and James D. Thompson and William J. McEwen, "Organizational Goals and Environments," in Amitai Etzioni, ed., *Complex Organizations: A Sociological Reader* (New York: Free Press, 1962), pp. 179-86. More promising are some of the models developed for the study of international relations. For example, see Richard C. Snyder, H. W. Bruck, and Burton Sapin, *Foreign Policy Decision Making* (New York: Free Press, 1962), pp. 14-185.

that is, the different patterns of action open to the administrative agency or court; (*b*) the goals, that is, the relevant objectives of the administrative agency or court; (*c*) the expectations, that is, the predicted outcome of the various alternatives; and (*d*) the integration process, that is, the overall relevant-decisionmaking process of the administrative agency or court. While this is a very simplified framework, it does enable the construction of the phases of a decision matrix, which identifies twelve elements of the interaction process between administrative agencies and courts. (See table 18-2.)

Table 18-2

Phase of Decision Matrix of Interaction Between Administrative Agencies and Courts

	1. Action by Administrative Agency	2. Reaction by Court	3. Counteraction by Administrative Agency
a. Alternatives	1*a*	2*a*	3*a*
b. Goals	1*b*	2*b*	3*b*
c. Expectations	1*c*	2*c*	3*c*
d. Integration	1*d*	2*d*	3*d*

The main findings with respect to these elements are as follows:

Action by Administrative Agencies

Alternatives (element 1a). Starting with the initial action of the administrative agency, we can distinguish two main alteratives open to the administrative agency: to initiate interaction with the courts concerning a certain case or issue, or not to initiate such interaction. A decision to initiate interaction with the courts necessitates a choice between two branched-off alternatives, namely, to initiate direct interaction with the courts by opening formal legal proceedings, or to behave in a way which increases the probability that some interested party will initiate administrative agency-court interaction by appealing to the courts against the administrative agency action. Similarly, a decision not to instigate action by the courts entails a number of branched-off alternatives. One of them is abstention from direct application to the courts and also from any action which might motivate an interested party to apply to the courts (this may involve various degrees of compromise with the interested party or a giving-in to his demands). Another of these alternatives is abstention from direct application to the courts combined with action to prevent an interested party from applying to the courts, action such as putting direct pressure on the party or hinting that "administrative sanctions" would be used against any party applying to the courts.[14] The administrative

[14]Dependence by private parties on the good will of administrative agencies often results in fewer applications to the courts because of the wish of the private party to preserve good relations with the administrative agency—even if the latter refrains from putting any explicit pressure on the private party—by not contesting he administrative agency in court.

agency often varies its strategies in different cases so that, if a certain issue is expected to become a subject for interaction between the administrative agency and the courts, the "test case" should present the administrative agency in as favorable a light as possible.

Goals (element 1b). In general, the administrative agency wants the court to contribute to the realization of the goals of the agency. More concretely, the administrative agencies can distinguish a number of functions fulfilled by the courts in their interaction with administrative agencies. From the point of view of the administrative agency, these functions have in different circumstances a positive or negative utility, their maximization or minimization, respectively, being the operational goal of the agency.

We can distinguish at least ten such functions: (1) to help enforce administrative agency orders and subpoenas; (2) to channel administrative actions into definite procedures; (3) to define administrative agency jurisdiction; (4) to provide substantive guides for administrative agency action; (5) to reexamine findings of fact by administrative agencies; (6) to strengthen the power of the administrative agency; (7) to enable the administrative agency to disclaim responsibility for "hot questions"; (8) to resolve internal conflicts within an administrative agency; (9) to limit the elasticity of administrative action; (10) to bring administrative agency action to favorable public attention. A discussion of specific ways in which these functions operate follows:

1. Administrative agencies need court help at two main stages of the administrative process: getting information and enforcing their decisions. Involved in the problem of getting information is the extent to which administrative agencies have investigatory powers: Do the agencies have authority to enforce subpoenas, or do they need to apply to the courts for help? Enforcement of decisions raises the problem of administrative sanctions and the extent to which administrative agencies can enforce their own orders without having to apply to the courts. These two variables determine the extent to which the achievement of the goals of administrative agencies involves application to the courts.

2. By determining the domain of applicability of Constitutional due process; by interpreting statutory procedural requirements as set down in the organic acts establishing the administrative agencies, and, in general, statutes such as the Administrative Procedure Act in the United States; and by requiring defined categories of findings to justify administrative decisions —in these ways the courts channel administrative activities into specific procedures and methods.

3. One of the important functions of interaction with the courts is definition of the jurisdiction of the administrative agency in relation both to private parties and to other administrative agencies. The special responsibility of

the courts for deciding jurisdictional problems is recognized in the doctrine of "jurisdictional facts."

4. Interaction between administrative agencies and courts has as its subject matter, in most cases, a substantive problem of policy and law; for example, What does a certain term in an act mean? Are the administrative agencies under an obligation to take into account all of the law or only the statutes explicity applying to them? What is the "legislative intent?" Hence, one of the functions of the interaction process is to provide the administrative agency with substantive rules for action.

5. Another function of interaction with the courts from the point of view of the administrative agencies is revision of conclusions of fact reached by the administrative agencies. Here, the emphasis is not on the methodology used by the administrative agency to establish a certain fact, as in function 1, but on the fact itself. Assuming the methodology is accepted by the courts, do the courts accept the finding of the fact as valid?

6. Administrative agencies operate in a power environment where they are subjected to conflicting pressures, many of which work in a direction opposed to the aims and ideologies of the administrative agencies. Passive resistance to administrative agency decisions, casting of permanent doubts on the legal validity of administrative agency orders, constant efforts to overturn these orders through appeals to the courts, accusations before the legislature branding administratve actions as "illegal" or "contrary to the Constitution"—all these are pressures which can undo administrative agencies' efforts. In societies in which the courts have more power than the administrative agencies and enjoy higher social prestige, a court decision upholding an administrative agency decision—or a court decision reaching independently the same conclusion arrived at by an administrative agency—strengthens to a considerable degree the power of the agency and helps it to overcome opposition. In other words, judicial review lends to an administrative agency action, and to the agency itself, the legitimizing authority and social power of the courts.

7. Interaction with the courts enables administrative agencies to withstand pressure in another way, namely, by passing on responsibility for a problem too "hot" to be handled by them to them to the courts. This may be done by arranging for an early test case, thus putting the responsibility for a certain decision—even if desired and worked for by the agency—on the courts. In Western democratic countries, courts are often better able to withstand public and social pressure and help the administrative agencies by taking upon themselves part of the pressure in this way.

8. Another interaction function of the courts is to help the administrative agencies resolve internal conflicts. Withdrawing an issue from the discretion of the agency and having it resolved once and for a long time by a court deci-

sion releases the administrative process from having to face time and again the same problem. This is especially important if the administrative agency is not formally bound by its own decisions and if the question has been a very controversial one within the agency itself.

9. At the same time, once the court adopts an administrative agency decision as its own (as distinct from approving it as a valid exercise of agency discretion), the matter is withdrawn from the discretion of the administrative agencies and, in most cases, the agencies will be bound in the future by the decisions of the courts. Thus, interaction with the courts can result in limiting the elasticity of the administrative agency even if its concrete action is upheld.

10. In many societies, decisions of the courts enjoy more attention than administrative agency actions. In these societies, including the United States, interaction between the administrative agencies and the courts results in communication of the agency actions to a much wider audience than the agency action would otherwise have. The results of such focusing of attention on administrative agency action vary from case to case. Opposition to the agency may be generated and intensified: the enemies of the agency sometimes use the wide publicity to organize their forces and attack the agency; or the agency may use the publicity to marshall its forces, organize support, and strengthen its positions; or both developments may occur, resulting in intensification of the struggle surrounding the agency's activities.

These are the main functions of interaction with the courts from the administrative agencies' point of view. Functions 1, 6, and 7 have a positive utility for the administrative agency's goals; function 9 has, in most cases, a negative utility for the administrative agency; while functions 2, 3, 4, 5, 8, and 10 have, under different conditions, positive or negative utility, depending on the expected content of the court decision, the self-image of the administrative agency, and the agency's operational goals.[15]

Expectations (element 1c). Turning our attention now to what an administrative agency anticipates in regard to the court reaction to different agency actions, we find that the main variable determining this expectation is the image of the courts held by the administrative agency. This image includes in all modern societies, though to different degrees, four main dimensions of

[15]One of these goals should be mentioned explicitly because of its political and social significance: the desire to uphold the rule of law. When this goal is held strongly enough, it allocates positive utility to every court clarification of a doubtful question, thus motivating the administrative agency to let doubtful points reach the court. An instrumental displacement of this goal, on the other hand, induces the administrative agency to maximize interaction with the courts in order to be sure to operate "according to the law." We have here an "overconformity" with the ideological requirement that all doubtful legal problems should be decided in court. Young and enthusiastic lawyers coming straight from graduate school tend sometimes in this direction and have to be restrained by their more sophisticated and experienced colleagues.

the courts: (1) authority; (2) power; (3) understanding of the administrative process and attitude toward it; and (4) social orientation. Variations in the administrative agency's image of these dimensions are the dominant factors determining the agency's expectation concerning future court reaction to administrative agency action. The image itself is determined by two sets of factors, the perception processes of the administrative agency and the objective state of these dimensions of the courts.

Not enough is known about the perception processes of organizations to permit any definite statements. They are influenced by earlier experience of any administrative agency, its memory structure, and the formal and informal intelligence and communication processes. Legal advisors play an important role in shaping the image of the courts and the expectations concerning their reaction, and so the professional characteristics of lawyers in general and the personal characteristics of the individuals filling the role of legal advisors in a specific administrative agency in particular are among the central factors shaping the image.

Although the significance of the organizational perception processes should be recognized, they are often of secondary overall importance. The objective characteristics of the courts are, in the long run, more important in shaping the subjective expectations, because any serious deviation of the image from reality leads to incorrect decisions. This, in turn, results in negative feedback, which usually brings about changes in the administrative agency's court image, bringing it more in line with reality.

Let us, therefore, now examine the relevant objective dimensions of the courts and their subelements.

1. *Authority.* Authority includes the formal right of the courts to give orders to administrative agencies and to private and public bodies which are interacting with the administrative agencies, and the ultimate authority of the courts to make use of the society's enforcement officers and armed forces to execute orders or impose sanctions for noncompliance with them. The extent of the courts' authority over administrative agencies, private parties, and the legislature is a crucial factor in shaping the interaction between administrative agencies and the courts. When the courts have authority to revise any and all agency action, to both give specific performance orders to administrative agencies and award damages against them, to re-examine witnesses and reach independent conclusions on questions of facts, to prevent legislatures from helping administratives agencies by declaring statutes unconstitutional—then the authority of the courts vis-à-vis the administrative agencies is at maximum. On the other hand, when the courts can give to administrative agencies only limited orders following certain predetermined forms of action, when the courts cannot grant damages against administrative agencies, when the courts are dependent on administrative agencies for

factual information and are bound by conclusions reached by the agencies, when the legislature is not limited by a rigid written constitution and judicial review of constitutionality of legislation—then the authority of the courts vis-à-vis the administrative agencies is at a much lower level.

2. *Power.* Formal authority is a part, but only a part, of the power of the courts. Other factors determining the power of the courts include the prestige of the judiciary, the effectiveness and speed of sanctions, and the position of a specific court within the general hierarchy of courts, and, hence, the chances of having the decision of the specific court overturned by a higher judicial body. More fundamentally, the power of the courts is determined by the general system of legitimation predominant in the society, the extent to which the social opinion of the judges are accepted by the general population, and the relations between the courts and other centers of political or other types of power.

3. *Understanding of the administrative process and orientation toward it.* Courts express opinions about administrative processes and develop orientations to them, and these, in turn, influence the images of the courts held by the administrative agencies. The training, background, and opinions of the judges determine, to some extent, the professional prestige of the courts in the eyes of the administrative agencies and the expectation of the administrative agencies as to whether or not they will meet in the courts persons who—in the opinion of the administrative agencies—understand the problems and needs of administration.

4. *Social orientation of the courts.* Very important, from the administrative agencies' point of view, is the social orientation of the courts: whether they are in sympathy with the administrative agencies' aims and outlook, are neutral or apathetic toward them, or are opposed to the objectives which the administrative agencies feel themselves called upon to serve.

Integration (element 1d) The overall action of the administrative agency in selecting one of the alternatives involves integration of the other elements within the inclusive decisionmaking process. Available literature on organizational decisionmaking leads us to expect this element to follow the patterns of "satisficing," "muddling through," and "incremental change"—involving limited search for alternatives and predominent influence by organizational precedents. Actually, however, the integrated decisionmaking process in administrative agencies with respect to interaction with the courts seems to be on a much better level: administrative agencies are aware of the main possible strategies and do carefully consider their possible pay-offs before adopting one of them. Indeed, it seems that the training of lawyers strongly encourages preferable decisionmaking within the domain of the legal order; it seems explicitly directed at maximizing output on a rather well-defined utility curve on which "winning the case" serves as the maximum pay-off, "losing the case" is the zero (or maximum negative) pay-off, and various compromises and intermediate judgments fall in between. While this utility curve does not cover all pay-off dimensions and while legal training also results in trained incapacity with respect to extra-legal alternatives and results, our material clearly shows that organizational decisions on interaction with the courts take place on a much higher level of preferability than assumed by contemporary administrative sciences literature.

Court Reaction

The second phase of interaction between administrative agencies and courts is court reaction to the action of the administrative agency. The material uncovered by our study does not justify detailed analysis of this phase, the tradition of judicial secrecy and the strength of verbal rationalizations preventing effective penetration into the elements of judicial decisionmaking. I will therefore limit myself to an indication of the main content of the elements and then proceed to the third interaction phase.

Alternatives (element 2a). The courts react to the actions of administrative agencies on three levels: the level of general orientations, the level of doctrines, and the level of discrete decisions. The orientations include basic attitudes which underlie the specific forms of reaction to administrative agency action; such an attitude is, for example, the view that the administrative agencies and the courts are cooperating institutions which should help one another. The doctrines are various judicially created principles which guide the concrete patterns of reaction followed in concrete cases; an example is the principle of "exhaustion of administrative remedy." The concrete decisions are the immediate reactions of the courts to specific actions of the administrative agencies, such as reversal and approval with or without reexamination on the merits. Reactions to the administrative agencies' actions take place simultaneously on these three levels which, while interdependent, can nevertheless be examined separately.

On the level of general orientation, at least three alternatives can be noted: cooperation, rejection, and competition. These three orientations in their pure form constitute three clear-cut extremes. In reality, the orientation of specific courts moves on the continuum bonded by the extremes and combines them to various extents.

On a second level of court reaction lie various doctrines developed by the courts in relation to their interaction with administrative agencies. As illustrations of such alternative doctrines, principles, and rules, we can mention, among others, the doctrines of exhaustion of administrative remedies, ripeness for review, primary jurisdiction, official bias, *omnia acta site esse praesumuntus,* and necessity. These doctrines constitute the court-developed guides to the concrete patterns of court reaction in specific instances of administrative agency action.

Alternatives on the concrete level of decision depend on the authority of the courts in various jurisdictions. In France, for instance, the Conseil d'Etat has wide authority to interfere with administrative agencies and to order compensations to be paid by them. In most Anglo-American jurisdictions, the authority of the courts is more limited. In all jurisdictions, the patterns of the court action include many variations and nuances which can be classified according to different criteria, such as the intensity of re-examination of the administrative agency action or application, the form of reaction, and the form of the court's order. Courts also react indirectly to administrative agency action through other institutions such as the legislature. For instance, a court may appeal to the legislature, through formal or informal channels of communication, to change laws dealing with some of the aspects of the interaction between the courts and the administrative agencies.

Goals (element 2b). The primary goals of the courts in regard to their interaction with administrative agencies include the following: (1) to uphold the law; (2) to preserve the power of the courts; (3) to advance social values held by the judges; (4) to enable the administrative process to operate.

While the first goal is regarded by the rule-of-law ideology as the only one, the other goals are in reality not less important, because they shape to a larger extent the interpretation given to the law. This point is well brought out by the Realistic School of Jurisprudence and the more recent behavioral studies of courts.

Expectations (element 2c). Predictions of pay-off seem to play a much smaller role in court decisions than in administrative agency decisions, court action being, in most cases, oriented mainly toward preserving the internal consistency of law as a closed system of norms. Especially striking is the difference in importance, to the administrative agencies and to the courts, of the role of anticipation of reaction. For the administrative agency, the potential reaction of the courts has important, and often critical, significance. For the courts, the potential counteraction of the administrative agency is in the large majority of cases of very minor, and even trivial, significance. This is one of the main reasons for the dominant position of the courts in the the administrative agency-court interaction process in most modern societies.

Integration (element 2d). Concerning the integrated overall decision process, the available material indicates five main differences between administrative agency decisionmaking and court decisionmaking: (1) administrative agency decisionmaking is mainly an organizational process, while court decisionmaking is more an individual or small-group process[16]; (2) administrative agency decisionmaking is relatively less structured by formal rules; (3) administrative agency decisionmaking involves more kinds of data and more comprehensive and elaborate data-processing procedures; (4) courts are, in most cases, more "professionalized" and homogeneous; (5) there seem to be important differences between the "judicial mind" common to judges and developed through special socialization processes, and the "public organization mind" developed through other socialization processes. These differences are all the more striking in view of the fact that the main decision-makers on administrative agency-court interaction in both actor-organizations are lawyers.[17]

Administrative Agency Counteraction

The third phase of interaction is counteraction by the administrative agency to the court reaction. Most the elements in this phase are similar to those in the first phase, but there are some differences which need examination.

Alternatives (element 3a). There are two primary levels of alternative counteraction by administrative agencies to court reaction: counteraction to the concrete decision of the court in the case before it, and counteraction to the new legal norm promulgated in the court judgment.

When the court renders a clear order to an administrative agency to act in a defined way in a specific case, the administrative agency has, in most cases, little choice. Exceptions are those occasional cases in which retroactive legislation is constitutionally and politically feasible. But often the courts remand cases to the administrative agencies with instructions to reconsider them in the light of the ruling set down by the court. The ruling might, for example, direct that a specific official must exercise his discretion, set down a rule of procedure to be followed by the agency, or establish a substantive rule of law to be applied by the agency. In such cases, the administrative agency can either genuinely reconsider the case and decide it in accordance with the ruling of the court, or engage in purely formal observance of the the ruling of the court while, in fact, leaving its earlier decision unchanged.

On the level of the legal norm, there are at least five possible counteractions by the administrative agencies to the court reaction: (1) full adjustment of administrative agency behavior to the decision of the courts; (2) partial adjustment of administrative agency behavior to the decision of the

[16]The only empirical study touching one facet of one type of such judicial group processes is part of the jury studies conducted at Chicago.

[17]Observation of a number of cases of transfer of lawyers from administrative roles into judicial roles indicates a rather sudden metamorphosis in behavior patterns and frames of reference. Here is a subject for research which may well provide new insights into role interchangeability and role-adjustment propensity, especially in the policy-making system.

courts; (3) evasive action designed to ignore or minimize the impact of the court decision; (4) counteraction designed to overcome the impact of the court decision; (5) counteraction designed to overcome or minimize the impact of the court action in general.

1. Full adjustment of administrative agency behavior to the decision of the courts is the administrative agency counteraction expected by the general ideology of the rule of law. Here, the administrative agency bona fide accepts the court decision *in toto* and changes its patterns of behavior to bring them into accord with both the words and the spirit of the court decision.

Nearly all administrative law and most public administration literature seems to assume that this is the only possible administrative agency counteraction to the ruling of the courts, but the case studies on which this chapter is based clearly show that this is a myth, and that, in fact, administrative agencies consider much more complex counteraction alternatives and, in many cases, adopt the other possible counteraction patterns.

2. The second possible counteraction is partial adjustment of administrative agency behavior to the decision of the court. Here, the decisions of the courts is not fully accepted as a guide to future agency action, but does have a significant impact on the administrative agency, bringing about changes in its behavior and actions.

3. Evasive action designed to ignore or minimize the impact of the court decision is a very important third alternative. Here, the agency is unwilling to accept the court reaction as a factor shaping its behavior. Through various devices, such as limiting the significance of the court decision to the special facts of the case before the court, the importance of the court decision is minimized and, in fact, ignored insofar as the future behavior of the agency is involved.

4. Because of the superior authority and power of the courts in most modern jurisdictions, it may be impossible for the agencies to evade the impact of court decisions for long without mobilizing support. Support can come, in most areas, from the legislature, either in the form of legislation abrogating the decision of the courts or—in those cases where the legislature cannot interfere because of the constitutional review authority of the courts—in the form of informal pressure on the judiciary or constitutional amendment.

Administrative agencies try, directly or indirectly, to convince the legislature and interested pressure groups that the consequences of the court decision endanger aims dear to the legislature or the pressure group, respectively, and that legislation is needed which will, in fact, annul the action of the courts. Depending on the facts of the situation, the administrative agency may use various forms of pressure and argumentation—resignation by key officials, promise of advantages to groups which help the efforts of the agency and threat of sanctions against groups which oppose the efforts of the agency, mobilization of public opinion, and so on—to move the legislature to act according to the wishes of the administrative agency.

Another form of such counteraction, which is fully in accord with the rule-of-law ideology, is appeal by the administrative agency to a higher level of the court hierarchy. This alternative has many similarities to initial commencement of interaction processes by the administrative agency, and our earlier analysis of this first phase of the interaction process applies in main lines here.

5. The fifth pattern involves counteraction designed to overcome or minimize the impact of court action in general by changing the relative authority and power of the administrative agencies and the courts. The most common form of this reaction pattern is appeal by the administrative agency to the legislature to limit the scope of judicial review and so grant the administrative agencies immunity against court action. This can be done by declaring the administrative agency decisions "final" or "final and conclusive," etc.; by granting the administrative agency wide powers which, in fact, exclude judicial review; by limiting the sanctions at the disposal of the courts; or by similar devices designed to exclude administrative action from the scope of authority of the courts. The effectiveness of such legislative action depends, to some extent, on the possible counteraction of the courts and especially on the extent of the constitutional review authority exercised by them.[18]

Goals (element 3b). The goals of the administrative agency at this phase are identical with those during the initial phase (element 1b).

Expectations (element 3c). The possibility of further counter-reaction by the court to the counteraction of the administrative agency is an important part of the prediction element, for the most part identical with the prediction element at the initial phase of interaction (element 1c). But two additional factors here enter the prediction element: the administrative agency's expectation as to the effect of the court action on the administrative process, and the administrative agency's predictions of the reaction by the legislature, interest groups, and media of communication to efforts at overcoming the effect of the court reaction through evasive counteraction.

The first of these predictions—the administrative agency's expectations of the effects of the court reaction on the administrative process—is a most important variable: when the administrators are convinced that faithful execution of the court decision will frustrate the administrator's goals, everything is done to evade the court decision and counteract it. On the other hand, when the administrative agency regards the court decision as com-

---

[18]In addition to these counteractions of administrative agencies to court reaction, the court reaction has a strong impact on the image of the courts held by the administrative agencies. This is an important part of the coninuous feedback among the various bits of the interaction process.

mensurate with its goals, or at last is convinced that the court is fully aware of the administrative problems, well qualified to deal with them, and eager to protect the administrative process as far as possible, the administrative agency generally tries to reconcile the court decision with what it regards as the needs of efficient administration. It will then execute the court decisions more faithfully than if it distrusts the qualifications and intentions of the court.

The second factor is conditioned by the prestige of the administrative agency; the strength of its supporters and opponents, especially in the legislature; the tendency and authority of the legislature to interfere with the interaction between the administrative agencies and the courts; the general ideology on the proper division of authority and functions among courts, administrative agencies, and the legislature; and the attitudes of various other social power centers. All these combine to form the power-and-authority map from which the administrative agency tries to construct its expectations concerning the outcome of selecting any of the different alternative counteraction strategies.

Integration (element 3d). The overall integrated administrative agency decision process at this point is similar in character to that during the first phase (element 1d), showing the same tendency toward preferization.

Conclusion

We could now proceed to a fourth phase of interaction, namely, the counter-reaction of the courts to the counteraction of the administrative agency, and so on; but no useful purpose would be served by doing so. Nevertheless, we must acknowledge the existence of additional interaction loops as character-istic of the continuous, crosscutting, and cross-influencing nature of the interaction processes between administrative agencies and courts. What we have done in this study is to make a sequential analysis of three main phases of an individual interaction bit, viewed in isolation from other interaction bits and from a variety of other social and political processes which significantly influence the interaction process. In reality, this is a continuous interaction process, including a flow of interaction bits between administrative agencies and courts.

When additional data become available, more complete and penetrating analyses of the interaction between administrative agencies and courts will become possible, including, perhaps, some quantification of the main para-meters and construction of semimathematical models. But even in its present form, the findings presented in this chapter do illustrate the possibilities of inclusive study of administrative behavior, integrating, to some extent, the juridical and psycho-sociological aspects. In addition, the findings seem to throw some light on a discrete interorganizational relationship of much theoretical and applied interest and significance, *inter alia,* for policy sciences.

This part adopts a different approach from the others: Instead of dealing with a component of policy sciences or some related discipline, it takes a policy issue and illustrates possible policy sciences contributions to its resolution. The issue taken up in this part is modernization, and the considered contributions of policy sciences are on the metapolicy level. The first chapter discusses the improvement of policymaking as an essential condition of successful accelerated modernization. The second chapter presents in more detail a specific proposal for the improvement of policymaking in modernization countries, namely, a course for politicians. Training of politicians is, I think, urgently needed in all countries, modern countries not less than modernizing countries. This is a need ignored in contemporary normal sciences. For instance, contemporary political science pays no attention whatsoever to the problems of preparing politicians for their increasingly difficult and demanding tasks. May I, therefore, invite the reader to pay particular attention to the second chapter and to try to consider it not only as good advice for "primitive countries", but as dealing with an issue of the utmost importance for the so-called modern and highly developed countries as well—if not even more so.

PART VI

A Policy Sciences View of Modernization

CHAPTER 19

Accelerated Modernization and Policymaking Improvement[1]

COMMENTS

This chapter presents the case for changes in metapolicy as essential for successful accelerated modernization. In addition to reasons why the improvement of the policymaking system is important and even essential for accelerated modernization, this chapter also includes seven more operational suggestions, which illustrate possible directions for such improvement. It thus somewhat applies main policy sciences ideas to the particular circumstances of modernization countries.

Introduction

During the early stages of modernization studies and modernization policies, the rather optimistic assumption was often accepted that socio-economic development can be achieved independent of weaknesses in the political and administrative system. With progress in the study of modernization processes and with the accumulation of frustrating experiences, this simple assumption was revised to somewhat take into account the interdependence of social, economic, and political phenomena, and some necessary political and administrative requisites of accelerated overall development were identified.

Political stability, strong symbols of identification, the ability to recruit support, implementation capacities, some professionalization of the bureaucracy, and some acceptance of a merit system—these illustrate the characteristics of the political and administrative system, recognized as requirements for accelerated socio-economic modernization (though insufficient by themselves). Many modernization aid activities are directed at encouraging these and related characteristics—from civil service training to strengthening the armed forces so as to resist subversion, from improving organization structures and procedures to encouraging widespread distribution of the instruments of mass communication as an essential tool for "nation building." These are, without doubt, highly desirable activities; clearly all the above-mentioned political-administrative characteristics are, indeed, essential for accelerated

[1]Based on a paper first published in *Civilizations* 19, no. 2 (1964): 209-15.

modernization. But it seems to me that at least one critical aspect of the political-administrative system, which constitutes one of the most important variables for shaping all facets of development, is very neglected in theory and action alike: this is the *policymaking* function.

Not that policymaking is completely neglected: quite some attention is paid —in theory and even more so in practice—to central planning organizations, budget procedures, and monetary controls. Often, also, serious efforts are made to improve operational policies in respect to some selected subject, such as education, agriculture, specific industrial projects, and water management. But the main components of central public policymaking are usually neglected in the study of modernization processes and excluded from intensive self-improvement efforts and from international and bilateral aid activities.

The omission of treatment of the public policymaking system, despite its constituting a critical factor in determining the probabilities of success in accelerated modernization endeavors, is not too difficult to understand. Three clusters of reason do explain, at least in part, this situation:

1. The study of policymaking and systematic approaches to policymaking improvement are new even in the modern nations. Policy sciences knowledge is still in its infancy; proved policymaking-improvement suggestions are scarce; and qualified professionals in the policy-relevant disciplines (or, more correct, interdisciplines) are scarce and are much in demand in their home countries, in addition to being difficult to identify and often disliked by more traditionally trained administrations, academicians, and by many politicians.

2. Effective policymaking improvement involves changes in the main components of the policymaking system, that is, in the political institutions. Patterns of decisionmaking by the senior ministers and by the Cabinet, information flow to the legislature, the social roles of intellectuals and universities— these are just a few illustrations of the foci of attention of any serious efforts to improve policymaking. Much can be done to adjust recommendations to prevailing power structures, indigenous values, and personal styles of the dominant political figures. But even after all possible adjustment, improvement of policymaking involves significant changes in the political institutions. It therefore is a very sensitive area, particularly hostile to foreign experts and external aid, which tend simultaneously to be absolutely essential and completely unacceptable. The result is that experts and aid concentrate on more technical activities, which are very useful but are often completely frustrated because of weaknesses in public policymaking.

3. In order to achieve worthwile improvements in the policymaking processes of modernization countries (and of modern countries as well), a whole set of interrelated improvements is necessary, which, together, reach the critical mass needed for making any real impact on so complex, diffuse, and aggregate a process. True, the apparently more simple structure of the public policy-

making system in modernization countries may lower the relevant threshold, and relatively fewer changes—in comparison to a modern country—may influence the quality of policymaking. But appearances may be misleading, with many complexities being invisible to the insensitive eyes of the foreign observer, only to reveal themselves when interfered with; also, the resources in qualified personnel, political support, span of attention, information, and the like, needed for improving policymaking are extremely scarce in most modernization countries, often making even a small critical mass impossible to achieve without very effective new types of aid, which, at present, are unavailable.

Each one of these three clusters of barriers to the improvement of policymaking in modernization countries is, by itself, sufficient to explain the absence of activities in this direction. Each of the first two reasons also explains the neglect in theories of modernization of the role of the public policymaking system. Taken together, those factors reinforce one another and constitute in combination most serious hindrances to policymaking improvement in the modernization countries.

Nevertheless, policymaking improvement seems highly necessary for accelerated modernization. There is evidence to indicate that parts of the modernization process are quite independent from conscious, goal-directed social direction, being more the result of basic socio-economic, psycho-cultural, and cross-national evolutions. There are also indications that parts of the modernization process can be stimulated through a series of "shock policies," any one of which will do, so that careful selection of a policy is not necessary. Even granted these assumptions (and not all will equally subscribe to them), still the quality of policymaking is very important: better policies can make quite a difference for the rates, directions, and sequences of accelerated modernization, and bad policies can radically increase the human and socio-economic costs of modernization and strongly retard it. Because of the broad scope of public policymaking and its widespread impacts on different facets of modernization, it constitutes a high-leverage variable, improvements of which will often have widespread and far-reaching impacts (though difficult to measure). Therefore, investments in policymaking improvement may be very efficient in terms of benefit-cost, being often one of the preferable uses of limited energy and resources, both internal and aid-supplied.

My conclusion is that in modernization efforts major emphasis should be put on improving the policymaking system—in research, theory, and practice.

One of the characteristics of efforts to improve policymaking is that a pragmatic approach is inadequate. Weaknesses in policy machines have no clear-cut immediate symptoms which permit diagnosis by the time-honored method of obvious "pains where the shoe presses" and treatment through "debugging," that is, removal of the external manifestations of trouble. The policymaking system is too complex and its features too submerged for such a "practical" approach. Instead, we need careful study of a given policymaking system and sophisticated redesign. Such study and redesign require, in turn, a thorough theoretic understanding of the operations of the policymaking system as an open-ended, complex and dynamic, social and political decisionmaking institution, one one hand; and explicit models of preferable policymaking modes and structures, including creative invention of designs moving in the direction of the preferable models and still being feasible under given political-social-human constraints, on the other hand. In respect to the improvement of policymaking at least, good theory is thus an essential foundation for good practice. A main operational conclusion of my analysis is, therefore, that intensive effort should be made to advance as rapidly as possible research and study on policymaking in modernization countries and on designs for its improvement.

This I regard as an important conclusion, having immediate implications for the allocation of attention and the distribution of resources. But we can proceed one step further.

As already mentioned, policy sciences—which focuses on the study and improvement of policymaking—is still young, even in the most modern nations. Nevertherless, the present state of knowledge in policy sciences, in combination with available knowledge in the various modernization study disciplines, does already permit some recommendations in respect to the improvement of policymaking in modernization countries. These recommendations are tentative and must be revised in view of the conditions and needs of each country. But they serve the double functions of (*a*) concretizing the contents of the terms *improvements of policymaking* and *redesign of the policymaking system* in respect to modernization countries, and (*b*) supplying immediate operational suggestions for policymaking improvement, implementation of which can and should start immediately, without waiting for the results of future study and research. (Such implementation activities, in turn, are a main source of added knowledge and, as a result, better operational suggestions—experimentation and collection of field experience being essential for building up policy sciences knowledge relevant to accelerated modernization conditions.)

Available knowledge seems to support, among others, the following illustrations of operational recommendations for improvement of policymaking in modernization countries:

1. The operations of the highest political decisionmaking organs, such as the president, prime minister, and cabinet, should be improved through (*a*) restructure of information input; (*b*) provision of staff aids for analysis; (*c*) monitoring of implementation results; and (*d*) changes in deliberation preparations (e.g., background papers and briefings).

2. The macro-structure of the government should be subjected to recon-

sideration, including the number of ministries, the composition of the cabinet (e.g., ministers without portfolios), the relations between different levels of government, the role of quasi-government agencies, etc. This reconsideration should look at the picture as a whole and from above, focusing on basic features and not the details of substructure and procedure.

3. The higher civil service patterns should be reconsidered, with special attention to their policy functions. For instance: easy interchange between governmental, other public, quasi-public, and, perhaps, private organizations, and compulsory rotation in the civil service seem essential for preserving imagination and readiness to innovate. Fixed-term appointments and freedom to engage in various forms of political activity may well meet better the needs of some modernization countries than the British-type career civil service traditions. Academic training in behavioral sciences and analytic methods may be preferable for the policy-level civil servants, requiring radical changes in the management- and administrative-technique orientations of many of the training centers in and for modernization countries.

4. Behavorial sciences and policy analysis professionals should serve as central staff officers for policy issues, in addition to and instead of the traditional civil servants, budget officials, and economic feasibility examiners. A special profession of "modernization policy analysts" (see chapter 21) may be required, for heading staff analysis units working on the higher policy level in the main ministries, on the cabinet level, and for the legislature (if the latter has autonomous policymaking functions).

5. Policy-oriented research and study in the involved country should be encouraged by establishment of special interdisiplinary policy analysis units and by motivating local universities to focus on national policy-relevant research. The policy analysis units should enjoy considerable freedom in their studies, but maintain confidential relations with the government (for an illustration, see chapter 27).

6. Innovative action must be initiated to improve the qualifications of the politicians. This is clearly possible within many given basic values and ideologies, for instance, by encouraging politicians after their election and/or appointment to engage in studies, paid for by the government or by external aid. The design of suitable courses for politicians from modernization countries is one of the urgent needs. (See chapter 20, next, for the design of such a course.)

7. New orientations and modes for considering policy alternatives under conditions of accelerated modernization must be designed, tried out, and conveyed to the main policymakers—politicians, civil servants, and professionals alike. These orientations and modes should be adjusted to the high degrees of uncertainties involved in efforts to direct accelerated modernization —for example, through contingency planning, sequential decisionmaking, self-insurance, sensitivity testing, social experimentation, etc. (in contrast to pre-

vailing modernization planning models, most of which tend to repress or at least ignore uncertainty).

These seven illustrations are intended to concretize the main ideas of this chapter and demonstrate their importance. These illustrations also clearly bring out the difficulties of realizing any advances in policymaking improvement. Intense, dedicated, and innovative efforts are necessary if we want to meet the challenge of contributing to better accelerated development through improving public policymaking in the modernization countries.

CHAPTER 20

Improvement of Leadership in Modernization Countries[1]

COMMENTS

As already indicated in the introduction to Part Six, improvement of leadership is a metapolicy suggestion distinguished by its absence in contemporary normal sciences and democratic practice alike. This chapter deals with the improvement of leadership in modernization countries and includes a course design for doing so. While oriented toward the needs of modernization countries, the needs for improvement of leadership are nowadays even more urgent in modern countries, because of the higher dangers of global catastrophe stemming from failure of leadership in the more modern and more powerful countries. Improvement of leadership *is a broad term, including many moral and value contents outside the scope of policy sciences. But improvement of leadership also includes increasing their rational and extrarational capacities for better policymaking. In this dimension, policy sciences should be able to make a significant contribution.*

Modernization Theories and Modernization Policies

The examination of trends in theories of modernization on one hand and in applied modernization policies on the other hand reveals an increasing gulf between these two, which threatens to become an abyss. Increasingly, the complexities of modernization processes and their dependence on deep-rooted and multidimensional variables are recognized by modern theories of modernization.[2] No longer do we believe in any simple devices which will result in some dramatic "taking-off," with assured continuous and fast modernization. Instead, modern theories of modernization tend to identify clusters of critical "modernization crises,"[3] successful mastering of which is presented as an essential (though not necessarily sufficient) condition for accelerated mod-

[1]An earlier version of this paper was published in *Civilizations* 17, no. 112 (1967): 72-79.

[2]One of the better presentations of modern theories of modernization is still Benjamin Higgins, *Economic Development* (New York: W. W. Norton, 1959).

[3]E.G., see Lucian W. Pye, *Aspects of Political Development* (Boston: Little, Brown, 1966), pp. 62-66.

213

ernization. Often highly sophisticated, modern theories of modernization clearly constitute an important first step forward in our understanding of modernization processes. But, as yet, they provide very poor guidance for modernization policies. Certainly, there is little relation, if any, between modern theories of modernization and actual modernization policies as practiced in the modernization countries themselves, and as encouraged and furthered by international and intercountry aid arrangement.

Modern theories of modernization point out the critical importance of complex and multidimensional factors such as, for instance, levels of aspirations; political participation; population balance; societal communication networks; economic and political entrepreneurship; identification with the state; assurance of order and peace; mobility of elites; changes in bases of legitimations; and quality of public policymaking. Insofar as we accept these theories as approximate indicators of at least some of the realities of modernization processes, our search for preferable modernization policies should try to identify variables which satisfy two conditions: (*a*) they are operational, that is, they can be influenced by conscious action; and (*b*) they are significant, that is, they have significant impact on actual modernization processes through changing the basic relevant factors as identified by reliable modernization studies. (To be more exact, a third condition should be added, namely, efficiency in terms of benefits-costs. But at the present state of knowledge, when most policies are ineffective, this is perhaps too sophisticated a requirement—though I think it should be kept in mind.) In reality, modernization policies tend to concentrate on variables which are related more to the visible outer facades of underdevelopment than to the hard core of modernization processes and their basic factors; modernization policies therefore, tend not to meet the condition of significance (nor, in many cases, the conditions of operationability).

Leaving aside, as deserving separate analysis, concrete physical projects such as steel mills, water systems, and road networks, the following oversimplified picture presents much of contemporary modernization policies:

The external layers of underdevelopment reveal many shortcomings which seem to cry for speedy action. These include, for instance, lack of technical know-how and dearth of professionals; low levels of nutrition and health; slums near the urban centers; absence of investment capital; weaknesses of administrative structures and personnel; soil erosion; tendencies towards local separatism and often some types of insurgence. These shortcomings are well recognized and receive intense treatment through international aid and through efforts by the involved modernization countries themselves—with little results in terms of the basic modernization processes. This is not to say that action directed at these and similar shortcomings has no effect whatsoever. Medical facilities are improved, teachers are trained, agricultural technologies are changed, and so on. Indeed, technological innovations can sometimes be of critical importance, as illustrated by the "green revolution."[4] But often these results are isolated islands, which, at best, change little, are often eroded away by the stormy waves of deeper processes, and sometimes even aggravate the situation (for instance, by increasing the net birth rate beyond any possible rate of increases in G.N.P.; or by creating a strata of school graduates who cannot be usefully employed).

A number of possible conclusions can be drawn from this diagnosis. One possible view is that, because of the complexities of modernization processes and the limitations of our knowledge and other resources, the best we can try to do is to engage in some incremental improvements, as is done, to some extent, in reality. These incremental improvements at least provide some help, promise better modernization policies for the future to be arrived at through learning from accumulating experience, and may perhaps achieve in the aggregate a critical mass effect which will result in changes in more basic features of society. Another possible view is that the best we can try to do is to expose underdeveloped societies to a series of less intense or more intense shocks, through radical changes in a number of more easily accessible variables—hoping that, at best, the shocks may stimulate movement in the direction of modernization, while, at worst, no real harm can result. A third possible view is that new modernization policies should be designed on the basis of modern theories of modernization—policies which should aim at the critical factors through influencing variables which satisfy the conditions of operationality and significance (and, later on, efficiency) as explained above.

Among these three views, the third has much to recommend itself. The involved risk is not high because present policies are quite ineffective and will continue, in any case, untill the search for new policies identifies alternatives with a superior expectation of desirable results. And the gulf between modern theories of modernization and most contemporary modernization activities, taken together with the niggardly results of most contemporary modernization policies, clearly justifies very intense efforts at designing new modernization policies.

Chapter 19 included a broad examination of required changes in metapolicy. In this chapter, I want to demonstrate the necessity and feasibility of innovations in modernization policies by exploring one such proposal, namely, the improvement of leadership.

The Need for Improvement of Leadership

One of the most critical resources for modernization is the high-level political elite, that is, leadership. The "nation-building" aspects of modernization,

[4]See Lester R. Brown, *Seeds of Change: The Green Revolution and Development in the 1970's* (New York: Praeger, 1970).

the need for widespread, active popular participation and enthusiasm, the necessary broad scope of governmental activities—all these (and additional) needs combine to make the role of political leadership in modernization countries a critical one and a very difficult one. The qualities required for successful leadership in modernization countries are as demanding as those needed in modern states. (Indeed, until recently, the tasks of the political elite in modern states were easier because they did not attempt far-reaching directed social change and were not involved in social upheavals—but now the situation is quite different.) At the same time, conditions in modernization countries are hardly conducive to spontaneous growth of a political elite having the required qualities. (This, again, becomes more and more true also for the modern countries.) The resulting inadequacies constitute one of the most difficult barriers to modernization, which frustrate many contemporary modernization policies.

This diagnosis is well recognized both by modern theories of modernization and by modernization advisors and modernization-encouraging agencies. Nevertheless, practically nothing is being done to try to improve leadership in modernization countries.

Three of the main reasons for this serious omission in modernization-aiding activities are not difficult to identify.

1. *A taboo effect.* In Western democratic countries, the political elite is not regarded as a legitimate object for conscious shaping and development. Any efforts to interfere with the spontaneous processes shaping the political elite are regarded as contradicting basic democratic values and are therefore outside the scope of legitimate alternatives for public policy. There is some experience available on training for political elites in Western democratic countries, especially in labor parties which often had no ready-made supply of suitable prepared candidates for leadership. But this experience is spotty and has made no impact on the taboos surrounding discussions of the subject.

2. *Political sensitivity.* Training for leadership constitutes a much more sensitive interference with the politics of modernization countries than, say, the training of engineers or technical assistance for improvement of administrative management. Necessarily, such training deals with highly controversial nontechnical issues and can easily be misused for indoctrinization and brainwashing, rather than leadership development. Participation in leadership training can easily stamp a politician as belonging to one or another "camp" which provided him with training; this can have disastrous results for his political career. International agencies are naturally wary of initiating such highly suspect activities, which can easily get them involved in acute political controversies. Aid-giving countries are similarly cautious and are suspected as being too interested in gaining political support and "selling" their values to be permitted to engage in leadership training.

3. *Lack of methods.* Improvement of leadership is at best a difficult and hard process, requiring much effort and a long-range point of view. Few ready-made methods are available and much learning through trial and error is necessary. New types of teaching material must be developed. Even after optimal action, many skeptics will doubt the benefits of the improvement efforts, which will be very difficult to evaluate and prove.

Lack of reliable methods compounds the taboo effect and political sensitivity, resulting in the contemporary lack of action for improvement of leadership for modernization countries. Thus, one of the more serious omissions in modernization policies is not very difficult to explain and understand. But explaining an omission is one thing, while justifying and continuing that omission is another. As long as an optimistic view of the prospects of accelerated moderization was justified by events, there was perhaps some sense in trying to help modernization through more conventional types of action. But now the futility of many types of modernization attempts, if unaccompanied by changes in the political processes of the relevant countries, is quite clear. Therefore, incrementalism and "muddling through" in modernization policies lose their justification, and more innovating, more imaginative, and even more daring action becomes necessary. Concerted action for improvement of leadership is in no way a panacea and not too much should be expected from it. Nevertheless, improvement of leadership, if feasible, is relevant to modernization processes, and thus satisfies the earlier-presented condition of significance. If feasible at all, improvement of leadership is probably also highly efficient—maximum costs being quite small in comparison with expected benefits. What we still have to examine is whether and to what extent improvement of leadership in modernization countries is feasible.

Possibilities for the Improvement of Leadership

Recruitment to the political elite and advancement in it involves a large number of stages. Most of these are not susceptible to directed improvement within medium and intermediate time periods. Being motivated to engage in politics, finding a patron, building a first power base, passing various screening and selection mechanisms—these and other critical stages are shaped by a large number of constantly changing variables which seem, in the main, in modernization countries, nonoperational for purposes of directed, improvement-oriented action. Furthermore, overt interference with the selection and advancement of political elites—even when feasible—is too dangerous a tool and too value-sensitive a tool to be encouraged for systematic use. What we are looking for are ways for improving leadership and not a totalitarian *Kaderpolitik*[5] which may defeat modernization by stifling

[5]A fascinating description of such a totalitarian *Kaderpolitik* is Joachim Schultz, *Der Funktionär in Der Einheitspartei* (Stuttgart: Ring-Verlag, 1956).

innovation and smothering political entrepreneurship. Therefore, by necessity and by choice, improvement of leadership will have to be a postentry activity, directed at persons who are already active in politics. Directing improvement efforts at already active politicians is also timesaving, by promising faster impact on political behavior, and more efficient, by concentrating on persons who have already passed some tests of practical politics.

My suggestion is to establish courses for politicians, where they will spend between four and twelve months undergoing a very intensive experience designed to improve their performance as political leaders. Tentatively, some main features of such leadership improvement courses can be summed up as follows:

1. *Participants.* The courses are designed for practicing politicians. Optimal participants are bright politicians who still occupy junior positions (and thus may be able to leave their jobs for an extended period) and who show promise for advancement to senior positions. The term *politicians* is used broadly, covering the wide spectrum of political positions in modernization countries—including parties, trade unions, military officers in countries with military regimes, political civil service positions, etc.

2. *Main objectives and curriculum.* The overall goal of the courses is to improve political leadership capacities and qualifications. More specifically, the course is directed at better preparation for the main types of political activities, including, *inter alia,* (1) policymaking and decisionmaking; (2) support recruitment, coalition building, and conflict treatment; (3) interpersonal relations; and (4) management of organizations and broader systems. Improvement of these activities requires educational efforts directed at all levels of human capacities and qualification, including, *inter alia,* (*a*) intellectual capacities; (*b*) explicit knowledge; (*c*) tacit knowledge and patterns of behavior; (*d*) personality and values. By cross-tabulating these two main dimensions, we get a matrix of training objectives which permits us to identify the main components of the curriculum and organize them according to purpose. This is done on a tentative basis in table 20-1.

3. *Teaching methods and material.* Teaching methods and teaching material must be adjusted to the unique objectives and participants of the courses. Much can be learned from modern courses for government administration, business executives, senior military officials, planners, etc. But in the main, the teaching methods and teaching material must be specially designed for the course. The lack of academic background by many of the participants, the need to unlearn a lot, and the necessity to influence various levels of capacities and qualifications—these are some of the characteristics which require a special mix of conventional and new teaching methods and teach-

Table 20-1

Suggested Main Objectives and Curriculum of Courses for Improvement of Leadership in Modernization Countries
(With Reference to Main Relevant Teaching Methods)

Types of Activities	Levels of Capacities and Qualifications			
	a. Intellectual Capacities	b. Explicit Knowledge	c. Tacit Knowledge and Patterns of Behavior	d. Personality and Values
1. Policymaking and Decisionmaking	1a. Abstract thinking; conceptualization; detachment from wishful thinking; data processing and evaluating capacities; analysis of complex situations; capacities for realistic appraisal of emotional situations (main teaching methods: C, D, E, F, J)	1b. Policy sciences; planning studies; economics; intelligence studies; knowledge of involved society (main teaching methods: A, B, D, E, I)	1c. Intuition; feeling for the possible; tacit knowledge of involved society; capacity for teamwork (main teaching methods: C, F, G, H, I)	1d. Creativity; high energy level; high tolerance of ambiguity; high propensity for change and learning capabilities; realistic idealism; moral integrity; patience; self-confidence (main teaching methods: G, H, I)
2. Support recruitment, coalition building, and conflict treatment	2a. As in 1a	2b. Behavioral sciences and development studies; political science; psychology; coalition theory and conflict studies; knowledge of power structure of involved society (main teaching methods: A, B, D, E, F, G, I)	2c. As in 1c plus rhetorical abilities; tactical skills; capacity to know and understand others (main teaching methods: as in 1c plus K)	2d. As in 1d plus charisma; capacity to evoke trust; tolerance for others (main teaching methods: as in 1d)

Table 20-1 (*continued*)

Types of Activities	a. Intellectual Capacities	Levels of Capacities and Qualifications		
		b. Explicit Knowledge	c. Tacit Knowledge and Patterns of Behavior	d. Personality and Values
3. Interpersonal relations	3a. As in 1a	3b. Psychology; organization theory, group dynamics (main teaching methods: A, B, C, D, E, I)	3c. Empathy; human relations skills; capacity to know others (main teaching methods: G, H, I)	3d. Charisma or "pleasant personality" (main teaching methods: F, G, H, I)
4. Management of organizations and other systems	4a. As in 1a	4b. Administrative sciences; systems theories (main teaching methods: A, B, C, D, E, I)	4c. As in 3c plus group-dynamic skills (main teaching methods: as in 3c plus F)	4d. As in 2d

Key to Teaching Methods (including training and personality-development methods):

A = Lectures
B = Guided reading
C = Case studies
D = Individual and group reports
E = Projects
F = Political gaming
G = Role Playing
H = T-Groups and sensitivity training
I = Individual counseling and tutoring
J = Special subjects (e.g., mathematics, logics)
K = Special exercises (rhetorics)

ing material. In addition to variations of more conventional passive and active teaching methods (such as lectures, guided reading, case studies, and individual and group reports), a number of more novel methods must be utilized. These include, for instance, complex projects, political gaming, role playing, sensitivity training, and individual counselling. A number of subjects may also have to be taught not as an integral part of the curriculum, but as auxiliary tools (e.g., fast reading) or as training tools (e.g., mathematics and logics). The relationship of different teaching methods to the various elements of the curriculum are indicated in table 20-1, in brackets in each cell of the matrix.

4. *Work load and course culture.* In order at least to move in the direction of the objectives of the course, more is required than specially designed and well-prepared curricula, teaching methods, and teaching material. The courses have to achieve a breakthrough into quite deeply rooted assumptions, opinions, perception sets, and dogmas of hardened politicians, who will initially be on the defensive. This requires an intense and focused impact to be achieved by a "total learning experience." The work load should be maximal, taxing the participants to the utmost. By mixing different teaching methods, fatigue can and should be controlled. Also, efforts must be made to adjust demands to the individual participants and to minimize negative feedback resulting from dropout during the course. But each participant must be worked to the utmost. This requires residential arrangements with special attention to the families, who should accompany the participants for longer courses. (It may be a good idea to arrange some training for the wives of the participants, both to gain their assistance in the intense effort demanded from the latter and to prepare the wives better for their supporting roles for the policymaking activities of their husbands.) The course culture should be one of intense cooperative effort and high intellectual tension, with hard give-and-take between the instructors and the participants and among the participants themselves. Frustrations, periods of self-despair, steep drops in the learning curve—all these are natural parts of such a course which the participant should be helped to handle and which will become an important and much cherished part of his learning experience.

5. *Faculty.* The proposed courses require a top faculty, which works for an extended period on the preparation and running of the courses. No fast collection of experts and university teachers brought together for a short period will do. For some subjects, guest lecturers can be used, but a permanent, high-quality core staff is essential. This is indeed the most scarce resource needed for the course, which may prove to be very difficult to get. The necessity to get together a top-quality staff, which also enjoys political and academic credibility among prospective participants, constitutes a specific constraint which must be carefully taken into account when the

organizational setups and locations of the courses are determined.

Beyond these five features, many problems remain to be faced and many details must be filled in. But these are of secondary importance. First, it is necessary to recognize the need for improvement of leadership in modernization countries as an essential part of realistic and innovating policy for accelerated modernization (and as an illustration of possibilities for designing new development metapolicies, which are operational, significant, and efficient). Then it is necessary to accept in principle the idea to establish courses for politicians from modernization countries,[6] to work out basic principles for these courses, and to mobilize the necessary resources. Only at that stage should a more detailed program for action be elaborated by a workshop, with the participation of experts in relevant disciplines and selected outstanding politicians from modernization countries.

[6]This is not to say that courses and other improvement activities are not needed, perhaps even more so, for politicians in modern countries. But this is a different subject, requiring separate treatment.

Policy analysis is an approach and methodology for design and identification of preferable alternatives in respect to complex policy issues.* It provides heuristic aid to better policymaking, without any presumption to provide optimization algorithms. Based on systems analysis and behavorial sciences and embedded in policy sciences, policy analysis should become a main contribution to the improvement of policymaking. Even though policy analysis is still very underdeveloped, enough is already known to improve reality by significant jumps. But this requires a number of innovations, starting with the training and development of highly qualified policy analysts, continuing with the location of policy analysts near all main decision centers of the societal direction system, and winding

PART VII

Policy Analysis

*For more detailed treatment, it is necessary to distinguish between 'policy design," which deals with the invention and construction of new alternatives, and "policy selection," which deals with the identification of preferable policies, from among available alternatives. I include both processes under the term *policy analysis,* but the differences and the interdependencies between them should be recognized. The extent to which both these processes should be located in the same units, and how— these are important questions in need of study. (See also footnote 7, p. 230.)

up with changes in the political culture, so that policymaking becomes more responsive to innovation and rational selection of alternatives.

This part presents some aspects of policy analysis. The first chapter discusses the characteristics of policy analysis and some implications for institutionalization of policy analysts in government. The second chapter takes up a rhetorical barrier to the development and utilization of policy professionals, including policy analysts, in government—namely, the "specialists versus generalists" mis-question. The third chapter illustrates the methods and contents of policy analysis by reproducing a policy analysis memorandum prepared for a political clientele.

CHAPTER 21

Policy Analysts:
A New Professional Role in Government[1]

COMMENTS

The existence of systems analysts and widespread efforts to utilize it for resolution of complex social issues is both an advantage and a disadvantagt for policy analysis. It is an advantage, because systems analysis is a main foundation for policy analysis and because available experience with systems analysis provides important lessons for policy analysis, both by its successes and not less so by its failures. It is a disadvantage, because systems analysis may unduly prestructure the development of policy analysis and because the failures and overclaims of systems analysis generate resistance to policy analysis and, indeed, to all intellectual and rational approaches to policymaking.

A main need, therefore, is to clarify exactly the relations between systems analysis and policy analysis and the differences between them. This chapter tries to do so. In addition, it examines some implications of policy analysis— in particular, in respect to institutionalization of policy analysis positions in government.

One of the main reform movements in public administration in the United States (and in other countries, as well) is based on an economic approach to public decisionmaking. The roots of this approach are in economic theory, especially micro-economics and welfare economics, and quantitative decision-theory; the main tools of this approach are operations research, cost-effectiveness and cost-benefit analysis, and program budgeting and systems analysis; and the new professionals of this approach are the systems analysts. Together, these elements constituted main components of the Planning-Programing-Budgeting System, as first developed in the Department of Defense and later extended to other departments and units of government. Even though somewhat on the retreat, this approach is still widely accepted and believed in, constituting a main intellectual underpinning of many improvement attempts.

[1]An earlier version of this chapter was published in *Public Administration Review* 27, no. 3 (September 1967): 197-203. The author is indebted to comments and criticisms by Gerald E. Caiden, Burton H. Klein, Moshe Shani, and Edward S. Quade of an early draft of this chapter.

In essence, this approach constitutes an invasion of public decision-making by economics. Going far beyond the domain of economic policymaking, the economic approach to decisionmaking views every decision as an allocation of resources between alternatives, that is, as an economic problem. Application of suitable tools of economic analysis should, therefore, in this opinion, contribute to the improvement of decisionmaking, whatever the subject matter of the decision may be. This was a main innovation of the Planning-Programing-Budgeting System, which was, in essence, a restatement of earlier budgeting theory combined with systems analysis and put into a coherent and integrated framework. This is also reflected in the growing number of "economic models" of political and administrative institutions and phenomena, all of which are greeted with much respect and/or awe by many scholars.

The invasion of public decisionmaking by economics is both unavoidable and beneficial, but fraught with danger. It is unavoidable, because economics provided, until recently, the only highly developed theoretical basis for improvement in highly critical decisionmaking processes. It is beneficial, because the economic approach in the systems analysis form can contribute to the improvement of public decisionmaking, if carefully ultilized. It is fraught with dangers because of the inability to deal adequately with many critical elements of public policymaking and the possible distortion in decisionmaking resulting therefrom.

A main question, therefore, is how to reap the full benefits of the economic approach and to utilize it for the improvement of public decisionmaking and policymaking while avoiding its pitfalls.

Systems Analysis and Decisionmaking

In considering the dangers of systems analysis, we must keep in mind an important consideration. I accept as a fact that systems analysis has made very important, though limited, contributions to better decisionmaking up to now, especially in the Department of Defense; but much of this contribution may have been due more to the wisdom, sophistication, and open-mindedness of the few outstanding practitioners of systems analysis and their readiness to fight organizational inertia and muddling-through tendencies than to their defined professional tools. But in order for systems analysis to become a profession with defined job responsibilities throughout government and to be practiced by a larger group of specially trained staff officers, we cannot rely any longer on the tacit qualities and multiple backgrounds (including, for instance, law, mathematical logic, physics, and engineering, in addition to economics) of the small number of highly gifted individuals who pioneered systems analysis. Instead, we must develop institutional arrangements, professional training, and job definitions which will provide the desired outputs with good, and hopefully very good, but not always outstanding, personnel.

When we look at the basic characteristics of systems analysis as a professional discipline (as distinguished from the personal wisdom of some of its pioneers), a number of weaknesses can be identified. These weaknesses are not transitory features of a new discipline, but seem to be endemic to the nature and origin of systems analysis and are introduced through it into PPBS.

Some of the more important weaknesses of systems analysis from the point of view of public decisionmaking can be summed up as follows:[2]

1. Strong attachment to quantification and dependence upon it, including both the need for quantitative models and for quantitative parameters for the variables appearing in the models.

2. Incapacity to deal with conflicting noncommensurate values (other than through neutralizing the issue when possible, by seeking out value-insensitive alternatives).

3. Requirement of clear-cut criteria of decision and well-defined missions.

4. Neglect of the problems of political feasibility and of the special characteristics of political resources (such as the power-producing effect of using political power).[3]

5. Lack of significant treatment of essential extrarational decision elements, such as creativity, tacit knowledge, and judgment.

[2]Many of the pioneers of systems analysis are aware of some of these weaknesses. A number of them have left systems analysis and devote themselves to development of broader tools, mainly in the area of strategy and conflict studies (e.g., Herman Kahn and Albert Wohlstetter). Others, at the Rand Corporation, continue to broaden systems analysis by developing sharper conceptual tools. Some important and able efforts have also been made to examine explicitly the relations between systems analysis and the political process, though without adequate and detailed attention to required and possible changes in the methods of systems analysis, so as to adjust them to broader political issues. See, for instance, James R. Schlesinger, *Systems Analysis and the Political Process* (Santa Monica, Calif.: The Rand Corporation, P-3464, June 1967); and Aaron Wildavsky, "Rescuing Policy Analysis from PPBS," *Public Administration Review* 29, no. 2 (March 1969): 198-202. These are important, though too timid, steps on the way from systems analysis to policy analysis, but systems analysis, as usually presented, does not share the benefits of these first-step advances. Highly relevant in this context is an excellent insiders' discussion of the roles and problems of analysis in the United States Department of Defense, namely, Alain C. Enthoven and K. Wayne Smith, *How Much is Enough?* (N.Y.: Harper and Row, 1971).

[3]The overwhelming influence of economic ideas causes even highly sophisticated political scientists to view political power as similar to economic resources, while ignoring the critical differences—such as the often immediate power-producing effect of using political resources in the form of favors or coercive moves. The economic models of resources which, for instance, can either be consumed or invested with continuous, concave, production possibility frontier curves, do not apply to political power.

6. Inability to deal with large and complex systems other than through suboptimization, which destroys the overall *Gestalt* of the more difficult and involved issues.
7. Lack of instruments for taking into account individual motivations, irrational behavior, and human idiosyncrasy.

This list of weaknesses of the economic approach to systems analysis should be supplemented by a rather overlapping list of weaknesses typical of the engineering approach to systems analysis (but also widespread in the economic versions of systems analysis):[4]

1. Lack of any attention to the findings of organization theory and the problems of organizational conditions for effective analytical work.
2. A narrow definition of quantitative analysis as a main contribution to treatment of complex issues (excluding, for instance, working out "concept packages" for social problems).
3. Inadequate treatment of improvement of intuition as a main mission of analysis, for instance, through broadening the frame of appreciation of senior decisionmakers.
4. No examination of the possibilities of introducing behavorial sciences' findings into systems analysis.
5. Ignorance of analytic methods and approaches especially appropriate for complex issues, such as sequential decisionmaking and impact evaluation studies.
6. Lack of attention to the political dimensions of problems and to possibilities of their explicit treatment by analysis, for instance, through political feasibility testing.

One can add to this list inadequate consideration of methods for new systems invention, no treatment of the special problems of long-life cycle systems (such as educational systems), and many other omissions. But I think my main argument on the weaknesses of typical systems analysis is clear.

As a result of these weaknesses, systems analysis as such is of doubtful utility for dealing with political decisions, overall strategic planning, and public policymaking. This does not disparage the importance of systems analysis for project and management planning and control or the essential contributions of systems analysis as one of the bases of a broader professional discipline of policy analysis. But, by itself, systems analysis cannot deal with issues and situations where the problem is to move on from one appreciate system[5] or multidimensional space to another.

[4]See Yehezkel Dror, "Review of Systems Analysis for Effective Planning, by Bernard H. Rudwick," *IEEE* Spectrum, January, 1970, p. 104.
[5]For the concept of "appreciative system" and its importance in public decisionmaking, see Sir Geoffrey Vickers, *The Art of Judgment: A Study of Policy Making* (New York: Basic Books, 1965), chapter 4.

Possible Boomerang Effects

Even so, a good prima-facie argument can be made for taking systems analysis as it is and applying it to public decisionmaking. The principal claim in favor of this position is that systems analysis will, at least, permit some improvements in public decisionmaking. To paraphrase one of the founders of modern systems analysis, even in the situations where technology and objectives change very swiftly, good systems analysis will at least try to get on an entirely different curve and not look for a peak of a rather flat curve.[6] Furthermore, with the help of systems analysis—so the argument may go—at the very least, we will begin to get out of the rut of inertia and incremental change onto the highway of doubting conventional wisdom and introducing desirable innovations.

These arguments would be valid if one condition is met, namely, that both the professional systems analysts and the senior staff and line of the agencies in which they serve are highly sophisticated in respect to the possibilities and limitations of systems analysis. But this is a completely unrealistic requirement. The successes of systems analysis in some domains of the Department of Defense, the brilliance of its main pioneers and first practitioners, and the exaggerated claims of some of its advocates and proponents combined to create an unrealistic level of expectation. Being evaluated in terms of such an unrealistic level of expectation, systems analysis was often judged as a failure. As a result, there is a great risk that the strong antiinnovation forces are vindicated, are more deeply entrenched, and are better able to oppose signifiicent reforms in the future. Unsophisticated reliance on systems analysis in this way may have impaired and, indeed, nullified the potential benefits of other important parts of PPBS, such as future-orientation and multiple-year programing.

From Systems Analysis to Policy Analysis

What is needed is a more advanced type of professional knowledge, which can be used with significant benefits for the improvement of public decisionmaking. This professional knowledge should do for public decisionmaking in various issue-areas what systems analysis did in some areas of defense decisionmaking. To fill this rather difficult order, the various orientations, ideas, and tools of systems analysis must be developed to be applicable to complex and nonquantifiable issues and systems. Furthermore—and this is more important and more difficult—politics and political phenomena must be put into the focus of analysis. The term *policy analysis* seems to be suitable for the proposed professional discipline, as it combines affinity with systems analysis with the

[6]See Albert Wohlstetter, "Analysis and Design of Conflict Systems," in E. S. Quade, ed., *Analysis of Military Decisions* (Chicago: Rand McNally, 1964), p. 106.

concept of policy in the broad and political sense.[7]

In essence, what is required is an integration between revised disciplines of political science and public administration, on the one hand, and systems analysis, decision theory, and economic theory, on the other hand, within the broad framework of policy sciences. This combination should be in the form of a compound rather than a mix, to provide a more advanced form of knowledge, rather than an eclectic collection of unrelated items. Care must be taken to achieve a real synthesis, rather than an uncritical subordination of the political to the economic models, in which the specific features of politics may be lost.

To clarify the idea, let me point out some main features of policy analysis, as compared with systems analysis.

1. Much attention should be paid to the political aspects of public decision-making and public policymaking (instead of ignoring or condescendingly regarding political aspects). This includes much attention to problems of political feasibility, recruitment of support, accommodation of contradicting goals, and recognition of diversity of values. Especially important are the development of theories and construction of models which do full justice to the special characteristics of politics and political behavior and do not try to force them into a Procrustean bed of economic terminology and theory.

2. A broad conception of decisionmaking and policymaking should be evolved (instead of viewing all decisionmaking as mainly a resources allocation). Many types of critical decisions cannot be usefully approached from an economic resource allocation framework, for example, determining the content of diplomatic notes or changing the selective draft to a randomized process. Here, qualitative exploration of new alternatives is necessary, beyond quantitative analysis and cost-benefit estimation.

3. A main emphasis should be on creativity and the search for new policy alternatives, with explicit attention to encouragement of innovative thinking (instead of comparative analysis of available alternatives and synthesis of new alternatives only as one of the elements of analysis). A good example is the problem of reducing smoking—where the problem is clearly one of inventing new promising alternatives, rather than cost-benefit analysis of different known alternatives, none of which is effective. The requirement of creativity

[7]One weakness of the term *analysis* is its calculative-logical connotation. In policy analysis, a very important part of the job is to invent new alternatives and to engage in creative and imaginative thinking. Nevertheless, I prefer a concept which somewhat understates the role rather than too presumptuous, too "political," and too frightening a term. As already mentioned (see footnote on p. 223), it may prove necessary to break the required function into subparts, in particular, by distinguishing between "policy design" in the sense of inventing new alternatives and "policy selection," in the sense of choosing the preferable alternative. Here, I include both these functions under the term *policy analysis*.

and innovation of alternatives has far-reaching implications, as there may be some incompatibility between the personality traits, training, and organizational arrangements optimal for analysis (in the strict meaning of the term) and those optimal for the invention of alternatives. The latter requires more "creative" personalities, structural tools for search for new ideas (for instance, through knowledge-surveys), pro-innovating organizational arrangements (e.g., cross-fertilization and stimulation through brain trusts and interdisciplinary teams), an imaginative and pro-risk entrepreneurship atmosphere, and changes in overall organizational climate (e.g., raising organizational levels of aspiration). Combining systems analysis with budgeting, as in PPBS, may be good for quantitative analysis, but is not a way to encourage and stimulate new and risky and expensive-looking policy ideas.

4. There should be extensive reliance on tacit understanding, *Gestalt*-images, qualitative models, and qualitative methods (instead of exclusive emphasis on explicit knowledge and quantitative models and tools). This involves imaginative thinking, systematic integration of trained intuition into policy analysis (e.g., through the Delphi Method),[8] development of qualitative tools (such as metaphor construction, scenarios, counterfactual thinking), and construction of broad qualitative models of complex issues in cooperation with behavioral scientists and other professionals (instead of ignoring the latter, in effect, or regarding them as passive sources of quantitative data).

5. There should be much more emphasis on "futures" thinking with long-range predictions, alternative states of the future, and speculative thinking on the future as essential background for current policymaking.

6. The approach should be looser and less rigid but, nevertheless, systematic. It should recognize the complexity of means-ends interdependence, the multiplicity of relevant criteria of decision, and the partial and tentative nature of every analysis (instead of striving for a clear-cut criterion and dominant solutions). In policy analysis, sequential decisionmaking and constant learning are dominant, and clarification of issues, invention of new alternatives, more consideration of the future, and reduction of primary disagreements to secondary disagreements are main goals.[9]

Policy Analysts as Government Staff Officers

To introduce urgently needed improvements in public decisionmaking, while avoiding the possible boomerang effects of systems analysis, policy analysis must become an important new professional role in government service. Policy analysis staff positions should be established in all principal adminis-

[8]See Olaf Helmer, *Social Technology* (New York: Basic Books, 1960).

[9]For further examination of the nature of policy analysis, see Yehezkel Dror, *Design for Policy Sciences* (New York: American Elsevier, 1971), chapter 9.

trative agencies and establishments, near the senior policy-determining positions, operating, in general, formally as advisory staff to top executives and senior line positions and actually establishing with them a symbiotic relationship. Certainly, all professional staff dealing in analysis and PPBS should be trained in policy analysis.

Policy analysis does not presume to bring about a radical change in policymaking. It does not presume to create omniscient units, which exist outside any socio-political-organizational framework and operate by a "downward and disaggregative flow" of top policy and policy directions. Good policy analysis can, at best, become an additional component in aggregative policymaking, contributing to that process some better analysis, some novel ideas, some futures orientation, and some systematic thought. Policy analysts are one of the bridges between science and politics,[10] but they do not transform the basic characteristics of "the political" and of organizational behavior. In order to contribute to the improvement of policymaking, policy analysts should be dispersed throughout the higher echelons of government service (and, indeed, throughout the societal direction system), as part of the effort to improve aggregate policymaking through introducing into the clash and interaction between competing partisan interests an additional element. Such redundancy will increase the aggregate effect of policy analysis on policymaking, while also providing a safeguard against trained incapacities, one-sided value bias, and professional prejudices.

The main role of policy analysts in the policymaking system as parts of PPBS—in distinct high-level staff units, in separate, independent policy research organizations, and in various other locations (including extra-establishment advocacy groups)—is to contribute to public decisionmaking a broad professional competence, based simultaneously on systems analysis and quantitative decision-theory and on a new outlook in political science and public administration, founded on policy sciences. The aim of policy analysis is to permit improvements in decisionmaking and policymaking by allowing fuller consideration of a broader set of alternatives, within a wider context, with the help of more systematic tools. No metamorphosis of policymaking is aimed at, but improvements of, say, 10 to 15 percent in complex public decisionmaking and policymaking can be achieved through better integration of knowledge and policymaking with the help of policy analysis—and this is a lot. This, I think, is certainly much more than can be achieved by systems analysis, outside relatively simple issue areas and subsystems.

It is premature to try to set down in detail the characteristics of the new professional role of policy analysts in government. These must be evolved

---

[10]For the concept, see Don K. Price, *The Scientific Estate* (Cambridge: Harvard University Press, Belknap Press, 1965), esp. pp. 123-26.

largely through a careful process of learning and sequential decisionmaking. Nevertheless, some suggested features can be presented tentatively in the form of a comparison between systems analysis and policy analysis (see table 21-1, page 234.)

Some Implications

Present tensions and issues in the United States—and all over the world—make all the more essential maximum utilization of systematic knowledge, structured rationality, and organized creativity for better policymaking. One of the required steps in this direction is a change in conception in respect to systems analysis, with explicit recognition of the necessity to move fast in the direction of policy analysis. As already pointed out, the main pioneers of systems analysis are highly sophisticated in their substantive work and often actually practice some policy analysis. Thus actual sophistication must be put into the formalized system and institutionalized directives. More important still, suitable programs to train and develop policy analysts must be established, preferably as parts of broader policy sciences curricula. Also, policy analysis units of different forms should be established at focal decision centers throughout the societal direction system.

The development of policy analysis depends on a number of transformations in the disciplines of political science and public administration. The one-sided invasion of public decisionmaking by economics was caused largely by the inability of modern political science and public administration to make significant contributions to governmental decisionmaking. Economics developed a highly advanced action-oriented theory and put it to the test of innovating economic policymaking. At the same time, the modern study of political science and public administration became sterilized by an escape from political issues into behavioral "value-free" research and theory, exhausted itself in suggestions for insignificant incremental improvements on the technical level, or exhausted itself in nonintellectual "involvement" patterns.

These trends must be revised. A new approach in political science and public administration, oriented toward the study and improvement of public policymaking, constitutes, in the longer run, a main avenue for the improvement of public decisionmaking. The new supradiscipline of policy sciences is urgently necessary to provide a sound theoretical and institutional basis for policy analysis knowledge and policy analysis professionals. In the meantime, serious boomerang effects and damage can and should be avoided, and the foundations for such a study and profession can and should be laid, by changing attempts to utilize systems analysis of complex issues in the direction of policy analysis.

Table 21-1

A Tentative Comparison of Some Features of Systems Analysis and Policy Analysis

Feature	Systems Analysis	Policy Analysis
Base discipline	Economics, operations research, quantitative decision sciences	As systems analysis, plus political science, public administration, parts of the behavioral sciences, and, in particular, policy sciences
Main emphasis	Quantitative analysis	Qualitative analysis and innovation of new alternatives plus quantitative analysis where possible
Main desired qualities of professionals	Bright, unconventional, high analytical capacities	As systems analysis, plus maturity, explicit and tacit knowledge of political and administrative reality, imagination, and idealistic realism
Main decision criteria	Efficiency in allocation of resources	Multiple criteria, including social, economic, and political effectiveness
Main methods	Economic analyses, quantitative model construction	As systems analysis, plus qualitative models and analyses, imaginative and futuristic thought, and integration of tacit knowledge
Main location	In PPBS—in Bureau of the Budget and agency budget units; in analysis units	As systems analysis, plus throughout the societal direction systems, in different forms
Main outputs when applied to public decisionmaking	Clearly better decisions with respect to limited issues; possible boomerang effect if applied to highly complex political issues	Somewhat better decisions on highly complex and political issues; educational impact on political argumentation and long-range improvements in operation of public policymaking system
Requisites for development of knowledge and preparation of professionals	Already operational; further development requiring some changes in university curricula	Changes in orientation of political science and public administration as academic disciplines—establishment of new university curricula and of new policy science supradiscipline

CHAPTER 22

Specialists versus Generalists—A Mis-Question[1]

COMMENTS

This short chapter takes up one of the big retarders to clear thought on the role of professionals in policymaking, namely, the "specialists versus generalists" dichotomy. This dichotomy is broken down into a number of dimensions, which clearly bring out its fallacious character. In particular, a policy analyst illustrates a new type of professional, who is a "specialist in a general approach and method," and who, therefore, does not fit into the specialists-generalists dichotomy, which should be completely abandoned.

Introduction

Every profession and discipline is troubled from time to time by some questions which mislead efforts to illusionary problems and feed controversy on meaningless issues. Policy sciences will be epecially prone to the disease of mis-questions, because of its characteristics as an undefined mix between diverse activities, a variety of professionals and practitioners, and an eclectic academic basis.

Whatever the exact causes may be, illusionary problems—usually posed in the form of dichotomies—are sure to upsurge to plague policy sciences and retard its development as a profession and as an academic discipline. One of the more misleading questions may be whether policymaking is a science or an art; an old question is "policy versus administration." Some may adopt a more sophisticated and somewhat less misleading form, such as "staff versus line." Others will persist in all their glamor, serving as barriers to significant improvements in practice and theory alike. One of the most misleading questions in policy sciences, which may show especially stubborn survival capacity and is being seriously discussed today, is "specialists versus generalists."[2]

[1]Based on a paper first published in *Public Personnel Review* 31, no. 1 (January 1970): 36-39.

[2]A recent collection of mainly old papers, most of which accept this misleading dichotomy, is *Specialists and Generalists: A Selection of Readings*, prepared for the Subcommittee on National Security and International Operations of the Committee on Government Operations, United States Senate (Washington: U.S. Government Printing Office, 1968). This Committee print became immediately a bestseller and received a lot of sympathetic attention in the media of mass communications. See, for instance, *Time*, November 29, 1968, p. 14.

235

The most critical stage in the advancement of knowledge and action is the formulation of more significant and more correct questions. Therefore, it is necessary for policy sciences to get rid, once and for all, of the "specialist versus generalist" mis-question. Instead, we need a new question, or a series of questions, which expresses in more adequate ways the real problems which hide behind the "specialists versus generalists" facade.[3]

To try to get some feeling for the real issues hiding behind the "specialists versus generalists" formulation, let us briefly consider the meanings in which these terms are used. Limiting ourselves to the more extreme positions, the following picture appears:

As generally used in controversy by the pro-generalists, *specialist* refers to a narrow, single-disciplinary professional, who has a lot of trained incapacity, views all problems from a very limited point of view, and is incapable of comprehending in a wholistic way the complexities of real-life problems. He is not only one who knows more and more on less and less, but what he knows more about is of decreasing significance. The *generalist,* by this same school of thought, is the well-trained person of superior capacity, who is able to bring to bear a fresh and sharp look and common sense[4] to a variety of problems, unencumbered by too much knowledge about any one of them.

There is also an opposite school which regards the *generalist* as a bungling amateur, intolerant of knowledge, proud of his irrelevant literati background, and self-confident in his idiosyncratic judgment. In its most extreme form, this school regards "experts" as the pioneers of science in government, who will substitute reliable facts and explicit algorithms for fallible human intui-

---

[3]I am leaving aside the interesting problem, why does the "specialists vs. generalists' formulation persist so strongly? My impression is that one of its sources of strength is its usefulness as a protective rationalization (in the psychological sense) for resistance against demands for more knowledge and faster professionalization. Insofar as some of these demands are exaggerated, this incorrect question, in fact, may fulfill, in part, useful functions. But those can be better served by a revised and improved view of the desirable roles of different types of knowledge, creativity, experience, and so on in policymaking.

[4]The term *common sense* also raises a variety of interesting issues. One strict meaning of that term refers to what is supported by the evidence of our ordinary senses—a criterion by which we should reject all modern knowledge in physics, micro-genetics, life-sciences, psychoanalysis, and economics. Indeed, it seems that one of the signs of advances in knowledge is that it gets beyond the obvious appearance of phenomena. Another strict meaning of that term may refer to what is accepted by "common"—in some statistical sense—opinions; this clearly is also unsatisfactory for anyone with some knowledge of the history of ideas. A third frequent meaning is that "common sense" is what I think, while "against common sense" is whatever I dislike or reject. The best way out of this maze of contradictory meanings and misleading uses may well be to drop this term altogether.

tion, if only undisturbed by politics and similar anachronistic carry-overs from the prescientific epoch.[5]

Some Relevant Dimensions

However overstated, these contrasting statements indicate the logical fallacy of the "specialists versus generalists" formulation. The fallacy reduces a multiplicity of attributes into two prototypes, assuming there is some necessary internal relationship which excludes (or at least reduces the probability of) other combinations.

Let me elaborate this point a little. Trying to break down the specialist and generalist prototype into components, at least four categories of characteristics can be identified, each one of which includes a number of dimensions, as illustrated in table 22-1.

Table 22-1

Some Components of "Specialists Versus Generalists" Prototypes

Categories	Dimensions of Each Category
Academic knowledge	None–much Narrow–broad monographic–nomographic Substantive (by areas)–methodological (by rationale)
Personal qualities	Closed-minded–open-minded Noncreative–highly creative Rigid–elastic Detail-oriented–general-picture-oriented
Experience	High level–low level One area–multiple areas Center–field
Tacit capacities	Good–bad human relations (in different situations) Good–bad intuitive judgment in few–many areas Good–bad managerial talents (in different types or organizations)

[5]Surprisingly enough, this view was, in part, accepted by a Royal Commission in the country which invented (after the Chinese) the pro-generalist ideology—England. The recent *Report of the Committee on the Civil Service* (The Fulton Report) includes the following statement about the generalist, which is quite revolutionary for England: "...the Service is still essentially based on the philosophy of the amateur (or "generalist" or "all-rounder"). This is most evident in the Administrative Class which holds the dominant position in the Service. The ideal administrator is still too often seen as the gifted layman who, moving frequently from job to job within the Service, can take a practical view of any problem, irrespective of its subjectmatter, in the light of his knowledge and experience of the government machine. Today, as the report of our Management Consultancy Group illustrates, this concept has most damaging consequences..." (London: HMSO, Cmnd. 3638, June 1968, Vol. 1, p. 11. The report of the Management Consultancy Group is reproduced in Volume 2.)

It may well be that a hundred years ago, and perhaps also fifty years ago, the class structure of a country in combination with its educational system and the structure of academic disciplines did, in fact, create a few clusters of these various attributes. Thus in England, academic training at Cambridge and Oxford in classics or mathematics often went together with an open mind, a broad view, elasticity, good intuitive judgment, broad experience, and similar features of the ideal generalist. But this was not the result of a direct causal relationship between the attributes (studying the classics resulting in an open mind, etc.), but rather of other variables (e.g., persons with an open mind tending to study the classics). Even less is there reason to assume an exclusive causal relationship, such as only studying the classics can result in an open mind, and so on.

I do not want to overstate my case, as if there are no causal relationships whatsoever. It may well be that—all other things being equal—some contemporary methods of teaching economics (but not all) tend to result in narrow-minded experts fulfilling many of the negative expectations of the "antiexpert" school. My only claim is that this is not necessarily so. Thus, a revised curriculum in economics can combine rigorous training of the mind with encouraging creativity and education in taking a broad "systems view" of social problems.

The changes in student interests and in the socio-economic origin of students, the changes in the structure of knowledge and in methods of teaching, and the changes in the public service itself—all these combine to add to the logical fallacies of the "experts vs. professionals" formulation, an even more important behavioral refutation.

Here, the most relevant developments are the changes in knowledge and its teaching which break up the division between general and narrow subject matters. Indeed, we can speak with some justification about trying to educate professionals who are experts in how to deal in a broad, innovative, and open-minded way with problems, a kind of "expert in generalism"—a contradiction only in traditional terms, but not in emerging reality. Policy analysts well illustrate such a new type of professional, who is a specialist in a general problem-solving approach and method.

Advances in the knowledge and teaching of behavioral sciences, systems analysis, general systems theory, decision sciences, and especially their convergence in overall policy sciences—all these may annihilate whatever basis the educational assumptions of the "specialist vs. generalist" formulation may have had in the past. Similarly, new patterns of civil service management—for instance, in respect to rotation, sabbatical leave of absence, and exchange with nongovernmental organizations—can do away with the rigid career patterns which are based on the expert-generalist assumptions and which serve to perpetuate them, through creating a closed circle in which these assumptions result in patterns of civil service management that tend to create and reinforce behavior which is in line with these assumptions.

The Modern Requirements

One further point will serve to bring out the richness of problems and possibilities hidden behind the "experts versus generalists" formulae. We have already broken up these two prototypes and recognized the multiplicity of attribute combinations. Now we must add to our overall view of the problem the pluralistic character of modern government and its increasing need both for top-level scientific and experience-based knowledge and for top-quality judgment and moral values.

Conventional thinking on the "experts versus generalists" formulation already recognized that it was a problem not of one or the other, but of the proper relation between them. But clearly the required qualities of government cannot be achieved by any mixture of experts and generalists in the traditional sense. Only by overcoming this dichotomy in action, as well as in discourse, can we achieve the qualities needed for handling new and difficult problems, and for absorbing new, very promising, and very frightening knowledge under conditions of accelerated social change. We must develop a breed of top policy professionals who are experts in a broad approach and in uses of diverse knowledge, and we must achieve a mix between various types of new professionals and administrators who are equipped for symbiotic teamwork.

The real question to be faced now (which, in turn, may become obsolete in the future) is not "specialists versus generalists," but "how to develop new types of policy professionals and achieve a synergetic mix between a large variety of differently qualified persons." This question is more difficult to deal with by sweeping generalizations and simple judgments, but is much more useful for understanding and handling the problems facing policymaking.

CHAPTER 23

Proposed Policymaking Scheme for the Knesset Committee for the Examination of the Structure of Elementary and Post-Elementary Education in Israel — An Illustration of a Policy Analysis Memorandum[1]

COMMENTS

Two of the main problems of improving public policymaking through the utilization of policy analysis are (1) how to analyze complex issues which are difficult to deal with through systems analysis and (2) how to introduce a more analytical approach into the considerations and proceeding of political bodies, such as legislatures.

The following memorandum has been rewritten to illustrate an effort to deal with these two problems. It presents a scheme for improved decision-making by a political body on a complex issue. This scheme is on the meta-analysis level: it does not analyze the policy issue itself, but tries to provide a design for doing such an analysis. In other words, the scheme tries to provide a policy analysis network[2] and a proposed structure for dealing with this network, with due allocation of critical events to the political units. Preparation of such schemes is, I think, essential if we want to move on from systems analysis by professional units to policy analysis as a mode (or mood) of real decisionmaking throughout the societal direction system. An effort was made in preparing this memorandum to adjust the language to the needs of achieving communication with politicians.

[1]This paper is based on a memorandum first prepared in June 1966 at the request of the Israeli Teachers' Union, in connection with the appointment of a Parliamentary Committee on the structure of elementary and post-elementary education. In accordance with the agreement with the Teachers' Union, this paper was prepared as an independent analysis and on the responsibility of the author alone. The present version has been rewritten to serve as a professional illustration of a policy analysis memorandum written for a political body, but the basic features of the original memorandum have been preserved.

This paper was first published in English in *Socio-Economic Planning Sciences* 3 (1969): 13-24.

[2]A policy analysis network is a morphological decomposition of an issue into sub-problems, bringing out the relations among them and with relevant variables. The structure of a policy analysis network should serve as a heuristic program for alternative innovation and preferable-alternative identification. Any policy analysis network is provisional, to be constantly iterated.

I should perhaps add that, due to some special circumstances, this memorandum was never formally submitted to the committee.

A. Introduction

1. This memorandum is directed at the Knesset Committee for the Examination of the Structure of Elementary and Post-Elementary Education, to which it proposes a scheme for policymaking. By making use of modern knowledge and experience in systems analysis methods, decisionmaking theories, and the emerging policy sciences, this memorandum tries to identify the main elements of preferable policymaking on the subject under consideration and to point to some main ways for the development of these elements. I have tried to take account of the limitations set to the Committee's work and to arrive at a recommended framework within the bounds of feasibility.

2. The proposed policymaking scheme represents an application of policymaking theories and policy analysis knowledge to a problem in the field of education. Of necessity, therefore, the proposed scheme is being designed on the basis of the ideas, and with the help of the methods, of theories and knowledge in policy analysis on the one hand, and the specific features of the subject under discussion on the other. Since the author of this memorandum specializes in policy analysis from the point of view of policy sciences and is not an expert in education, it is only natural that this memorandum should stress those components and elements that do not require specialization in the discipline of education.[3] Hopefully, this is not a serious weakness, because this memorandum deals with the basic network of the decisionmaking process by the Parliamentary Committee for the Examination of The Structure of Elementary and Post-Elementary Education (hereinafter referred to as "the Committee") and not with its details; I think that the design of such a basic network does not require deep penetration into the disciplines of education.

3. Needless to say, this memorandum does not presuppose any preferable solution to the problem faced by the Committee. Indeed, the basic assumption of the proposed scheme is that, in order to identify with reasonable confidence a preferable solution, a set of actions is required, involving—at different points—political judgment, research, creative inventions, analysis, expert opinions, etc. The scheme proposes a structured framework for identifying such desirable steps on the way to formulating a preferable solution, and some methods for implementing those steps.

4. While preparing this memorandum, I experienced great difficulties in

[3] I am particularly grateful to Dr. Rachel Elboim-Dror for her important professional help in educating the author to recognize at least some of the relevant and more critical features of the involved educational issues.

balancing the desire to provide a detailed and full explanation and justification of the various proposals, on the one hand, and the need to produce a short memorandum of maximum readability, on the other. In general, I have preferred brevity and readability, sacrificing when necessary full elaboration of the various ideas and of their professional base.

B. Principles for the Work of the Committee

5. Good policymaking requires, *inter alia,* the development of five main elements with regard to the subject under discussion:

    a. Formulation of the problem and delineation of its boundaries.

    b. Clarification of aims.

    c. Identification of main alternatives.

    d. Construction of forecasts.

    e. Integration and decision.

6. All these elements are closely interrelated. Therefore, policymaking comprises more than the development of these elements, each one by itself. Good policymaking requires a systematic and feasible process constructed in such a way as to assure a maximum integrated development of these elements with constant feedback and in a way that leads toward an optimal or, at least, a "preferable" policy.

7. For the development of the various elements there are different sources which can each, although in differing degrees, contribute to better policymaking on the subject under discussion by the Committee. The following sources should be mentioned, among others: political-public value judgment; specific and general know-how; research and experimentation; tacit knowledge and intuition; assumptions; and higher-level guidance. The use of all these sources requires different ways and means as illustrated below:

Source	Ways and Means for the Use of the Source
Political-public value judgment	The discussions and judgments of the members of the Committee themselves in conjunction with groups and organizations concerned.
Available specific know-how	The preparation of know-how surveys by experts; systematic canvassing of expert opinion (e.g., through the Delphi Method).
Tacit knowledge and intuition	The feeling of the Committee members themselves; the evidence and opinions of people with great personal experience in the matters under discussion.
Assumptions and political guidelines	Specific decisions by the Committee after critical examination with the help of other sources. Guidelines by superior political units (e.g., Knesset decisions).

8. The use of these different sources, with the help of various means, in a manner that should lead to the development of elements in a way required for good policymaking, necessitates, in my view, the early design of a carefully considered framework for the work of the Committee. The endeavor of the Committee to identify a preferable policy within the shortest possible span of time further enhances the necessity to structure the work of the Committee in a way that makes maximum use of time, by using various methods and means simultaneously. For this purpose, advance programing of the modus operandi of the Committee and the provision of the required auxiliary means at as early a stage as possible are necessary. The proposed network, therefore, intends to try to help the Committee in this respect while preserving required flexibility, so as to adapt the continuation of work in the light of the findings and conclusions drawn after the first stages.

9. The principal aim of the proposed scheme is to help the Committee in its task of good policymaking under conditions of lack of time. In addition to this principal purpose, it seems to me that a few other considerations should be taken into account:

a. The establishment of a parliamentary committee for a thoroughgoing discussion of an important complex subject and for identification of a preferable policy represents, from many points of view, a highly significant innovation in Israel's parliamentary life. It is, therefore, important that the Committee should create in its methods of work a precedent that will strengthen the role of Knesset Committees in policymaking on complex subjects and should open up avenues for increased reliance on parliamentary committees for the discussion of subjects which are of a mixed public-professional nature.

b. The modus operandi of the Committee should not only produce good policy; it should also contribute to an acceptability of the policy. For this purpose it is essential to make it visible in public that the conclusions of the Committee are based on the best know-how and judgment, and that the policies recommended are the result of the Committee's independent judgment, helped by the best experts. It is also important—as a matter of democratic principles and in order to enhance acceptability—that the principal bodies interested in the matter should feel that they are given an appropriate opportunity to present their views and state their case.

c. A further aim is to educate the public in the merits of well-considered policymaking. This purpose, too, requires full public examinations of the modis operandi of the Committee and the basing of its recommendations on specified considerations, and detailed data and judgments.

10. The proposed scheme is directed at the achievement of these auxiliary

objectives, together with the principal aim—good policymaking on the subject under discussion. We will now turn to a more detailed and operational exploration of the various elements of the proposed policymaking network. But first, we have to deal with a basic aspect of the Committee's work, namely, the problem of the minimum time required for good policymaking on the subject under discussion.

C. The Element of Time in the Committee's Work

11. In every process of policymaking there is a problem of reaching the point of optimum balance between the quality of the recommended policy and the length of time required for policymaking. This problem confronts the members of the Committee in a very acute form, because their terms of reference include a specific time constraint.

12. One of the keys for the analysis of the problem of optimum balance between the quality of policymaking and its duration lies in the nonlinear character of the relationship between these two variables. There is no direct proportion between the duration of time devoted to policymaking on any given subject and the quality of the policy so achieved. If we ignore other variables which affect the quality of the policy and the time required for its determination, it seems to me that the most general (though not necessarily universal)[4] relationship between time and quality in policymaking under conditions similar to those faced by the Committee can be represented by an S-shaped curve (see figure 23-1 on page 245.)

13. Making due allowance for the pressure of limited time under which the Committee operates, everything should obviously be done to shift the curve to the left, that is to say, to reduce the time required for reaching point C on the curve. For this purpose, as mentioned in paragraph 8 above, it is desirable to lay down at an early stage a scheme for the Committee's work and its various subactitivities (such as research, collection of data, hearing of witness, etc.), in order to permit scheduling of the proceedings so as to best utilize time.

14. Admitting the need for maximum efforts to speed up the work of the Committee, I nevertheless think this should not be done in a manner that might jeopardize the very possibility of good policymaking, that is to say, it should not be done at high expense in terms of developing the various required elements of good policymaking. It would not seem worthwhile to stop the work of the Committee arbitrarily at a predetermined deadline, if by that time the Committee is still somewhere between points B and C on

---

[4]Under conditions of very poor policymaking, the first bits of time devoted to better policymaking may have the highest marginal utility in terms of achieving better policies. Under other conditions, policy may be unimprovable, however much time is devoted to policymaking.

the curve, where the allocation of relatively little extra time yields high returns in terms of the quality of policymaking. Under such conditions, careful consideration should be given to the net desirability of changing the time limit, rather than accepting it as an absolutely rigid constraint.

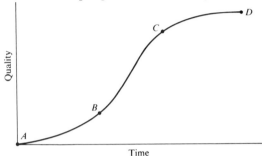

FIG. 23-1. Relationship between time and quality in policymaking. In the period that elapses between point A and point B, time is invested without contributing a great deal to raising the quality of the policy; between B and C, relatively small periods of time contribute much to quality; between C and D, time again contributes little to quality (sometimes there will again be a period of high marginal quality/time output, followed by a period of low marginal quality/time output).

15. I see no possibility for estimating in advance with certainty the minimum length of time required by the Committee to achieve good policymaking on the subject under discussion. The time requirements can be established only at a later stage, after it becomes clear how long a time is required for various levels of development of the different policymaking elements. Therefore, taking into account both the difficulties of breaking through the time constraints and the danger of regarding it as an absolute limit, it is recommended that the committee follows these two complementary guidelines:

A. The scheme of operations of the Committee and the scheduling of its proceedings are to be directed at shortening as much as possible the time required for good policymaking on the subject under discussion.

B. It is not desirable to stop the Committee's work as long as additional time invested contributes a great deal to raising the quality of the policy (that is to say, as long as its work is still somewhere between points B and C on the curve).

D. Policymaking Elements

16. After having examined the problem of time, we can now approach the core of this memorandum, in which we examine the policymaking elements mentioned in paragraph 5 above. We shall do so by working out some main aspects of these elements in relation to the policy subject under discussion

with a view to arriving at a number of operational recommendations with regard to the Committee's work.

a. Formulation of the Problem and Delineation of its Boundaries

17. Education constitutes a closely knit system in the fullest sense of the word. This means that the various components of the educational system are interwoven and intertwined and that it would be difficult, dangerous, and misleading to deal with any of them in isolation. Teachers, curricula, examination arrangements, premises and teaching aids, administrative staff, the structure of the educational hierarchy—all these are but single components of the educational system, which have no real meaning by themselves. Moreover, the educational system as a whole is but one—although a very important —component, or subsystem, of the social system. There are close interrelationships between the educational subsystem, on the one hand, and culture, economy, and technology (to count only a few other subsystems of society), on the other.

18. It follows that it is very difficult to formulate a meaningful issue in the field of educational policy that would be restricted to only one component of the educational system. When speaking of slight incremental changes which do not greatly affect the present situation, it is perhaps permissable to discuss a single component and to neglect partially the interdependence between that component and others in the educational system. However, when we speak of real innovation, then any narrow restriction in the formulation of the problem under discussion would assure in advance that policy-making is defective, and ignores the basic character of the system we are dealing with. At the same time, it is unavoidably true that every problem posed for decision must be delimited in such a way as to enable us to tackle it with limited understanding and resources.

19. The difficulties in useful formulation of the problem are particularly acute when we deal with the "formal structure" of the educational system, as indicated in the terms-of-reference of the Committee. Correctly viewed, structure is a variable of the third degree: first, we need some specifications of the purposes of the educational system in terms of the net output we want to achieve; then we should design curricula, teaching methods, staffing characteristics, and the other main variables connected directly with the process of teaching, in a way which, we believe, will lead to a maximum achievement of the explicated (and constantly changing) purpose; structure should enter consideration after these more critical variables are designed, or perhaps as one of them. Even when the point of departure for any analysis is structure, it is clearly impossible to evaluate the characteristics of various alternative structures without examining simultaneously the other components of the educational system with which structure closely interacts.

Furthermore, even if changes in structure are the only feasible main alternatives, many changes in other components are essential in order to get benefits from changes in structures.

20. The possibilities for formulating and delineating the policy issue before the Committee range between two extremes. At the one end the issue can be formulated in terms of reexamination of most, or at least many, of the main components of the elementary and the post-elementary education system and their interface with other systems—with a view to redesigning the system, to the extent that this should be useful for increasing the desired outputs of education. At this end, recommendations regarding the structure represent only one item of an integrated set of interdependent recommendations. At the opposite end the issue can be formulated narrowly as a problem of structure, completely ignoring both the necessary dependence of the preferred structure on other features of the educational system and the required changes in the other components following any changes in structure. The first possibility is in theory preferable, but may be difficult to follow with available knowledge. The second possibility is too narrow to permit significant results.

21. A less extreme, "in-between" possibility is to locate structure in the focus of inquiry, while at the same time examining the other components of the educational system, as far as they are closely interconnected with structure. This formulation may be preferable, as it is well within the clear mandate of the Committee, while being broad enough to adopt the essences of a systems approach. The boundaries of such a formulation of the issue must be flexible, because only as the Committee's work progresses will it be possible to establish which other components of the educational systems are so interconnected with structure, as to require their intense consideration as an internal part of the subject under discussion.

22. To conclude our discussion of formulation of the problem and delineation of its boundaries, I wish to point to two additional aspects, which are again interconnected:

A. It may well become clear at some stage of the inquiry that changes in other variables (such as curriculum and teacher training) may be more efficient for the achievement of the aimed-at goals of the educational system, rather than changes in the structure.

B. One of the important advantages of changing the structure may well be not the educational results of these changes themselves, but the shock that has been dealt to the educational systems. Such a shock may sometimes shake the entire system out of its routine and open up prospects for other more important changes which are unfeasible before the former system equilibrium has been disrupted.

b. Clarification of Aims

23. Clarification of aims is vital in order to provide standards for the appraisal of various alternatives. What I have in mind is not ultimate values on the level of the philosophy of education, but more concrete aims on a more operational level, such as the satisfaction of an undefined public demand for "change"; fuller development of the child's personality; greater attention to adolescent youth; increased output in terms of knowledge, higher mental capacities, artistic sense, intellectual independence, etc.; higher outputs in term of human capital; equal opportunity; acceleration of immigrant absorption; ideological socialization (in different directions); and so forth. An important goal on a different level is to preserve options for the future and increase capacity to adjust education to changes in goal preferences.

24. For the purposes of policymaking in our case, it is unnecessary and impossible to try to establish an "objective function," with marginal rates of exchange between the various aims. Aim priorities and rates of exchange are necessary for identification of the preferable alternatives only in respect to those aims which are alternative-sensitive, that is, those aims the extent of achievement of which will be significantly influenced by the choice between feasible alternative policies. Taking into consideration the difficulties (methodological and political) of scaling aims in terms of desireability, this task should be reduced as far as possible, at least by being deferred until the main alternatives are identified and their probable consequences in terms of different aims have been outlined.

25. What is nevertheless required in the early phases of the analysis is a goal-matrix which includes all reasonably relevant aims of the educational system, without any priorities. This goal-matrix constitutes the basic framework for ascertaining the relevant probable results of the various alternatives (and their later appraisal, insofar as necessary).

26. An instrumental goal which bisects the other aims and which needs special emphasis in the world of discourse of education is the striving for efficiency, that is to say, the achievement of maximum net output (i.e., output in terms of achievement of aims, minus input, expressed in terms of opportunity costs). The entire analysis therefore has to be made in terms of benefit-cost (in qualitative terms whenever quantification is impossible or distorts education-relevant aspects).

27. The futures orientation of any present policymaking in the area of education also need special emphasis. The outputs of any present decision on the structure of education and related components must be evaluated in terms of the aims of education at the time these outputs occur, that is, approximately the next five to at least fifteen years. The goal-matrix and aim priorities should therefore not express our present goals and aims, but

our best image of our goals and aim-priorities during the next 5-15 years. Also, elasticity to permit adjustment to unexpected goals is essential.

28. Working out a goal-matrix which includes, in effect, all socially significant goals, on the achievement of which contemplated changes in the structure of education and related components might have meaningful impact, is basically a professional job involving little value judgments. Some research on presently held values may be required, but as the initial goal-matrix should be all-inclusive rather than selective, the problem is more one of structuring the goal-matrix in a form convenient for policy-oriented uses than one of value-screening. Certainly, the Committee will make sure that no goals recognized by it are forgotten, and, indeed, careful interviewing of the Committee members by the professional staff may be a main method for filling in the goal-matrix. But, in the main, the goal-matrix should be worked out by professionals. An interdisciplinary university team might be a good group for preparing the goal-matrix on contract with the Committee.

29. The situation is completely different in respect to the value judgments involved in preferring the probable results (in terms of the goal-matrix) of one alternative over those of another alternative. This is a main function of the Committee. Careful staff work can facilitate this task by posing the judgment issues in operational terms (so-and-so-much more allowance for the adolescent child as compared to so-and-so-much teaching of know-how, and not "the soul of the boy" as compared to "know-how" generally; I want to stress that a much more operational terminology does not depend necessarily on the quantification of the various data and single-point predictions, but can be achieved with the help of a comparison of a detailed series of qualitative and probabilistically stated elements). Furthermore, the professional staff may aid the Committee in structuring its image of future goals of education and deciding among the different result sets in terms of those goals by running with the Committee a number of simulation exercises.[5] Such exercises may sensitize the Committee members to various issues and thus sharpen their value judgment, but they are no substitute for the political-public judgment of the Committee.

c. Identification of Main Alternatives

30. The quality of a policy depends to a large extent on our capacity to create new alternatives which are better than any of the alternatives already known. The great differences between Israel and almost all other countries from the point of view of its aims, its population features, its size, and its problems of society and economy make necessary an intense effort to invent

[5]E.g., see the methodology suggested in L. O. Helmer, "A Use of Simulation for the Study of Future Values" (Santa Monica, Calif.: The Rand Corporation, P-3443, September 1966).

alternatives. These alternatives must be based on the best international know-how and experience and the best Israeli experience together. There must be a willingness to accept change combined with an effort at original creation, based on know-how and experience, that will fit our conditions and specific needs. This general thought, it seems, is true particularly with regard to the educational system, in which traditional methods, which have grown out of conditions quite different from the present ones, confront new possibilities and novel needs which become ever more severe.[6]

31. The question therefore arises in all its severity whether the only alternatives with regard to the structure of the educational system are those which we already know or whether additional alternatives, considerably preferable to the known ones, can be invented.

32. This question is of great significance with regard to the Committee's work. It is recommended that the Committee should make a determined effort to go beyond the well-known alternatives and encourage creative thought for the invention of new alternatives. For this purpose, it is vital that the Committee's discussions should be directed at innovation and that too early a freezing of positions should be avoided. It is also necessary to forge tools that can help in the invention of new alternatives. A "brain trust" that includes the best and most imaginative persons available and that would be asked specifically to try to create new alternatives might be very useful here.

d. Construction of Forecasts

33. An essential element of good policymaking is explicit forecasts based on the expected results (positive and negative) of the various alternatives. This is a task for experts. Experts of various kinds have to construct forecasts on the basis of available data, comparative study, field research, experimentation, and intuition of people of experience, and so on.

36. Beyond the technical questions of constructing the forecasts (such as the methods for systematically processing expert opinions)—which are not within the purview of this memorandum—there are some main problems which have to be mentioned because of their importance and difficulty. These are the problems arising from conditions of uncertainty, that is to say, the impossibility to arrive at a reliable forecast with regard to the main results expected from the various alternatives. In respect to a complicated subject like the structure of the educational system, where the important results extend over many areas and a long span of time, the tools at our disposal (and perhaps the inherent nature of the relevant phenomena) do not enable us to make a reliable forecast of expected results. This is true,

[6]Radical changes in main societal variables and in the goals of education seem to require new inventions in education in all countries, including the United States.

though to a lesser extent, even if we were to content ourselves with the results most important to us within a relatively short time span. Insofar as this is the case, far-reaching uncertainty must be explicitly admitted, and we should decide on the basis of intuitive judgment whether we want, nevertheless, to make more radical changes with all the increased uncertainty and risk involved in doing so, or whether we prefer to limit ourselves to incremental change, where we sometimes can arrive at relatively more reliable (or less unreliable) forecasts. Together with explication of the degrees of uncertainty involved in the preferred approach—and, later on, the preferred policy—suitable steps should be decided upon to contain this uncertainty or compensate for it, including, for instance, careful testing of the sensitivity of the alternatives to different images of the relevant futures and explicit judgment on the preferred degrees of "gambling"; providing for policy change in view of feedback; and hedging against uncertainty by building into the adopted policy additional elasticity. However, a main effort should first be made to exhaust all feasible methods for the construction of reliable forecasts.

35. There is a widespread inclination in areas such as education, in the face of uncertainty, to postpone a decision and to recommend that field experiments be made in the interim; that is to say, in our case, that different educational structures should be introduced in different locations in order to learn from them and then to arrive at more reliable forecasts. (This method is sometimes called "decision by stages" or "sequential decisionmaking.") This method is only useful if there is a basis for the expectation that it will indeed be possible to draw reliable conclusions from the experiments. To the extent that the expected results cannot be measured or at least reliably estimated and to the extent that the results are very much influenced by specific local variables, the possibility diminishes of improving the forecast by means of experimentation. When this is the case, then it is pointless to postpone a decision until these experiments are made. The question whether and to which extent field experiments can help in the construction of more reliable forecasts requires a careful examination by experts.

36. The case is entirely different when the forecasts do not point to a real difference between the alternatives because there probably is none. Here, the failing does not lie in the weakness of the forecasts, but in the fact that alternatives may be similar in expected meaningful results. Thus, examination may show that according to international experience there is perhaps no considerable difference in main outputs between different structures of educational systems (all other things being equal). This is a most important and meaningful conclusion, which is radically different from a conclusion that there probably are significant differences in results, but we cannot predict them. It is necessary to differentiate sharply between these two situations, which are basically different.

37. Construction of forecasts is essentially a professional job as is identification of ways for containing uncertainty and compensating for it. Taking into account the nature of our policy issue, care must be taken to avoid exclusive reliance on more quantitative but less applicable forecasting techniques, such as extrapolation and analogue with other countries. Rather, there is much need for qualitative forecasting (such as construction of alternative scenarios and images of the future) and full utilization of the tacit intuitions of teachers, educators, and other persons closely involved in relevant experiences.

38. Construction of forecasts is analytically a different process from deciding on preferred "megapolicies" on how to regard uncertainties and how to evaluate the dangers and promises (unexpected results may be both undesirable and desirable). This is a matter for judgment by the Committee members. Professional staff can help in making the relevant judgments more explicit and structuring them more systematically, insofar as this does not disrupt the give-and-take dynamics of the Committee's work.

e. Integration and Decision

39. Integration of the various elements into a decision is a continual process, unfolding and iterative in nature. Close interconnection between the various points in the policy network is required. This means that close, continuous, and intense contacts between all the persons and units working on the problem are necessary throughout all the stages of the process. The final integration and final decisions are a central task and responsibility of the Committee. However, it appears that the integration of the various elements and the crystallization of the material toward the intermediate and final decisions require professional staff assistance of the highest quality. What is required is a senior staff assistant for the Committee. This person, in addition to the necessary personal characteristics, should have good qualifications both in the disciplines of education and in policy analysis.

E. The Committee's Methods and Instruments

40. From our brief discussion of the various elements of policymaking, preliminary conclusions can be drawn with regard to the Committee's methods and instruments of work. Without going into details, it seems that the development of the various elements requires methods and instruments as outlined in table 23-1.

41. With regard to the methods and instruments, I should like to add these remarks:

    a. The task of the Committee policy advisor is of especial importance because, as already mentioned, he should serve as senior staff assistant for the whole work of the Committee. He should be an independent personality of the highest professional caliber who can

Table 23-1

Elements of Policymaking and Methods and Instruments for their Development

Methods and Instruments for Developing the Elements	Desired Elements of Policymaking					
	Definition and Delineation of Problem	Design of Goal Matrix	Value Judgments (on Goals, on Orientation to Uncertainties, and more)	Identification of Alternatives	Construction of Forecasts	Integration and Decision
Discussion and examination in committee	‡	*	‡	*	*	‡
Structured proceedings in committee	*	†	‡	*	*	*
Opinions by men of experience	†	†	*	†	‡	*
Brain trusts	*	†	*	‡	†	—
Research teams and individual researchers (research in the country, comparative research, experiments)	†	†	*	†	‡	—
Committee policy advisor	†	†	†	†	†	‡
Expert evidence	†	†	*	†	†	*

*Minor contribution †Medium contribution ‡Major contribution Does not apply

      devote all of his time to the Committee's work.

    b. An interdisciplinary approach is necessary in order to examine the issue from all its aspects. It is essential to examine it at least from the points of view of psychology, sociology, economics, political science, and administration, in addition to the pedagogical aspects in the customary sense of the word.

    c. The political aspects of the problem should be explicitly dealt with. Expected reactions of relevant interest groups and the public at large may well be subjected to study.

42. The final product of the Committee should include three main parts:

    a. Recommendations (conditional or unconditional).

    b. Detailed reasons (in the form of a detailed policy analysis).

    c. Background (research findings, evidence and memoranda).

Since the form of the final product affects some of the Committee's methods, the Committee should tentatively decide roughly in he middle of its proceedings which form the final product is to take.

F. Conclusion

43. Let me conclude by pointing to the tentative character of this memorandum; it is only a preliminary attempt to help the Committee in its heavy tasks by means of a few proposals and remarks with regard to the framework for policymaking on the subject under discussion. The analysis and the recommendations included in this memorandum require development, extension, and elaboration.

Megapolicies, in the sense of master policies
providing guidelines for sets of policies, are
another main concern of policy sciences—all
the more important because of their neglect in
contemporary theory and practice alike. In
many respects, the concept of megapolicy and
examination of its main dimensions constitutes
one of the few already available innovations
of policy sciences, an innovation of
significance for behavioral research and
prescriptive study alike.
This part includes examination of a main
megapolicy issue in the first chapter, which
discusses the choice between incremental
change and innovation. The second chapter
provides a systematic application of the
concept of megapolicy and its different
dimensions to administrative reforms.

PART VIII

Megapolicy

CHAPTER 24

Muddling through — "Science" or Inertia?[1]

COMMENTS

This chapter takes up a main megapolicy controversy, incremental change versus policy innovation. Through critical discussion of a famous article of Charles E. Lindblom, a number of criteria for preferability of policy innovation instead of incremental change are developed. This chapter also presents in outline some elements of a preferable policymaking model, in between "muddling through" and "comprehensive rationality."

Introduction

In a much-quoted article published in the *Public Administration Review* in 1959, Charles E. Lindblom put forth a brilliant justification of policy and decisionmaking through "muddling through," that is, through incremental change aimed at arriving at agreed-upon policies which are closely based on past experience.[2] He presented a well-considered theory, as developed and expanded in other articles and books,[3] which was fully geared to the normal experience of practicing administrators in modern countries, till quite recently, and well designed to reinforce their actual behavior patterns by giving them the blessings of scientific approval.

[1] This chapter is based on an article first published in *Public Administration Review* 24, no. 3 (September 1964): 153-65. A reply by Charles E. Lindblom was published ibid. pp. 157-58.

[2] See Charles E. Lindblom, "The Science of 'Muddling Through'," *Public Administration Review* 19 (Spring 1959): 79-88. Unless otherwise noted, quotations from Lindblom included in the present chapter are taken from that article.

[3] See especially Charles E. Lindblom, "Policy Analysis," *American Economic Review* 48 (June 1958): 298-312; and Albert O. Hirschman and Charles E. Lindblom, "Economic Development, Research and Development, Policy Making: Some Converging Views," *Behavioral Science* 7 (April 1962): 211-22. Both these papers are more careful in their conclusions than "The Science of 'Muddling Through'," both recognizing some limitations inherent in the method of "change through incremental comparison" and its locality-bound assumptions. In some recent books, Lindblom further develops his ideas, but without changing this basic rationale. See David Braybrooke and Charles E. Lindblom, *A Strategy of Decision* (Glencoe, Ill.: Free Press, 1963); Charles E. Lindblom, *Intelligence of Democracy* (New York: Free Press, 1965); and Charles E. Lindblom, *The Policy Making Process* (Englewood Cliffs, N.J.: Prentice-Hall, 1968).

257

There can be no doubt that in comparison with the "rational-compre-hensive" models of decisionmaking commonly accepted in management sciences and their related diciplines, Lindblom's approach constitutes a very valuable contribution. It is more closely tied to reality, more sophisti-cated in theory, and more adjusted to human nature. Nevertheless, the question must be asked whether the favorable evaluation of incremental change and muddling through (in the sense of policymaking through succes-sive limited comparisons) does not, in many respects, constitute a danger-ous overreaction.

More specifically, it is necessary to reexamine the "Science of 'Muddling Through' " thesis both in respect to its inherent validity and its potential impact on actual policymaking and decisionmaking practices. The possi-bilities for constructing a mixed preferable model of policymaking, superior to both the muddling through and rational-comprehensive ones, also requires attention, especially because of the neglect of such a possibility in the professional literature.

Conditions Limiting the Validity of the "Science of 'Muddling through'" Thesis

Conceding the many insights in Lindblom's paper, there may, nevertheless, be a critical examination of two main elements of the "Science of 'Muddling Through'" thesis, namely, the incremental nature of desired changes in policy and agreement on policy as the criterion of its quality.

The basic strategy of incremental change, as stated by Lindbloom, is one of maximizing security in making change. All reliable knowledge being based on the past, the only way to proceed without risk is by continuing in the same direction, limiting consideration of alternative policies "to those policies that differ in relatively small degrees from policies presently in effect."[4] This is sound advice, provided certain conditions pertain—a requirement not adequately faced by Lindblom.

Unless three closely interrelated conditions are concurrently met, incre-mental change by successive limited comparison is not an adequate method for policymaking. These three essential conditions are—

1. the results of present policies must be in the main satisfactory (to the policymakers and the social strata on which they depend), so that marginal changes are sufficient for achieving an acceptable rate of improvements in policy results;
2. there must be a high degree of continuity in the nature of the problems;

---

[4]Lindblom, "The Science of 'Muddling Through'," op. cit. [in footnote 2], p. 84.

3. there must be a high degree of continuity in the available means for dealing with problems.

When the results of past policies are undesirable, it is often preferable to take the risks involved in radical new departures. For instance, in modernizing countries aspiring to accelerated socio-economic development, the policies followed by the former colonial policymakers clearly do not constitute an acceptable basis to be followed with only incremental change. Similarly, in modern countries when changes in values make formerly accepted policy results unacceptable, radical departures in policy are required despite the risk,[5] for instance in respect to the segregation problem in the United States.

When there are no past policies in respect to a discrete policy issue, incremental change is, in fact, impossible. For instance, many of the problems faced during the New Deal had novel characteristics making nearly every policy alternative (other than doing nothing) a radical departure from the past. The same is largely true, for instance, for contemporary environmental and pollution issues.

Changes in knowledge—technological and behavioral—put at the disposal of policymakers new means of action, which, unless ignored, lead to radically new policies. The best illustrations are provided in military technology, where incremental change results in the often noted tendency of a nation's armed forces to be excellently prepared for the last war. Similar illustrations can be cited in most spheres of social action where innovations in knowledge take place, such as medicine (policymaking in regard to smoking) and education (utilization of programed teaching-machines).

The three conditions essential to the validity of the muddling through thesis are most likely to prevail where there is a high degree of social stability. Under conditions of stability, routine is often the best policy, and, change being at a slow rate, incremental policy adjustment is often optimal. But, even in the most stable societies, many of today's qualitatively most important problems are tied up with high-speed changes in the levels of

[5] In 1970, this statement in respect to the United States seems obvious. When originally published in 1964, this statement of mine was strongly criticized. It is indeed amazing how stubbornly United States's behavioral scientists clung to the incremental change thesis. Quite representative, for instance, is a statement in an essay published in 1968, that "dramatic breaks with the past such as the atomic bomb, or the space program... can be treated as *random disturbances* in the otherwise stable and incremental policy-making process, only *momentarily* producing a fluctuation in the old patterns of policy-making which quickly reassert themselves." (Emphasis added.) See the otherwise excellent survey by Enid Curtis Bok Schoettle, "The State of the Art in Policy Studies," in Raymond A. Bauer and Kenneth J. Gergen, eds., *The Study of Policy Formation* (New York: Free Press, 1968), p. 179. Little wonder that, when faced with the realities of accelerated transformation, many United States behavioral scientists tend to jump to the other extreme of unbridled advocacy of ill-considered extreme positions.

aspirations, the nature of issues, and the available means of action, and require, therefore, a policymaking method different from muddling through.[6]

A similar conclusion may be reached from examination of the reliance on agreement on policy as the criterion of the policy's quality. Under conditions of stability, when all relevant parties have a more or less clear image of the expected results of a certain policy, with a high correlation of subjective and objective probability, a policy agreed upon will ordinarily involve little risk of catastrophe; also, under such conditions, it is, in fact, much easier to agree on a discrete policy than on abstract goals. In contrast, under conditions of high-rate change, ignorance can produce agreement upon a catastrophic policy; under such conditions, moreover, it is often much easier to agree on abstract or operational goals (e.g., raising the standard of living, and increasing the net per-capita product by 2% annually) than on policies, there being no background of shared experience to serve as a basis for consensus on policy. Lest the reader reach the conclusion that these comments apply only to modernization countries, let him consider military policy, where decisions agreed upon by experienced military personnel are often incorrect when new conditions are faced.

The formula that "agreement equals high quality" is the more dangerous because of its appeal to a value highly regarded in democratic ideology, as attested to by the abundance of "administration by consent" literature and the recent upsurge of interest in "participatory democracy." It is, therefore, highly necessary to emphasize that agreement should follow examination of the consequences of policy and not be substituted for it, in all save the most familiar and stable policy areas.

The conclusion is inescapable, therefore, that the "Science of 'Mudling Through' " thesis has limited validity. It may have been more valid for a larger number of policy areas in a relatively stable society, such as the United States some years ago, than in countries engaged in high-rate directed social change. But today in nearly all countries many of the most critical policy problems involve factors changing at a high rate of speed.

The Impact of "Muddling Through" on Actual Policymaking

Although Lindblom's thesis includes a number of reservations, these are insufficient to alter its main impact as an ideological reinforcement of the proinertia and antiinovation forces prevalent in all human organizations,

[6]In his "Policy Analysis," op cit. [in footnote 3], Lindblom explicitly recognizes that his analysis applies to the United States and other "stable, well-established, deeply rooted democracies" (p. 30). But he fails to pursue this limitation and does not realize that there is today no country, including the United States, "stable" enough to fit his analysis.

administrative and policymaking.[7] The actual tendency of most organizations is to limit the search for alternatives to the minimum; there is little danger in real life that organizations will become bogged down in an exhaustive search for all alternatives and full enumeration of consequences, in order to achieve "rational-comprehensive" policymaking. The rational-comprehensive model has at least the advantage of stimulating administrators to get a little outside their regular routine, while Lindblom's model justifies a policy of "no effort."

Taken together, the limited validity of the muddling through thesis and its inertia-reinforcing implications constitute a very serious weakness. This conclusion in no way diminishes Lindblom's pioneering role in pointing out the shortcomings of the rational-comprehensive policymaking model. This may well prove to be one of his most important contributions, since the countermodel of muddling through is itself open to serious doubts. A choice between these two models would be difficult, but, luckily, may be avoided through construction of a third model for public policymaking.

A Prescriptive Preferable Model for Policymaking

The bases for a preferable model for policymaking are the following assumptions:

1. Preferable policymaking involves an effort to increase rationality content, through more explication of goals, extensive search for new alternatives, conscious attempts to elaborate expectations, with an explicit cutoff point, and some formulation of decision criteria.

2. Extrarational processes play a significant role in preferable policymaking on complex issues. This is not only unavoidable because of lack of resources and capacity for complete rationality, but, in fact, makes a positive contribution to better policymaking. Intuitive judgment, holistic impressions derived from immersion in a situation, and creative invention of new alternatives are illustrations of extrarational phases of preferable policymaking. The importance of such processes is not only acknowledged by all experienced policymakers, but also by some modern research in psychology, for instance, the works of Carl Rogers and Michael Polanyi discussing "experience" and "tacit knowledge" as sources of insight and understanding. Even "altered states of consciousness" may at a later stage play some roles in good policymaking.

3. These extrarational policymaking phases can be improved by various

[7]Even more dangerous is acceptance of the incremental change attitude by behavioral scientists, as it reduces their functions as an innovating social factor. By limiting his suggestions to incremental change, the behavioral scientist also significantly reduces his utility to policymakers, the latter being well aware of incremental alternatives and looking to the behavioral scientist for new ideas.

means, such as case discussions, sensitivity sessions, and "brainstorming." Similarly, the rational policymaking phases can be improved, for instance, through increasing the input (especially time), through increasing the knowledge and qualifications of policy practitioners, and by setting up special "think" units for the improvement of conceptual analytical tools.

4. Actual policymaking in modern states has a tendency to follow precedents, incremental change, "muddling through," intertia, and routine. Compared with the rate of change in the problems faced by policy, in the levels of aspiration, in the available alternatives, and in knowledge about the policymaking process itself, most contemporary policymaking practices lag behind. This can and should be improved.

A reprocessing of both the "comprehensive-rationality" and the "successive-limited-comparison" models in light of these assumptions may result in a prescriptive-preferable model for policymaking which includes the following main features:[8]

—Some clarification is needed of values, objectives, and decision criteria.

—Alternatives should be designed, accompanied by a conscious effort to consider new alternatives (through survey of comparative literature, experience, and available theories) and to stimulate creative alternative innovation.

—A preliminary estimation should be made of the expected pay-off of various alternatives, and it should be decided whether a strategy of minimal risk or a strategy of innovation is preferable.

—If the first is preferable, the successive-limited-comparison model should be followed. If the latter, the next element is establishment of a cut-off for considering possible results of alternative policies and identification of main expected results, relying on available knowledge and intuition.

—One of the tests of preferable policy is that a policy analysis network is agreed upon by the various analysts after full and frank discussion of stages 1 to 4.

—A conscious effort is made to decide whether the problem is important enough to make analysis more comprehensive.

—Theory and experience, rationality and extrarationality are all relied upon, the composition of the mix depending upon their availability and the nature of the problem.

—Explicit arrangements are made to improve the quality of policymaking through systematic learning from experience, stimulation of initiative and creativity, staff development, and encouragement of intellectual effort.

[8]For a detailed discussion of this model, see Yehezkel Dror, *Public Policymaking Reexamined,* (San Francisco: Chandler, 1968), Part IV.

The Need Redefined

To state the problem of policymaking as a choice between the "rational-comprehensive" and the "successive-limited-comparison" methods is misleading and dangerous. It is misleading because other policymaking models can be devised. It is dangerous because it leads either to an effort to achieve the impossible or to an encouragement of inertia and a continuation of the status quo.

What is needed is a model which fits reality while being directed toward its improvement, and which can, in fact, be applied to policymaking while motivating a maximum effort to arrive at better policy. By all these criteria, the model presented in "The Science of 'Muddling Through'" is inadequate, having limited validity and constituting a barrier to the improvement of policymaking. Its favorable acceptance, the result, in part, of its many merits, reflected the widespread disposition of administrators and students of public administration to accept the present as a guide to the future, and to regard contemporary practice as a norm for the future.

The broad acceptance of the muddling through thesis indicates that inertia and the tendency to incremental change are, in fact, widespread phenomena. This, in itself, serves to emphasize the need for models of policymaking stressing the limits of such an approach and pointing out the needs and possibilities for better policymaking. The prescriptive-preferable model presented above is only one variation of such a model, many others being feasible.

It is time for policy sciences to enter the area of inquiry, illuminated by Lindblom, and take up the challenge of providing models for policymaking, as opposed to the preoccupation of normal management and behavorial sciences with managerial techniques and "Grand Theories," respectively. In doing so, the search should be directed at constructing prescriptive models for policymaking which combine realism and idealism. The models should be near enough to reality to serve as feasible guides for action; at the same time, the models should aspire to a higher quality of public policymaking and serve as a means to encourage the improvement of reality.

CHAPTER 25

Megapolicies for Administrative Reform[1]

COMMENTS

Administrative reforms are a main challenge for policymaking, particularly interesting because they deal with a metapolicy issue. Especially important for modernization countries, administrative reforms are becoming also an urgent necessity for modern countries, to meet new conditions and demands. Therefore, the issues of administrative reforms constitute an interesting test case to try out the megapolicy concept and examine whether it is useful.

This chapter does so, applying systematically the different dimensions of megapolicy to issues of administrative reform. As the issues of administrative reform are similar to those of policymaking reform and partly overlap the latter, this chapter is also relevant for implementation of other metapolicy improvements.

The Need for Explicit Administrative-Reform Megapolicies

I am using the concept *megapolicy* as referring to a defined series of master policies. Megapolicies establish the framework of guidelines and the boundaries of policy space within which operational and detailed policies are to be established and decisions are to be made. Megapolicies for administrative reform must, therefore, deal with issues such as overall goals of administrative reform; the boundaries of administrative reform; preferences in respect to time; risk acceptability; choice between more incremental or more innovative reform; preference for more balance versus more shock-directed reform; relevant assumptions on the future; theoretic (tacit or explicit) assumptions on which the reform is to be based; resources available for the administrative reform; and the range of feasible reform instruments.

These and similar dimensions of megapolicy can serve as a conceptual framework for behavioral study of actual administrative reforms, both historic and contemporary. The absence of any comprehensive conceptual framework is an important reason for the shallowness of most writings on

[1]Based on a paper first published in *Development and Change* 2, no. 2 (1970-71): 19-35. The author is very grateful to Professor A. F. Leemans for his helpful comments on an earlier draft of this paper.

administratitve reforms and their failure to penetrate beyond technicalities into basic features.[2] From a prescriptive point of view, a systematic comparative study of administrative reforms with the help of the proposed dimensions of megapolicy is, therefore, urgently needed to provide feedback from experience as an aid to better administrative reform megapolicymaking. But even in the absence of comparative empirical studies, the proposed megapolicy dimensions can and should be used for improvement of administrative reforms, at least by providing a policy analysis network for explicit consideration and decision of crucial reform features.

The preferable mix of administrative reform megapolicies is in the main a function of the concrete circumstances of each particular reform situation. Specific local needs, the availability of different resources, historic traditions, and indigenous political culture—these illustrate the unique variables which make impossible the existence of universal optimal administrative reform megapolicies. Some generalized recommendations regarding a number of megapolicy dimensions may be useful in respect to defined groups of situations, such as "modernization countries," "postindustrial societies." "threatened countries," etc. A few recommendations in respect to single megapolicy dimensions may even be of universal validity, resulting more from the very characteristics of administrative institutions than from their particular forms in different countries. But, in general, identification of preferable administrative-reform megapolicies depends on unique situations and, therefore, requires careful and detailed analysis on the basis of elaborate data.

Nevertheless, the concept of reform megapolicy and an explicated set of main dimensions of reform megapolicies can be of much applied usefulness as a framework for administrative reform policymaking. My main argument here is closely related to my use of the term *administrative reform.* By administrative reform I mean *directed change of main features of an administrative system.* This definition recognizes the existence of a continuum between administrative improvements and administrative reforms, the exact borderline between these two depending on one's perception of the main features of an administrative system. But, more important, this definition makes clear my concern with administrative reforms as a directive and conscious activity, rather than a postfactum classification of administrative-change phenomena, which may be the aggregate result of incremental changes or the undirected side effects of sweeping social movements and societal transformations (which, of course, often are also causes of directed main administrative system changes, i.e., "administrative reforms").

[2]Distinguished exceptions include, for instance, Dwight Waldo, *The Administrative State* (New York: Ronald Press, 1948); S. N. Eisenstadt, *The Political Systems of Empires* (New York: Free Press, 1963); and Gerald Caiden, *Administrative Reform* (Chicago: Aldine, 1969).

Given this conception of administratitve reform as consciously directed change of the main features of an administrative system, the general recommendation that explicit and carefully considered megapolicy determination will improve the quality of administrative reforms is a special case of a general theory of preferable policymaking. Full exposition of this general theory is out of place here. But the general principle that fuller and more explicit consideration of the main dimensions of a decision issue will usually contribute to better decisions is so strongly supported by both policy sciences and other types of knowledge and experience as not to require elaboration.

Let me, nevertheless, point out some caveats, to avoid the over-simple impression that more explicit megapolicy determination is always conducive to better administrative reform, and, at the same time, to indicate some difficulties of explicit administrative-reform megapolicymaking.

a. Administrative-reform megapolicymaking requires a high-quality staff. Unless good megapolicies are decided upon, it may be better to "muddle through," so that at least serious mistakes can be avoided. The same is not necessarily true for administrative reforms as a whole—in some situations, nearly any change is better than perpetuation of the present situation; also, megapolicymaking requires more sophistication than many other aspects of administrative reform.

b. Explicit administrative-reform megapolicymaking involves clear choice between a range of alternatives that are favored by different values, interests, organizations, and personalities. Therefore, megapolicymaking often involves significant political costs in terms of coalition maintenance, support recruitment, implementation possibilities, participation, and more.

c. Establishment of administrative-reform megapolicies may easily lead to overrigidity unless the megapolicies themselves are elastic, are related to clearly defined contingencies, and are subjected to periodic re-examination. This, again, assumes not only a highly qualified staff, but also advanced administrative-reform policymaking and monitoring.

In short, determination of good administrative-reform megapolicies presupposes to some extent a high-quality policymaking system—which is usually absent exactly when administrative reform is most urgently needed. Therefore, it is important to emphasize that my recommendation to explicitly decide administrative-reform megapolicies should not be regarded as a Procrustean bed, which provides a rigid framework to be followed equally in all cases. But I think that in practice the danger of too much administrative-reform megapolicymaking is unreal. Resistance to abstract thinking and to systematic policymaking is usually very strong; therefore, I think that administrative-reform megapolicymaking will not be overdone. Rather, the real danger is in the opposite direction, with concrete reform issues driving out of consideration the underlying megapolicy dimensions, resulting in ill-considered, inconsistent, overatomized, and too-short-range administrative-reform attempts. Therefore, the overall recommendation to pay more attention to administrative-reform megapolicies is justified and, consequently, a set of administative-reform megapolicy dimensions should be of practical help, at least by serving as a check list and as a sensitizer, and often by serving as a framework for at least some explicit consideration of the megapolicy dimensions of a contemplated administrative reform.

Having explored the significance of administrative-reform megapolicies, let me pass on to a discussion of eleven main megapolicy dimensions.

1. Overall Goals

A standard answer to the question, "Administrative reform for what?" is, "To increase efficiency." But this is largely a meaningless answer, because the real question is, "Efficiency, or effectiveness, in doing what?" Different administrative-system characteristics are more effective and efficient for fullfilling different functions and achieving different goals. Therefore, clarification of the overall goals of an administrative reform is a fundamental requisite for success. Usually, an administrative reform will be a multi-goal-oriented endeavor. This makes it all the more necessary to examine the consistency of the various goals and to establish necessary priorities.

To illustrate the parameters of this dimension, let me mention a few possible administrative-reform goal clusters:

a. Increasing traditional "administrative efficiency," in the sense of saving money through form simplification, procedure change, duplication reduction, and similar O.M. (organizations and methods) approaches.

b. Reducing perceived weaknesses, such as corruption, favoritism, political spoils, and so on. (This "debugging" goal is itself very heterogeneous, leading, therefore, to different preferable megapolicy combinations.)

c. Changing a particular main component of the administrative system to meet some ideal image. This again includes a large variety of main goals, such as introduction of a merit civil service; introduction of a planning-pro-graming-budgeting system; moving towards automated data processing and integrated data and information banks; increasing the utilization of scientific knowledge; and many more.

These three goal clusters are intra-administration directed, at least in their direct effects and their initial facade. Much more important and often tacitly underlying such intra-administrative goals are administrative-reform goals dealing with the societal roles of the administrative system and its interrelation with other components of the policymaking system and even of society as a whole. Goal clusters of this type include, for instance, the following:

   d. Adjusting the administrative system to advancing overriding societal objectives, such as accelerated modernization, or war.

   e. Changing the division of labor between the administrative system (and especially its higher levels) and the political system. For instance, in the direction of either reducing the power of the senior civil service and making it a more obedient servant of the political process or increasing the professional autonomy of the administrative system and strengthening its influence on policy.

   f. Changing the relations between the administrative system and the population or selected population segments. For instance, through relocation of decision centers (centralization vs. decentralization), "democratization" in the sense of participation, and "democratization" in the sense of making the personnel composition more reflective of various population segments and more responsive to them.

   Administrative reform can also serve purely political functions, such as making administration serve as a scapegoat, gaining support through distributing spoils, receiving a foreign loan, etc. While abhorred by traditional administrative theory, such functions are sometimes essential, and sacrificing the administrative system may sometimes be justified to avoid an even greater evil—though in most cases the longer-range costs of such a "reform" are by several magnitudes larger than the benefits.

   This list of six goal clusters, each one of which covers a variety of main goals, does not exhaust the list of possible and reasonable overall goals of administrative reforms. But it is, I hope, sufficient to concretize the concept of "overall administrative reform goals" and to demonstrate the dependence of preferable reform features on the overall goals of the respective reform, and, therefore, the necessity to clarify and clearly decide what goal-mix a particular reform should be aimed at, initially (while recognizing that the goals will change with time). This is a most important administrative-reform megapolicy dimension which is seldom more than touched upon in most actual cases of administrative-reform decisionmaking.

2. Reform Boundaries

Public administration is a complex system, which itself is a subsystem of a number of larger systems—such as the political system and the societal system as a whole. Simultaneously, various subsystems of the administrative system are also components of a variety of other systems. Thus, civil service staff schools are also components of the education system; professional staff members are also components of professional associations; administrative employees are also components of employee organizations and of the manpower system as a whole; and so on. Further to complicate the boundary issues, there are a multiplicity of units which are in between the administrative system and other systems. Thus, mixed corporations are in between public administration and private enterprise; private consultants who work for public administration, independent research facilities working on contract for government, private producers serving as main suppliers for public administration—these are additional illustrations of entities not easily classified as either inside or outside the public administrative system. The citizen in his role as an object of administration, as a client of administration, and (in the aggregate and in some senses) as the master of public administration, also is and is not a component of the public administrative system, depending on our definition criteria and boundary postulates.

All these abstract observations on the undefined boundaries of the public administrative system relate to a very real and practical administrative-reform megapolicy dimension: What are the boundaries within which an administrative reform is to be confined? In other words, what is the domain of institutions to be considered as appropriate objects for an administrative reform?[3]

A brief exploration of some concrete boundary issues often met in administrative reforms will serve to operationalize this megapolicy dimension and demonstrate its applied importance:

a. *Politicians and political institutions.* The interface between politicians and political institutions, on one hand, and the administrative system, on the other hand, is so close that many aspects of the administrative system cannot be changed without also changing some political institutions. Thus, spoils system and corruption cannot be dealt with through changes limited to administration. Furthermore, in respect to many other aspects of the administrative system, interaction between it and political institutions is so intense that change limited to the administrative system is useless and often even counterproductive. Thus, upgrading the professionalism of senior administrators while leaving the capacities of politicians and political institutions low will change the balance of power between administration and politics in directions which may often involve undesirable alienation and de-democratization. Especially when the goals of administrative reform involve improvement of policymaking, administration and politics must be regarded as intensely interacting components of the policymaking system which must be subjected to directed change as a whole. (See chapter 19.) Indeed, one of the widespread weaknesses of administrative reforms is the neglect and

---

[3] A different question also involving a boundary issue is, Within what domain shall we look for relevant reform consequences? Related are such questions as, What shall be regarded as first order consequences? As second order consequences? As third order consequences? These are important problems, but they would carry us too far into general policymaking theory to be treated in this chapter.

inability to bring about adjustments in closely linked aspects of politics, without which the administrative reform cannot achieve its goals.

b. Academic institutions. A main factor shaping the quality of civil servants is the qualification of candidates for recruitment. The qualifications of candidates for recruitment, in turn, are largely shaped by the output of academic institutions (and competing demand). Here is a main interface between the administrative system and academic institutions, which demonstrates the importance of sometimes considering academic institutions as within the boundary of administrative reforms. Similarly, possible functions of academic institutions as centers for postentry training, research, and consultation provide additional reasons for carefully determining how far academic institutions should be regarded as within the boundary of an administrative reform.

c. Legal institutions. Quite important are the roles of legal institutions *vis-á-vis* the administrative system. Usually recognized are the functions of legal institutions in (1) controlling administrative discretion, especially when the rights of individuals are involved; and (2) enforcing rules of conduct, such as criminal sanctions against corruption. Not less important, though less discussed, is the transferability of important social functions between courts and administration. Thus, control of utilities, medicines, food, etc., can either be entrusted to the administrative system or to the legal institutions, or to some mix between these two. Therefore, clarification of the extent to which an administrative reform can also involve changes in the legal institutions is important. Such changes can include both new statutory laws and/or new court structures—such as establishment of administrative tribunals and quasi-judicial units. Therefore, the importance of legal institutions as one of the boundaries of administrative reforms should be recognized. But it is necessary, at the same time, to reject the tendency in some countries to view all administrative reforms mainly from a legal perspective. A purely legal perspective is much too narrow and shortsighted to be useful for administrative reform.

d. The public. More diffuse, but more important, are the problems of including some aspects of "the public" within the boundaries of an administrative reform. Introducing new procedures involving much contact with the public (such as computerization of income tax or social security), fighting corruption, involving the public more in participatory decisionmaking, changing the recruitment base of the civil service—these are only some illustrations out of many, of administrative changes, the success of which depends *inter alia* on changes in the public. Ideological and political considerations usually cause us to be suspicious of attempts to influence the public. Therefore, very careful treatment of the boundaries of an administrative reform with related aspects of public behavior, opinions, and attitudes is essential.

This megapolicy dimension is closely related to another, which I will discuss later, namely, range of reform instruments. Together with overall goals, the boundaries of an administrative reform really constitute a most basic decision shaping all features and elements of the reform. Therefore, it is so important not to take any a priori image of boundaries for granted, but explicitly to consider and reconsider this megapolicy and decide and redecide it on the basis of careful analysis before and while more detailed reform issues are taken up.

3. Preferences in Time

The question of the target time—when does one wish the main results of administrative reform to be produced?—is another main megapolicy issue. There is a fundamental difference between a reform that wants to achieve savings, or more subordination to politics, or better realization of accelerated modernization "immediately," and a reform that wants to upgrade the capabilities of an administrative system over the next ten to twenty years. This dimension clearly brings out a characteristic shared by all megapolicies, namely, the necessity for iteration and reconsideration of megapolicies in light of detailed reform plans and reform results. Thus, often the a priori desire will be for fast results, while more detailed reform plans will make obvious that significant results need more time, with consequent reformulation of the time preferences. Nevertheless, the often positive correlation between achievable results and required time and its sensitivity to availability of reform resources and reform instruments is quite clear, and it is wasteful to relearn through bitter experience what is already well known. Also, external variables (political feasibility, critical survival needs, etc.) often establish rigid constraints on time availability. Therefore, early establishment of clear time preferences in respect to various reform outputs is essential as a directive for detailed reform plans. Even more important, the early identification of rigid time constraints is essential for megapolicy consistency, as overall reform goals must often be reduced because of nonelastic time preferences.

4. Risk Acceptability

This megapolicy dimension involves the degrees of risk to be accepted in the administrative reform. Closely correlated with the next megapolicy dimension, the issue is largely whether one is ready to accept the higher risks associated usually with more innovation, or whether one prefers the lower risks often associated with incremental changes (though one should bear in mind that the risks of maintaining the present situation may sometimes be higher even than those of radical reform). In theory-of-games terminology, the choices here are between maximax, on one hand, and maximin or minimax, on the other hand. Also involved are preferences in respect to "average expected value," "lottery value," and similar choice principles between different forms of risk parameters.[4] However abstract, this is a very important choice, especially in view of the tendencies of risk avoidance commonly found in organizations, on one hand, and the tendencies toward recklessness often found in administrative reforms motivated by sweeping social movements and political changes, on the other hand.[5] Therefore, explicit judgment on acceptable risks significantly improve reform decisionmaking. Furthermore explication of acceptable and expected risks carries with it important implications for detailed reform plans by encouraging suitable hedging, contingency planning, and similar risk-absorbing methodologies.

5. Incrementalism versus Innovation

This dimension deals with the choice between various degrees of changes in the administrative system (defined in terms of extent of change, scope of change, and time), ranging from small incremental change of a few administrative details over a long period to far-reaching, comprehensive, and rapid administrative system redesign and even nova-design (i.e., design anew). One main variable in this choice is risk acceptability: the more innovation, the higher often are the unpredictable consequences. What is often forgotten is that a higher probability of far-reaching improvement in outputs is also positively correlated with far-reaching innovation, the latter being an essential (though, by itself, insufficient) condition for the first. Also, often forgotten is the already mentioned possibility that the status quo and limited change may, in some countries, be even more risky than far-reaching change. Strong organizational tendencies toward incremental change and scarcity of good administrative inventions make explicit megapolicymaking on this issue all the more essential for innovative administrative reforms. Significant and carefully considered innovations (as contrasted with convulsive jumps) usually are not a natural organizational phenomenon and, therefore, need specific encouragement, which, as a rule, does not come forth without an explicit megapolicy. While thus often leading toward more innovation, specific consideration of the pros and cons of innovation in administrative reforms and the related risks may sometimes also serve to restrain recklessness and encourage more careful megapolicies. This may involve either a more incremental megapolicy or an effort to combine innovation with risk-reducing methodologies such as pilot experimentation and sequential decisionmaking (i.e., decisionmaking by phases on the basis of parallel attempts coupled to constant learning).

[4]For a stimulating and readable treatment, see Howard Raiffa, *Decision Analysis: Introductory Lectures on Choices under Uncertainty* (Reading, Massachusetts: Addison-Wesley, 1968).

[5]Nevertheless, appearance may be misleading. Thus, upon closer study, it is clear that the Nazi leadership was very careful not to disrupt German bureaucracy as a whole, but rather focused their resources on selected ministries, especially police and youth.

6. Comprehensiveness versus Narrowness

This megapolicy dimension involves the degree to which the administrative reform should deal with a broad range of administrative system components or should focus on a few components or even a single one. Conditioned by the reform boundaries on one side and determining the range within which reform instruments may be searched for on the other side, the degree of comprehensiveness versus narrowness is, nevertheless, a distinct megapolicy dimension. Thus, a reform dealing with personnel policy and organizational structure and information processing will be comprehensive (even though within the traditional boundaries of an administrative system), while a reform dealing with recruitment for the senior staff will be narrower, even if it adopts broader boundaries and includes academic institutions and recruitment-influencing public images within its scope. (This illustration also shows that "more comprehensive" does not necessarily mean "more important" or more significant.")

This dimension is conceptually important for an additional reason: together with the degree of innovation, it categories an instance of directed administrative change as an "administrative reform," as defined by me. We can now postulate that to qualify as an administrative reform, a case of directed administrative system change must either (*a*) be of at least medium comprehensiveness plus high innovativeness, or (*b*) be of high comprehensiveness plus at least medium innovativeness. (A third, soon to be discussed, case is far-reaching change of a single component, but one which has overriding influence on the administrative system as a whole—for instance, novel recruitment patterns for the senior civil service.) (See figure 25-1.)

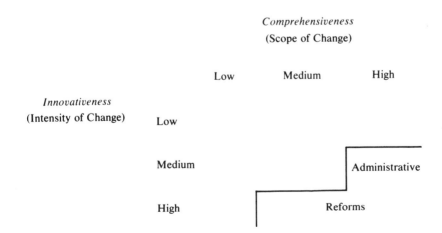

FIG. 25-1. The concept of administrative reform.

Still left open is the operational definition and measurement of *low*, *medium,* and *high,* and the development of more advanced classification scales (ordinal or nonmetric) than the "administrative reform/administrative-change-short-of-administrative-reform" binary classification. Our megapolicy dimensions permit some progress in this direction. With the help of the two dimensions conditioning the scope and intensity of administrative change, we can at least order administrative change on a five-point ordinal scale: low-low; low-medium or medium-low; medium-medium; high-medium or medium-high; and high-high.

7. Balance Oriented versus Shock Oriented

The question faced by this dimension is, to what extent should a reform be directed at changing a number of administrative system components together in a mutually coordinated (balanced) way? or, should a few components, or single components only, be subjected to change, with the purpose of shocking the system into a new state-of-existence, including increased openness to change and transformation?

This megapolicy dimension is closely related to the comprehensiveness versus narrowness dimension, in the sense that only a comprehensive administrative reform can be balance oriented and only a narrow administrative reform can be shock oriented. But it is a separate dimension, because not every comprehensive reform is or should be balance oriented, and not every narrow administrative reform is shock oriented. This megapolicy dimension is especially important because it raises for explicit examination the widely accepted notion that every "good" administrative reform must be balance oriented in the sense of striving for synchronized change of a multiplicity of components. This a priori assumption is strongly reinforced by much of general systems theory, systems analysis, and planning theory (where the term *comprehensive planning* means both "comprehensive," in the sense of broad scope, and "balanced").

While the idea of balanced administrative reform appeals to our preferences for harmony and is reinforced by a number of influential tacit theories (e.g., biological analogues of the administrative system) in addition to the just-mentioned decision approaches, it suffers from a number of serious fallacies. (See also chapter 11.) Often very harmful is the innovation-damping effect of an effort to achieve balanced reform, because radical change will often appear to be incompatible with balance. Furthermore, to preserve balance, we must be able to predict the consequences of directed change—and this, again, pushes us to limit change to incrementalism, which permits more reliable predictions than far-reaching innovation. When what is aimed at is radical transformation of the adminstrative system, shock effects which first disbalance the system so as to open it up for redesign and novadesign may often be the optimal strategy, though admittedly a risky and expensive one[6]. Again, explicit consideration of this megapolicy dimension should be useful in two directions: (a) by helping to overcome the a priori preference for balanced change in situations where administrative reform is approached from a conservative point of view; and (b) by explicating the risks of shock change and bringing out the need for risk-reducing measures in situations in which administrative reform is approached from a radical and even revolutionary point of view.

8. Relevant Assumptions on the Future

The dependence of preferable administrative systems on a large number of exogenous variables results in the necessity to base every reform on assumptions concerning the expected state of those variables. To illustrate, the state of administrative technologies (such as automated data processing), availability of qualified personnel, internal pressures and wars, and changes in societal goals and functions to be served by the administrative system—these are some of the variables, the future of which must be taken into account when a preferable reform plan is being developed.[7]

This problem is especially important in administrative reforms with a longer-range time preference, but exists even when the main time preference is for the near future. The usual practice is to ignore possible alternative futures of relevant variables and not to engage in systematic efforts to try to study them, but rather to assume that what exists now will continue in the future and to engage in arbitrary guesses on futures based on accidental information and personal bias. This is a result of the absence in most countries (including nearly all modernizing countries) of any efforts to predict alternative futures, and of the lack of any interconnection between lookout efforts and administrative-reform decisionmaking in the few countries where some lookout mechanisms (in government or outside it) do exist. Here we run again into the already mentioned dilemma, namely, that good administrative reform requires a highly developed policymaking system, which, in turn, usually depends on prior far-reaching administrative-system redesign and novadesign. Nevertheless, much can be achieved even without establishment of highly sophisticated outlook institutes. Present neglect of consideration of relevant assumptions on the future is so far-reaching that some sensitization of administrative-reform policymakers to the need to explicate their under-

[6]It is interesting to consider the role of a comprehensive and innovative administrative reform as a shock instrument directed at society as a whole. This is a possibility to be considered as another overall goal for administrative reform.

[7]When we regard some of the futures of some of the variables as endogenous, that is, as themselves objects for administrative-system operations directed at influencing the future, then we get into one of the possible goals of administrative reform—namely, increasing the capacity of an administrative system to shape the future.

lying assumptions on the future would itself already constitute a break with contemporary reality. Furthermore, available futures studies are good enough to provide some substantive contents for an attempt to improve assumptions on the futures underlying a proposed administrative reform, without the need first to set up special lookout institutes.

9. Theoretic Bases

The importance of bringing hidden assumptions which are critical for an administrative reform out into the open, to subject them to conscious re-examination and, if possible, to improve them with the help of systematic knowledge, structured rationality, and organized creativity—this is one of the main intellectual justifications for proposing megapolicy dimensions as a framework for administrative-reform decisionmaking. Nowhere is this motive more important than in respect to the theoretic bases of an administrative reform. Psychology brings out the fact that decisions and judgments are strongly influenced, among other factors, by the tacit theories held by decisionmakers. Organization theory supports this finding in respect to organizational decisionmaking, where collectively held tacit theories shape group and organizational decisions. "Tacit theory" here means unexplicated believed-in explanations of behavior and other phenomena; in short, subjective images on "what makes the world tick." Widespread elements of tacit theories in respect to administrative reforms include, for instance, the belief that a merit civil service makes a lot of difference; the belief that civil servants are motivated by monetary incentives, by appeal to patriotism, etc.; a view of administration in which some components, with which one was personally involved, are regarded as important reality-shaping variables; prototype images of politicians and clients; and so on. What distinguishes all tacit theories is (a) by definition, that they are not subjected to the tests of explicit consideration; (b) that many of them are rejected by the persons who hold them, once they are explicated; and (c) that they lag behind available scientific findings, comparative knowledge, and conclusions of distilled experience. Therefore, this megapolicy dimension serves, first, to bring into the open at least some of the tacit theories underlying proposed reform plans, and, second, to try to improve them by self-consideration and by trying to relate them to explicated theories, to available knowledge, and to distilled experience.

10. Resources Availability

On a different level is the megapolicy dimension of resources available. Here, too, explication is needed and useful, to bring up for consideration the often unrealistic hidden assumptions concerning resources which will be available for the reform, or, still worse, to expose widespread lack of concern for many cost elements of a proposed reform. This applies not only to money, but—even more so—to qualified personnel, information, equipment, and so on.

In respect to this megapolicy dimension, some clear decisions are called for, concerning the resources to be allocated for the reform. Both indirect and direct costs must be taken into account and the time distribution of resources availability must be worked out, as important constraints on reform. While iteration may result in some revisions in available resources, more often constraints on resources are quite rigid, and clear establishment of reform budget ceilings will have strong influence on the reform plans. In particular, it may avoid sudden ruptures of reform activities, because the tacitly expected resources do not become available. True, sometimes explicit resources-availability megapolicies may prevent a reform which otherwise may have been executed through step-by-step allocations but I think that, all in all, more realistic administrative-reform planning will result in more cases of successful administrative reforms.

11. The Range of Reform Instruments

This last of the megapolicy dimensions to be discussed in this chapter sums up, in a sense, all other megapolicies, while adding to them an additional perspective. Rational reform planning means adoption of a mix of reform instruments which, within the given instruments, provides the highest probability of better approximating the overall dynamic reform goals. It is therefore in the selection of reform instruments and their setting that the megapolicies are transformed into reform plans and reform action. An essential requisite for selecting a preferable mix of reform instruments and of their settings is to work out first a list of available reform instruments with their main characteristics, in terms of benefits-costs. A distinct effort to develop a taxonomy and characterization of administrative-reform instruments as one of the megapolicy decisions is all the more necessary for three main reasons: (*a*) the tendency to ignore many available reform instruments because of tacit theories, limited information, and inertia; (*b*) the potential benefits of identification and invention of ignored or unknown reform istruments, some of which may prove to be very effective and efficient; and (*c*) the important feedback from the reform-instrument evaluation to other megapolicy dimensions, for instance, by showing the necessity to broaden reform boundaries to include additional sets of instruments within the domain of reform planning.

The last megapolicy dimension serves to re-emphasize the relations between policy sciences as a whole, administrative sciences research, and reform endeavours. The identification of policy instruments for directive human action is one of the main tasks of policy sciences. The evaluation of that subset of policy instruments which may be available for administrative reforms in terms of relevant benefits-costs belongs to administrative sciences. Reliable mappings of possible administrative-reform instruments with condition-sensitive evaluation of their benefits-costs (both each instrument by itself and in various mixes) will be very helpful in concrete administrative-reform endeavors.

Even in the present underdeveloped states of policy sciences and administrative sciences, the concept of administrative-reform megapolicies should be useful—as a sensitizer, as a heuristic aid, and as a guideline. This, I hope, has been demonstrated (though not proved) with the help of the eleven administrative-reform megapolicies discussed in this chapter. What is urgently needed is intensive study and research, which will permit elaboration of various megapolicies in terms of applicability, effectiveness, and efficiency under different conditions. For such prescription-oriented and policy-sciences-directed administrative sciences research, the concept of reform megapolicy may serve as a main focus.

This last part of the volume takes up what may well be considered the most important level of policy sciences, namely, the metapolicy level. Because of its concern with the operations of the policymaking system, the metapolicy level dominates policymaking on specific issues and megapolicymaking. Therefore, metapolicies deal with the most critical issues of the improvement of policymaking.

This part starts with a set of suggestions for the improvement of public policymaking in Israel, which illustrates some concerns of metapolicy. The second chapter presents in detail one metapolicy proposal which is of particular importance, namely, for the establishment of a policy research organization. The third and last chapter discusses broad issues of urban metapolicy, applying some of the main ideas presented throughout this volume to the context of urban affairs—thus suming up this volume within a specified context.

PART IX

Metapolicy

CHAPTER 26

Improvement of Public Policymaking in Israel: A Set of Suggestions

COMMENTS

This chapter presents twenty-three suggestions for the improvement of policymaking in Israel, organized in six sections. Summing up the findings of an extensive study carried on during 1953 to 1970, this set of proposals illustrates some of the range of possible metapolicy improvements, as applied to a particular country.

1. Improvement of Crisis Management

a. Past experience with crisis management should be studied as a basis for improvements. A structured crisis-management system should be designed, with special attention to the highest political levels and to the introduction of longer-range considerations into crisis decisionmaking.

b. Crisis exercises and crisis games should be conducted on the Cabinet and sub-Cabinet level—to run in the crisis management system, to aid in contingency planning, and to sensitize top policymakers to additional considerations and alternatives.

2. Improvement of Current Decisionmaking

a. Policy analysis and policy planning staffs should be established in the Prime Minister's Office, to deal with main superministerial issues.

b. Cabinet decisionmaking should be improved through suitable information input, briefing system, and supportive studies. Policy analysis memoranda should serve as background material for consideration of all major issues. A monitoring system to provide feedback should be established.

c. Introduction of the planning-programing-budgeting-system should be accelerated and combined with establishment of small planning and policy analysis units in all ministries. Those units should constitute a compact interdisciplinary staff, working on main policy and decision issues.

d. The establishment of policy research units should be encouraged in all components of the societal direction system (e.g., parties, trade unions, main municipalities).

e. The Knesset Committees should appoint professional staff and increasingly utilize expert testimony and opinions.

3. Improvement of Medium-Time-Range and Long-Time-Range Decisions

a. An Institute for Policy Analysis should be established, at which about 25 interdisciplinary scientists will engage in policy-oriented study of main policy issues. This institute should enjoy both independence in its professional work and access to government information and senior policymakers. Senior policy practitioners and academicians should participate in the work of this Institute.

b. The Economic Planning Authority should be transformed into a "National Planning Authority," dealing in an integrated way with economic, physical, and social planning. The professional composition of its staff should be suitably broadened.

c. Foreign policy and strategic planning (beyond the highly developed military level, which is not dealt with in this set of proposals) should be strengthened through establishment of a National Policy Planning Board, with a staff including both experienced practitioners and academicians.

d. The National Planning Authority and the National Policy Planning Board should operate within a reconstructed Prime Minister's Office and/or Cabinet Secretariat, and maintain close contact with the ministerial planning and analysis staffs. Its more basic and long-range work is to be based in part on studies prepared by the Institute for Policy Analysis.

e. Among the tasks of the National Planning Authority and the National Policy Planning Board is the preparation of alternative operational goals for the country for the year 1975. Among the tasks of the Institute for Policy Analysis is the preparation of alternative future images of Israel for the year 2000, with the help of various teams and panels of experts, politicians, senior officials, and public persons.

f. In all these activities—and also in the current decision-making-improvement activities—"brain trusts" should be intensely utilized, both on an individual basis and as organized groups. Suitable persons from abroad should be closely involved in some of these "brain trusts."

4. Improvement of Research and Information

a. The collection of information, in particular in respect to social issues, should be significantly improved. For these purposes, a social accounting system should be introduced and current opinions study should be strengthened.

b. Research and publications dealing with the problems of the country should be encouraged and supported. In particular, incentives should be provided to orient academic research toward national policy problems. Also, an independent periodical dealing with analysis of Israeli policy problems should be established.

5. Improvement of Policymaking Personnel

a. A new policy for developing the senior civil service should be designed, including the following elements: intense courses in policy sciences and policy-relevant areas, combined with personality training (e.g., T-group method); rotation within the government and between the government service and the public and private sectors; accelerated advancement for innovative and capable young entrants, together with early retirement for some others; short-term appointments to senior positions of university academicians, businessmen, etc.; and restructuring of recruitment for senior positions.

b. Elected politicians should be encouraged to study and develop through the granting of "sabbaticals" paid for by the public, the arrangement of special courses for politicians, and study tours.

c. Highly qualified personnel for policymaking positions should be provided by establishing graduate teaching programs in policy sciences at the universities, directing parts of behavioral sciences teaching toward policy advisory positions, and granting government fellowships for advanced graduate and postgraduate studies in these areas.

d. A National Policy College should be established to take over in a more comprehensive and effective way the functions of the former National Defense College. In particular, it should provide intense 6-week to 3-month seminars for senior officials, defense force officers, politicians, academicians, newspaper commentators, and similar policy-involved persons on national problems—emphasizing integrated and comprehensive analysis of defense, foreign, economic, and social problems.

e. Special learning opportunities should be provided to mass media professionals—such as correspondents and commentators—to get them acquainted with policy sciences and encourage better presentation of policy issues to the public.

6. Improvement of the Role of the Public in Policymaking

a. The teaching of civics, history, and social sciences in the schools should be reformed, to train pupils in information search, analysis, and position formulation. Special attention should be paid to study of current public issues in a way advancing the autonomous judgment capacities of the students. Teachers should be suitably trained and retrained.

b. Discussion of policy issues in the mass media of communication should be improved to provide the audience with deeper insights into the problems and a better understanding of the involved values, facts, interests, and alternatives.

c. Participation in decisionmaking should be encouraged, mainly on the community level and in work teams (on the lines of "overlapping management" instead of, or in addition to, distant representation).

Implementation Comments

a. Several of the proposed units and activities may be combined. In particular, a central Israeli Institute for Policy Analysis could combine the functions of the units discussed in sections 2a, 3a, parts of 3b, 3c, and 5d.

b. The total cost involved in the proposals is very small in comparison with potential benefits. In particular, the proposals for an Institute for Policy Analysis, a National Planning Authority, a National Policy Planning Board, Ministerial planning and policy analysis units, "brain trusts," and professional staff for the Knesset Committees would not involve more than the equivalent of about 100 full-time professionals per year.

c. The various proposals are synergetically related, but they can and should be implemented by stages. Appropriate first steps should include (1) establishment of an Israeli Institute for Policy Analysis and (2) establishment of teaching and training programs in policy sciences at one of the universities.

CHAPTER 27

The Israeli Institute for Policy Analysis: A Proposal[1]

COMMENTS

Policy research organizations are a main modern invention in government, directed at improving symbiosis between power and knowledge.[2] Establishment of policy research organizations is one of the main recommendations which seem well supported already at the present underdeveloped stage of policy sciences. The detailed features of policy research organizations must be adjusted to the characteristics and conditions of each country and its specific needs; but the basic features of policy research organizations are quite universal, as they result from the very nature and functions of applied policy sciences.

This chapter includes a revised English version of a proposal prepared by the author at the request of the late Prime Minister of Israel, Mr. Levi Eshkol, and released for publication in August 1967. More detailed proposals were prepared and submitted at later dates; but the version presented here brings out the more universal features of policy research organizations, while indicating some of the problems of adjusting these features to specific conditions.

In February 1971 this proposal was in principle realized, through establishment of a Policy Analysis Division in the World Institute, Jerusalem.

Introduction

1. The proposal to establish an *Israeli Institute for Policy Analysis* constitutes an attempt to apply to Israel modern knowledge and experience on independent policy research organizations as contributors to better public policymaking. The development of new knowledge and methods which can help in better policymaking on complex issues requires new institutional arrangements for integrating such knowledge and methods into actual policymaking. One of the important structural innovations directed at applying such knowledge and methods to complex policy issues are "think tanks," which specialize in interdisciplinary application of policy sciences to medium-

[1] An earlier version of this proposal was published in *Civilizations* 17, no. 4 (1967): 435-441.
[2] For an excellent discussion, see Roger E. Levien, *Independent Policy Analysis Organizations—A Major Social Invention* (Santa Monica, Calif.: The Rand Corporation, P-4231, November 1969).

285

range and long-range problems. Israel urgently needs such an organization to help in handling the increasingly complex and difficult problems facing the country in the foreseeable future.

2. In this preliminary memorandum, no definite position is taken with regard to the preferable structural setup for the proposed institute. Mention is merely made of several alternatives together with the principal criteria that should determine the choice between these alternatives. Neither does this memorandum contain budgetary estimates, nor does it deal with staffing problems. Its principal purpose is to present in outline a proposal for discussion, consideration, and decision in principle. Detailed examination of operational questions would, therefore, be premature.

3. It should be pointed out that the activation and running-in of an Israeli Institute for Policy Analysis, as proposed in the fallowing, is a difficult undertaking and requires a great deal of time. Personally, I am convinced that the establishment of the proposed Institute will yield high returns to Israel in terms of contributions to improved policymaking. However, no meaningful analysis or significant recommendations should be expected before the professional staff have undergone a period of acclimatization and training and have acquired experience in the exploration of several subjects. The period of running-in depends on the timing of the establishment of the Institute and varies from one subject to another according to their degrees of novelty, complexity, and difficulty. Even under very favorable conditions, about a one-year lead time may be required before significant findings can be arrived at or meaningful recommendations can be offered. Speed is therefore imperative if the potential outputs of an Israeli Institute for Policy Analysis are regarded as important.

Main Purposes

4. The main purpose of the Israeli Institute for Policy Analysis is to intensify the application of scientific knowledge to the improvement of public policymaking in Israel. Its main function is research into policy issues of importance to Israel and offering of contributions to the improvement of policymaking on those issues by means of redefinition of issues, search for new alternatives, better consideration of the future, fuller examination of consequences, careful preparations of policy analyses, and formulation of recommendations.

5. Secondary objectives include the following:

a. Advanced training for policy analysts and for policy practitioners (both Israeli and possibly foreign, especially from modernizing countries), by their inclusion in mixed work teams and by special workshops, seminars, and briefings.

b. Contributions to knowledge in policy sciences.

c. Cooperation with modernizing countries and provision of help in analyzing some of their main policy issues.

d. Participation in international policy studies in which Israel is interested and can make a significant contribution.

6. The objectives mentioned above reinforce one another. For instance, the establishment of mixed work teams of scientists and policy practitioners is simultaneously an important method for applied policy research and a preferred method in advanced training for public officials. Also, it is desirable that the Institute should work, in part, on subjects of importance both for Israel and for other countries, where the exchange of experience can be of mutual benefit.

7. The proposed Israeli Institute for Policy Analysis may be able to achieve further important pay-offs by influencing political argumentation and the frames of reference of public debate, by encouraging policy research by other organizations, by stimulating export of knowledge, and so forth. These are additional expected benefits which strengthen the case for the establishment of the proposed Institute.

Principal Methods of Operation and Organization

8. The proposed Israeli Institute for Policy Analysis will employ methods quite unlike those used by existing research and consultant bodies in Israel. Without going into details, five main characteristics of these methods should be mentioned here:

a. In the work of the Institute, there will be far-reaching integration between *pure* knowledge and *applied* knowledge. A main criterion of policy sciences is its potential contribution to actual policymaking, while the study of real policy issues is one of the main sources of relevant knowledge (in addition to tacit sources of knowledge, contemplation, and rigorous empirical research).

b. The Institute's work is of an interdisciplinary nature, its aim being to improve policymaking by using all fields of knowledge likely to make a substantial or methodological contribution. The main fields of knowledge essential for the Institute's work include (not necessarily in order of priority) the following: psychology, sociology, economics, political science, geography, demography, mathematics and statistics, law, some of the natural sciences (depending on the subject of research), parts of history (depending on the subject of research), and parts of philosophy (mainly for the examination of the value sensitivity of various policy alternatives). Many of the modern interdisciplines are basic to the work of the Institute, such as operations research, decision theory, organization theory, systems analysis, systems engineering, conflict theory, futures studies, and information theory. Policy sciences constitutes the framework in which the contributions of these different disciplines and their application to policy issues is to be integrated and further developed.

c. In the work of the Institute, there will be close contact and mixture between scientists and experienced policy practitioners in order to achieve a synthesis between scientific knowledge on the one hand and tacit knowledge on the other.

d. There will be a large measure of interdependence between individual and team studies by the permanent staff; continuous staff rotations and development; and instruction and training of senior policy practitioners and advanced students attached to the Institute for fixed terms.

e. The Institute engages in advanced thinking, analysis, and paper study. It uses complex methods, such as gaming and Delphi studies and requires advanced computation facilities; but the Institute does not engage directly in large field studies, laboratory experiments, and the like, subcontracting them, when necessary, to other research organizations.

9. The organization of the Institute must be adjusted to its functions and its characteristics. It is essential that the permanent staff should number at least about twenty-five full-time professionals and scientists. (A limited number of positions at the Institute can perhaps be combined with regular university and academic teaching appointments.) These professionals and scientists should represent the main fields of knowledge enumerated in paragraph 8b. Additional professional and scientific manpower will be employed on a part-time basis for defined projects, or as consultants. In addition, there will be attached to the Institute on a full-time and fixed-term basis a number of policy practitioners and advanced students. (The two latter categories will also be able to attend selected courses at institutes of higher learning during their work in the Institute.) The Institute will further enlist the help of national and international brain trusts, panels, discussion groups, and similar organs. In respect to specific studies, the Institute may work in cooperation with other organizations, subcontracting to them part of the study, setting up mixed teams, etc.

10. As to working arrangements at the Institute, I wish to stress one basic principle, namely, the need for maximum flexibility. Applied policy research and policy analysis differ from traditional academic or other research activities. This is evident from the characteristics mentioned previously. It is, therefore, imperative that the Institute's work should not be fettered by traditions incompatible with its tasks and objectives.

The Scope of Activity and Illustrative Subjects

11. The scope of activity of the proposed Institute comprises the entire range of public policymaking and all policy issues which, because of their complexity, importance, and character, can be treated and improved through

the application of the orientations, frames of mind, and methods of policy sciences and policy analysis. The choice of subjects for research depends on the size of the staff, their knowledge, and their interests, and on the priority given to various subjects by the clientele (mainly the government). It is important that the order of priority should, in part, be independently assessed by the Institute, and that the Institute should be free to redefine the subjects of study submitted to it by the clientele.

12. To explain better the functions of the proposed Institute, I list here five illustrative policy issues suitable for study by the proposed Israeli Institute for Policy Analysis:

a. Demographic policy. This subject includes the problems of birth rate, changes in the age composition of the population and the problems of urbanization and of regional population dispersal. In its Israeli context, this subject includes also (1) the population dispersal policy, with a calculation of its cost and an explicit consideration of alternatives with regard to the timing of the stages of this policy, taking into account economic and political feasibility; and (2) the immigration policy and some aspects of family planning and birth rates.

b. Research and Development (R&D) policy. Most of the literature and present experience in the field of Research and Development policy refer to large countries, particularly the United States. This knowledge is not directly applicable to small countries. This is a problem with which Israel is wrestling a great deal. Here, special attention must be paid to problems of technological forecasting and predictions of markets.

c. Policy for the encouragement of national culture. Many countries (including modernization countries on the one hand and some of the Scandinavian countries, for instance, on the other) find it difficult to formulate a policy for the encouragement of the development of local culture (literature, poetry, cinema, drama, art, etc.). This problem is of the greatest importance for Israel and is nearly completely untouched by research and analysis.

d. Administrative policies adjusted to accelerated and directed social change. Most administrative policies in Israel are partly based on policies taken over from the Western countries; and partly they are a patchwork of improvisations designed under the heavy pressure of acute current problems. A substantial part of the difficulties encountered in accelerated social change stems to some degree from the unsuitability of these administrative policies to the new tasks and the real conditions. The proposed study aims at developing better patterns for governmental administrative policies fitting conditions of accelerated and directed social change in Israel.

e. Social accounting system. Israel faces serious difficulties in social policy-making, one of the reasons being the absence of tools comparable to economic national accounting, in respect to social aspects of society. Leaning on recent work in other countries, an important task for the proposed Institute could be the design of a social accounting system meeting the needs of social policy-making in Israel.

14. The aforementioned five subjects are merely examples, intended to demonstrate the broad field of activity of the proposed Israeli Institute for Policy Analysis. Probably some of these subjects will turn out to be unsuitable, while others, which I have not listed (including some dealing with foreign affairs and strategy) will be found more suitable. Also, the proposed Institute may devote some of its time (but not more than about 25 percent) to help the shorter-range critical policy issues facing Israel.

Organizational Setup

15. As stated above, this preliminary proposal is not intended to lay down detailed specifications for the institutional setup and the organizational location of the proposed Institute. There are a number of possibilities, such as the following:

a. An independent nonprofit institute, operating in rather close contact with the Government (on the model of The Rand Corporation in the United States) or having a more private status with a more mixed clientele (as the Hudson Institute in the United States).

b. A governmental institute, enjoying much independence in its current work (such as the Swedish Defense Research Institute).

c. An interuniversity institute, maintained by a number of institutions of higher learning (such as the Institute for Defense Analyses in the United States).

d. An institute integrated with the activities of and owned by one of the institutions of higher learning (such as the Syracuse University Research Corporation).

There are additional possible forms and combinations, which may better suit Israel's conditions, such as a government corporation with a public board of directors.

16. A choice between the various alternatives necessitates a detailed comparison of advantages and disadvantages, which is beyond the limits of this preliminary proposal. I shall, therefore, restrict myself here to laying down the four main criteria for the evaluation of the alternatives and selection of the preferred organizational setup for the proposed Institute:

a. The organizational setup should assure professional independence so as to minimize the dangers of adjustment of subject matters, analyses, findings, and recommendations to the wishes of the clientele or other interests.

b. The organizational setup should assure relationships of mutual trust between the various bodies engaged in policymaking and the Institute, so as to enable access to necessary data and to increase the probability of impact on actual policymaking.

c. The organizational setup should assure close mutual relations and cooperation with other scientific and research institutions and with institutes of higher learning, so as to permit and encourage fullest use of the country's scientific and professional potential.

d. The organizational setup should assure sufficient administrative independence from the Government and from academic institutions alike, so as to permit creation of conditions which will draw top-quality personnel to the Institute and permit it to develop its unique functions and orientations without interference by rigid Government procedure on one hand and by departmental university traditions on the other.

It is important to give careful thought to the organizational setup of the proposed Institute so that it should satisfy a preferred mix of these four criteria. At the same time, it is clear that the success of the Institute will, in many respects, depend more on the quality of its staff, their personal and professional characteristics, and their commitment than on the formal organizational basis of the Institute. One of the essential conditions for success is, therefore, meticulous care in the selection of the staff members.

CHAPTER 28

Urban Metapolicy and Urban Education[1]

COMMENTS

This last chapter repeats and sums up, within the urban context, the main ideas presented in this book. It pays particular attention to innovations in education which are essential for the realization of some suggestions for better metapolicies particularly relevant to the maintenance and reinforcement of democracy.

I hope by now the reader is equipped to reconsider the ideas presented first in Chapter 1 and to decide on his personal response to the challenge of policy sciences.

A Short Appraisal of Urban Policymaking

"Urban problems"—however ill-defined this concept may be[2]—are one of the main concerns of modern society. The transition to a "saturated society," in which many of the material and service necessities of life become free goods, the population growth, anticipated innovations in technology, and many of the possible (though unpredictable) transformations in culture and values—all will result in urban configurations and urban problems even more difficult to manage and resolve than the contemporary ones. Therefore, when we compare our incapacities to handle present urban issues with the problems of urban conglomerates of tomorrow, which will be more difficult by several orders of magnitude, one cannot but be somewhat afraid about the future.

Two typical reactions to present and expected problems are (1) to try to deal with them by pushing harder for solutions which are supposed to have

[1]This chapter is based on an article first published in *Educational Technology* 10, no. 9 (September 1970): 15-21. Copyright Educational Technology Inc.

[2]My impression is that the term *urban problems* is used as referring to a vague cluster of social problems, with different emphasis on various issues—depending on the interests of the user. Even in its narrower uses, the term *urban problems* is significantly broader than the term *city problems,* though there is much overlapping between them. For the purposes of this chapter, I will use the term *urban problems* without further definitions. My main jusification for doing so is that my analysis and conclusions are quite insensitive to various uses and meanings of that term.

292

work in the past (e.g., more police in the streets to control crime), and (2) to look for new ideas in respect to concrete and acute problems faced today. But very little is done to improve urban policymaking and decision-making capabilities, so as to be better able to handle dynamic problems and changing situations.

The search for better solutions to present problems is both essential and useful, and much more needs to be done to move from "muddling through" to explicit policy innovations. But I think that efforts limited to resolving defined problems are doomed unless they are accompanied by far-reaching attempts to improve the urban policymaking system (which includes components in all levels of government—federal, state, and local—as well as special interest groups, the local communities, etc.). The case for this rests mainly on three reasons:

1. Innovative policy proposals have little chance of being carefully considered, adopted, implemented, and revised unless the urban policymaking system develops new capacities for creativity, policy analysis, implementation, and feedback. Also required are significant relaxations of present constraints on policies, including, in particular, political and organizational constraints. New patterns of decisionmaking are needed which in turn require changes in most of the elements of the urban policymaking system—including personnel, structure, rules of the game, equipment, and, perhaps most important of all, policymaking culture.

2. Many problems can be better resolved before they are made visible by assuming crises dimensions. Therefore, the prediction of problems and the allocation of resources to treatment of future problems are needed, requiring in turn changes in urban policymaking so as to make it more future-sensitive.

3. For many present and expected problems no useful policies can be identified through contemporary policymaking knowledge. What is required, therefore, are new types of policy knowledge, policy research, policy invention, and policy professionals.

Urban planning does little to change the picture. To be more exact, there exists no urban planning, but only city planning—which is something quite different. Not only is city planning constrained by the above-mentioned limitations of contemporary urban policymaking as a whole, but it suffers from a number of additional inadequacies of its own, such as the following:

1. Strong orientation to the physical features of cities, despite much lip service to more comprehensive approaches. Social problems in particular are ignored in most real-life city planning.

2. Poorness in policy instruments. Thus, despite recognized extreme weaknesses, "master plans" and zoning continue to be regarded as major policy instruments of city planning.

3. Far-reaching isolation from most facets of urban policymaking, includ-

ing nearly all acute problems, the treatment of which in fact significantly shapes urban futures. Attempts to tie in city planning with on-going decision-making through PPBS have as yet achieved very little.

4. Value-loadedness. Most city planners not only prefer one image of "ideal city"[3] over all others, but regard their preference as science-based; and they therefore avoid explicit value-sensitivity testing. The recent undermining of many "ideal city" images causes much bewilderment and heart-searching, but as yet has contributed little to a clearer conception of the roles of city planning in relation to urban policymaking and in respect to value judgments.

Most, if not all, of these weaknesses are recognized by some more advanced city-planning scholars and practitioners, who slowly move toward a conception of urban planning in the full sense of that term. But, as yet, actual city planning is little influenced by the newer ideas and it is hard to see how even a sophisticated urban planning approach could have significant impacts within the present urban policymaking system.

To sum up my short appraisal of contemporary urban policymaking, I see the main problem not as one of weaknesses of present urban policies alone. I think the problem is a more fundamental one: the present urban policymaking system is incapable of handling present and future urban issues. Not only do we not have an urban policy,[4] but a good urban policy cannot be formulated and implemented without redesign of the urban policymaking system.

In short, my main thesis is that in order successfully to face urban problems, we must innovate metapolicies, that is, policies on how to make policies.

Approaches to Urban Metapolicy

Governmental reform is not a new idea and there has been quite some talk in the United States on required adjustments in public institutions to meet urban problems[5], and even some action in this direction[6]. But the idea of

[3]For an illuminating discussion of "ideal cities," see C. A. O. van Nieuwenhuijze, "The Ideal City or the Varieties of Metasocial Experience: A Typology," in C. A. O. van Nieuwenhuijze, *The Nation and the Ideal City* (The Hague: Mouton, 1966), pp. 74-148.

[4]Compare Daniel P. Moynihan, "Toward a National Urban Policy," *The Public Interest,* no. 17 (Fall 1969), pp. 3-20.

[5]E.g., see Theodore J. Lowi, *The End of Liberalism: Ideology, Policy, and the Crisis of Public Authority* (New York: Norton, 1969); and Robert Wood, "When Government Works," *The Public Interest,* no. 18 (Winter 1970), pp. 39-51.

[6]For instance, establishment of the Urban Institute and of the Domestic Council in the White House.

metapolicy goes beyond individual reform proposals. Its basic framework is a systems view of policymaking. Policymaking is regarded as an aggregative process in which a large number of different units interact in a variety of part-stabilized but open-ended modes. In other words, urban policy is made by a system, the urban policymaking system (which is very closely related to the public policymaking system, as urban policy is related to public national policy).

This system is a dynamic, open, non-steady-state and includes a large variety of different and changing multirole components interconnected in different degrees and through a multiplicity of channels; it is closely interwoven and overlapping with other policymaking systems and with social macro-systems (e.g., the production system, the demographic-ecological system, the technological and knowledge system, and the cultural system), and it behaves in ways which defy detailed modeling.

Even such a very simple systems perspective of urban policymaking leads to three important improvement-relevant conclusions:

1. As urban policy is a product of complex interactions between a large number of various types of components, similar changes in the output (or similar "equifinal states") can be achieved through many alternative variations in the components. This means, for our purposes, that different combinations of a variety of improvements may be equally useful in achieving equivalent changes in the quality of policymaking. This is a very helpful conclusion, because it permits us to pick out of a large repertoire of potentially effective improvements those which are more feasible under changing political and social conditions. This view also emphasizes the wide-open nature of any search for improvement suggestions: there is, in principle, unlimited scope for adventurous thinking and invention.

2. A less optimistic implication of a systems view of urban policymaking is that improvements must reach a critical mass in order to influence the aggregative outputs of the system. Improvements which do not reach the relevant impact thresholds will, at best, be neutralized by countervailing adjustments of other components (e.g., a new urban planning method may be reacted to in a way that makes it an empty ritual). At worst, these improvements may in fact diminish the quality of overall urban policy (e.g., through a possible boomerang effect, reducing belief in the capacity of human intelligence, with the chance of retreat to some types of mysticism, leader ideology, etc., or by implementing wrong policies more "efficiently," and thus reducing an important social protective mechanism—inefficiency as diminishing the dangers of implementation of wrong decisions and as permitting slow and tacit learning).

3. The third, and again optimistic, implication of a systems view of urban policymaking is that, thanks to the interactions between different system com-

ponents, it may be possible to achieve the threshold of overall system output effects through a combination of carefully selected changes in important sub-components, each one of which by itself is incremental. In other words, a set of incremental changes can in the aggregate result in far-reaching system output changes. Furthermore, because we are speaking about changes in the urban policymaking system, there may be a good chance that a set of relatively minor and quite incremental changes in the urban policymaking system will permit—through multiplier effects—extensive innovations in the specific policies made by that system. This possibility is of much practical importance, because of the much greater feasibility of incremental change than of radical change in United States urban politics (though I think the readiness to innovate is increasing by step-level functions, as a result of shock effects of highly perceived crises symptoms).

The systematic design, analysis, and evaluation of policymaking-system improvements is the main subject of metapolicy. Urban metapolicy is there-fore concerned with improving the urban policymaking system. Such improve-ments involve all dimensions of the urban policymaking system, including environment, inputs, policy knowledge, personnel, structure, process pat-terns and stipulated output.

Let me concretize the idea of innovative urban metapolicy with a number of illustrative interrelated ideas:

1. Innovative policy research on urban problems must be encouraged, as a part of emerging policy sciences. This involves novel research methods (such as social experimentation), novel research tools (e.g., acceptance of tacit knowledge of politicians and senior executives as an important source of knowledge), and novel research structures (e.g., inter-disciplinary policy-oriented teams). Also necessary are the study and utilization of experience with urban problems in other countries. Especially relevant are European and Japanese experiences, which are very little known in the United States. A main aim of such urban policy research should be development of an overall conception of urban policy, which can be of much help, initially by operationalizing the meaning of "urban problems" and then by providing heuristic search patterns for possible resolutions.[7]

---

[7]The absence of any integrated conception of urban policy in the United States is not surprising, but is very disturbing. This omission is well demonstrated by the differences between foreign affairs and urban affairs. Foreign affairs are heterogenous and multi-dimensional; nevertheless, some integrating conceptions exist, as well illustrated in President Nixon's First and Second Annual Foreign Affairs Messages. But were one to decide to put together an Annual Social State of the Nation, it would have to be either very eclectic or very abstract—because even a useable concept package for urban affairs does not exist. Also, relatively simple issues, such as the relation between the "urban problems" cluster and the emerging "environmental problems" cluster, are quite unexplored.

2. New urban policy tools, ranging from monitoring and information processing tools to new policy instruments, must be invented and developed. Such tools and instruments may include, for instance, urban indicator systems, to permit early identification of problems and to encourage feedback on policy results; cable television, to provide multiple communication channels with citizens; home computer consoles, for systematic contingency opinion polling; differential scheduling of work hours, weekend days, and holidays, to deal with rush-hour and rush-day traffic; and many more.

3. The urban policymaking system must be enabled to engage in megapolicymaking in respect to basic assumptions, problem perceptions, value hierarchy, strategies, etc. Thus, explicit megapolicies (including mixed megapolicies) are needed on the following issues, among others: degrees and locations of acceptable innovations in policies; extent of risk to be accepted in policies and choice between a maximax posture and/or maximin posture and/or min-avoidance posture;[8] preferable mix among comprehensive policies, narrow-issue oriented policies, and shock policies (which aim at breakthroughs accompanied by temporary disequilibration); and preferable mix among policies oriented toward concrete goals, toward a number of defined future options, and/or toward building up resources better to achieve as yet undefined goals in the future. Such megapolicy decisions in turn require a variety of methodological innovations, such as construction of alternative comprehensive urban futures and policy analysis networks.

4. New institutions must be designed and established as influential components of the urban policymaking system. Especially urgent is the need for "think-tank" research institutes to work specifically on urban policy issues. The short experience of The New York City Rand Institute demonstrates the importance of such services for urban government and their difficulties to survive contemporary urban politics. Establishment of The Urban Institute is another important step in this direction. But a whole set of such institutes to serve all centers of urban policymaking is required. Other possible institutional innovations include Lookout Institutions for early identification of emerging problems, and allocation of urban policy research roles to universities.

5. Urban policymaking personnel must be improved. This includes, for instance, intense efforts to improve qualifications of urban politicians. Thus, urban politicians should be encouraged to participate in courses and seminars in policy sciences, to be designed for this purpose. Also needed is reform of urban senior civil service policy, including requirements for better qualifications, encouragement of rotation with other governments and with business, and incentives to draw top-quality candidates. More important are

[8]As already explained, I use the term *min-avoidance* to refer to policies directed at avoiding the worst of all possible situations.

activities to train presently nonexisting urban policy scientists and urban policy professionals. All this involves the relations between urban metapolicy and urban education, to which I will return soon.

6. Also closely related to urban education is another main direction of urban metapolicy improvement, namely, advancement of citizen participation in urban policymaking. Here, modern technology may be very helpful, by providing tools for a much better presentation of urban issues before the public (e.g., policy analyses of controversial issues on television and citizen education through active participation in urban games through cable television) and for more intense involvement of the public in decisionmaking (e.g., as already mentioned, systematic opinion polling with the help of home computer consoles).

Having clarified the concept of metapolicy, we are now ready to take up our next and final subject, which I already touched upon in the last two metapolicy directives—namely, some relations between urban education and urban metapolicy.

Urban Education and Urban Metapolicy

One rather obvious application of our general analysis to education concerns the necessity for reform of the urban educational policymaking subsystem of the urban policymaking system, as a requisite for improving urban educational policies. All our analysis on the dependency of better policies on improved metapolicy applies to education, as do the various illustrations of needed metapolicy directions. Some adjustments are necessary to meet the special characteristics of educational policymaking.[9] But the general conclusion is I think quite clear without further details: the urban educational policymaking subsystem must be improved through innovative metapolicy, as a condiiton for design, evaluation, adoption, and implementation of urban educational policies that can meet contemporary and future needs.

One point that should be emphasized is that improvement of the urban educational policymaking subsystem cannot take place in isolation. Because of the strong interconnections and overlappings between the urban educational policymaking subsystem and the urban policymaking system as a whole, the first cannot be changed without changes in the latter. Furthermore, because of the diffuse nature of education and the multiple forms of educational institutions,[10] any sharp distinction between education and other policy issues is a doubtful one. Education constitutes a main policy instrument for the achievement of nearly all urban policy goals, and the states of

[9]See Rachel Elboim-Dror, "Some Characteristics of the Education Policy Formation System," *Policy Sciences* 1, no. 2 (Summer 1970): 231-53.

[10]See Michael Marien, *The Education Complex: Emergence and Future of a Macro-System* (New York: Free Press, 1971, in press).

nearly all aspects of urban life influence urban education. Therefore, educational policies must be closely fused with urban policies as a whole; and the educational policymaking subsystem must be considered and improved as an integral part of the urban policymaking system.

Less obvious are the implications of our analysis for the functions of urban education as an essential instrument of metapolicy innovations. This is still a very neglected subject. Let me therefore point out a few main directions of changes in urban education required in order to reform the urban policymaking system. Such changes are needed on at least five levels:

1. The education of adults for more active roles in urban policymaking.
2. The preparation of children for even more active future roles in urban policymaking.
3. The training and retraining of urban policy practitioners for new patterns of urban policymaking.
4. The training of new types of urban policy professionals.
5. The development of urban policy scientists.

I will discuss these five levels one by one.

1. *The education of adults for more active roles in urban policymaking.* I already mentioned the intensification of citizen participation in urban policymaking as one of the directions of urban metapolicy improvement. But in order for increasing citizen participation to constitute in fact an improvement, changes in the quality of that participation are needed. At the very least are needed more knowledge of urban problems, better understanding of the interrelations between different issues and various resolutions, and fuller realization of the longer-range consequences of different alternatives. Also highly desirable are better value explication and sensitivity to value trade-offs, increased propensities to innovate, and capacities to face uncertainty.

The slogan of "enlightened citizen" as a requisite of democracy has been with us for too long to be taken seriously. Nevertheless, increasing demands for citizen participation based on both ideological reasons and functional needs combine to make "citizen enlightenment" a hard necessity. Indeed, because of the growing complexity of urban issues, increased quality of citizen contributions to urban policies is essential in order to preserve the present level of citizen participation in urban policymaking. In other words, if the quality of citizen inputs into urban policymaking remains as it is now, meritocracy may well become the only chance for survival. Therefore, building up the policy-contribution capacity of citizens is essential for continuous viability of urban democracy.

This is the challenge facing adult education from the point of view of urban metapolicy. When we add the many other reasons making adult education into an increasingly important social and individual activity (such as learning as a main leisure-time pursuit), then we arrive at a really first-class challenge for adult education. To meet this challenge, radical novadesign of urban education is required.

To illustrate, let me mention these main plausible directions of novadesign of urban adult education:

a. The mass media of communication must develop new formats for presenting and analyzing public issues in ways conductive for informed individual opinions formation. For instance, policy issues should be presented in the form of policy analysis networks, with clear alternatives, explicit sensitivity analysis, uncertainty explication, and assumption visibility. Present techniques are adequate for presentation of such programs on television in ways which combine audience appeal with improvement of citizen comprehensions of complex issues.

b. Training tools which are simultaneously interesting and beneficial must be developed. Such tools include, for instance, cases, projects, urban games, and individual policy-exploration programs. In particular, urban games and individual policy-exploration programs are very promising. Based on computers and brought to each house through cable television and home computer consoles, suitable games and policy-exploration programs can combine education for better urban policymaking with inputs into urban policymaking—while also providing fascinating leisure-time activities. (The same equipment can serve other multiple purposes in respect to broad educational goals, urban metapolicy improvements, leisure-time use, communication, etc., thus justifying their costs.)

c. Incentive for participation in policy-oriented educational activities must be provided. Hopefully, increased opportunities to participate in urban policymaking together with availability of clearly relevant learning opportunities will provide basic motivation. This may be the case all the more because of the possibility—illustrated by the proposed techniques—to combine the useful with the attractive. But additional incentives may be necessary. Competitive games and exercises may provide one set of incentives; public attention and dramatization may provide a second set of incentives. If this does not work out, reservation of some special opportunities to participate in urban policymaking (other than the basic rights of voting, expression of opinion, etc., reserved of course for all) for those who do undergo a set of learning activities might prove necessary in some circumstances in the longer run. But adoption of suitable programs in schools—as soon discussed—should make such distasteful distinctions unnecessary.

These are only some illustrations which point out the possibility for redesign of urban education to serve, *inter alia,* the needs of increasing citizen participation in urban policymaking. This is a problem in need of much research and creativity.

2. *The preparation of children for future roles in urban policymaking.* On a more fundamental level, preparation for increased participation in urban policymaking must take place before maturation. The best location to prepare the citizen for increased policymaking roles is in school, when the necessary knowledge and capacities should be developed as a basic part of the equipment needed by every citizen in a modern urban democratic society.

The necessary knowledge to be conveyed and capacities to be developed at school include, among others, some knowledge and understanding of the urban system and of urban dynamics; a feel for alternative urban futures; the ability to handle uncertainty and probabilities; basic skills in logic and semantics; an understanding of the elements of policy analysis and the capacity to handle problems with the help of policy analysis networks; a tolerance of ambiguity; an appreciation of the main concepts of behavioral sciences, economics, and decision theory and their application to urban issues; and the ability to search for information on new problems and issues and absorb that information within one's frame of appreciation.

This is a formidable list which may look prohibitive, unless we bear in mind that no technical skills and professional knowledge are aimed at. Some familiarity with fundamental concepts, some appreciation of their use, and, most important of all, some skill in application of the knowledge and concepts to concrete issues as a main mode for making up one's mind—this is all that is aimed at.

Even so, this is an ambitious program which can only be approximated through far-reaching changes in school teaching. Much of the required knowledge and capacity should be developed through new approaches and novel teaching methods in traditional subjects. Thus, the study of history should include the history of urban life, should be problem oriented, and should be supplemented by treatment of alternative urban futures. As another illustration, mathematics should be taught as a problem-solving approach, with emphasis on probability theory, Boolean algebra, and theory of games. Some new subjects also have to be added, devoted explicitly to urban problems and policy analyses. In the new subjects and in the new contents of the traditional subjects, new teaching methods play a major role. Such new teaching methods include, for instance, gaming, computer interaction, and internships. Existing methods such as projects and essays can also be very useful, if suitably adjusted.

These few pointers provide no solution to the nearly insurmountable difficulties of reforming school education, which are beyond both my competence and the scope of this paper. But I do want to emphasize that preparation of the future citizen for his future roles in urban policymaking while still in school is essential for managing the urban clusters of tomorrow democratically. This is only one of many demands upon school education resulting from the changing patterns of urbanism, but it is a demand deeply rooted in the requisites of improved urban metapolicy.

3. *The training and retraining of urban policy practitioners.* The need to train and retrain urban policy practitioners for the changing requirements of urban policymaking is a clear and straightforward one, which would not require much elaboration were it not for the taboos surrounding parts of it.

The need to re-equip urban civil servants is more and more recognized. With changes in the main functions of urban management from administrative efficiency to urban problem solution and directed social change, the classic contents and skills of public administration become relatively less important (though they should not be forgotten). Instead, policy sciences, applied behavioral sciences, and modern organization theory must be the foundations for urban management. Even though it is a hard and slow process, suitable changes do go on at universities, at new schools for urban affairs, at redesigned schools of public administration, and at schools of management. These changes can be expected to take care of training and retraining urban civil servants (not including policy analysts), though this trend should be accelerated.

The situation is completely different in respect to the most important component of urban policy practitioners and of the urban policymaking system as a whole, namely urban politicians. As a result of naive misunderstandings of democratic theory and of institutional carry-over from simpler periods, the idea that elected politicians ipso facto of their election are qualified (in addition to being legitimized) to fulfill crucial roles in policymaking is usually accepted without questioning. This is a wrong conclusion, ideologically as well as factually.

Ideologically, democracy does imply that candidates do not have to pass any educational qualification test and that every person duly elected is legitimately entitled to exercise all the prerogatives of office. But there is no reason in democratic ideology for ignoring the need that politicians be suitably qualified and for abstaining from establishing institutions to encourage politicians to develop the necessary knowledge and capacities. Factually, the dangers of politicians either overrelying on experts and meritocrats or of underutilizing modern knowledge, as a result of lacking sufficient knowledge and capacities to correctly utilize systematic knowledge and structured rationality, are obvious today. These dangers will be aggravated in the future when both relevant knowledge and problems are even more complex and difficult to handle.

My conclusion, therefore, is that improvement of politicians through learning is essential (though, by itself, insufficient) for qualifying them to handle present and future urban problems. The need can be handled within the tenets of democracy, if we are innovative enough in designing suitable institutions. In particular, needed are special courses, seminars, and curricula for politicians, ranging from one week to a year, devoted to conveying to politicians appreciation, knowledge, and skills in policy sciences applied to urban issues.[11] While politicians cannot and should not be forced to participate, better politicians will welcome short and well-designed seminars which may help them in fulfilling their duties. At the same time, sabbatical leave for politicians to engage in longer courses of study, paid for by the public, should become universal. Hopefully, participation in courses and training will be recognized by the electorate as desirable, thus providing a powerful incentive for politicians who are looking, as they should, for votes.

Here, some synergetic relations between different proposals become visible, namely, the interdependence between adult education for better urban policymaking, the preparation of pupils for future participation in urban policymaking, and popular support for policy relevant studies by politicians. But let me wait with further emphasis of the mutually reinforcing bonds between various policy-oriented changes in urban education till we examine the training of new types of urban policy professionals and the development of urban policy scientists.

4 and 5. *The training of new types of urban policy professions and the development of urban policy scientists.* The development of reliable policy sciences knowledge applied to urban issues is a precondition for all other proposed improvements both of urban metapolicy and of urban policy-relevant education. Only reliable and relevant policy sciences knowledge can serve as a basis for better urban metapolicies and for urban policy-relevant teaching material. To develop policy sciences systematically on a massive scale, a new generation of scholars and researchers are needed who avoid the trained incapacities of existing disciplines and are able to work out the innovative paradigms of policy sciences. And in order to apply policy sciences to concrete urban metapolicy and urban policy problems, a new profession of urban policy analysts is necessary to fill new roles in the urban policymaking system.

It is convenient to discuss the education of policy sciences scholars and of policy analysis professionals together, because (*a*) there should be no clear distinction between these two roles, as movement between and fusion of abstract research and concrete applications is among the specific characteristics of policy sciences; and (*b*) similar innovative academic arrangements are necessary for both of them. What is required are teaching programs on the postgraduate level which are characterized by the following

---

[11]Special institutes providing short courses to elected urban politicians exist in some countries. The *Kommunskolan* in Sweden is a good illustration.

features[12]: (1) an interdisciplinary basis, with special emphasis on decision theory on one hand and behavioral sciences on the other; (2) strong emphasis on training through applied work, to develop capacity to transform abstract knowledge into concrete recommendations and to develop abstract knowledge on the basis of real-life applications; (3) encouragement of creative innovation, together with strict analysis; (4) strong emphasis on methodology, combined with extensive problem-area knowledge; (5) sensitization to involved values, with education for a "clinic-rational" approach; and (6) very demanding programs, which only limited groups of carefully selected students can successfully undertake.

Such programs need new locations at universities; it may even be the case that such programs have a better chance to succeed not at established universities, but at policy research organizations which can combine applied policy sciences work, production of new policy sciences knowledge, and advanced teaching in policy sciences.[13]

Additional variations come easily to mind. For instance, some elements of policy sciences should be included in all university curricula—to broaden preparation for citizen participation (undergraduate programs), to prepare different professions for urban policy-relevant work (e.g., medicine, social work, social science, and engineering), and to initiate future urban politicians (e.g., law). But, as in all other sections, my intention here is not to exhaust the subject, only to indicate some guidelines for thought, research, and action.

It is important to recognize the interdependencies of the different analyses and proposals. Not only are different metapolicy proposals interdependent and different urban education proposals interdependent, but better urban metapolicy depends on the improvement of urban education, and the improvement of urban education depends on better urban metapolicy. This does not imply that everything can or should be done simultaneously. But it is correct to draw the conclusion that isolated incremental changes here or there will make no worthwhile contributions. A massive and multidimensional effort is needed to improve urban metapolicy and urban education, so as to meet the urban challenge for the present and of the foreseeable future.

---

[12]For a detailed discussion, see Yehezkel Dror, *Designs for Policy Sciences,* (New York: American Elsevier, 1971), chapter 14.

[13]The new Teaching Program in Policy Analysis initiated at the Rand Corporation in 1970 well illustrates this possibility. See Charles Wolf, Jr., "Policy Sciences and Policy Research Organizations", *Policy Sciences* 2, no. 1 (1971): 1-6.

Author Index

(Entries followed by n indicate information given in a footnote.)

Subject Index

(Entries followed by n indicate information given in a footnote.)